A New Star-Rating System & Other Exciting News from Frommer's!

In our continuing effort to publish the savviest, most up-to-date, and most appealing travel guides available, we've added some great new features.

Frommer's guides now include a new **star-rating system.** Every hotel, restaurant, and attraction is rated from 0 to 3 stars to help you set priorities and organize your time.

We've also added **seven brand-new features** that point you to the great deals, in-the-know advice, and unique experiences that separate travelers from tourists. Throughout the guide look for:

Finds	Special finds—those places only insiders know about
Fun Fact	Fun facts—details that make travelers more informed and their trips more fun
Kids	Best bets for kids—advice for the whole family
Moments	Special moments—those experiences that memories are made of
Overrated	Places or experiences not worth your time or money
Tips	Insider tips—some great ways to save time and money
Value	Great values—where to get the best deals

Grand Canyon National Park

3rd Edition

by Alex Wells

Hungry Minds

Best-Selling Books • Digital Downloads • e-Books
Answer Networks • e-Newsletters • Branded Web Sites • e-Learning
New York, NY • Cleveland, OH • Indianapolis, IN

ABOUT THE AUTHOR

Alex Wells has written for magazines including *Condé Nast Traveler, Men's Journal, Outside,* and *Skiing.* When not on assignment, he enjoys backcountry skiing and mountain-biking near his home in the Tushar Mountains in southwestern Utah. His idea of heaven is an eternal backpack through the Grand Canyon—with weekly breaks for pizza and showers.

Published by:

HUNGRY MINDS, INC.

909 Third Ave.
New York, NY 10022

ISBN 0-7645-6583-4
ISSN 1093-9784

Editor: John Vorwald
Production Editor: Heather Wilcox
Photo Editor: Richard Fox
Cartographer: Roberta Stockwell
Production by Hungry Minds Indianapolis Production Services

SPECIAL SALES

For general information on Hungry Minds' products and services, please contact our Customer Care department; within the U.S. at 800-762-2974, outside the U.S. at 317-572-3993 or fax 317-572-4002. For sales inquiries and reseller information, including discounts, bulk sales, customized editions, and premium sales, please contact our Customer Care department at 800-434-3422.

Manufactured in the United States of America

5 4 3 2 1

Contents

List of Maps

AN INVITATION TO THE READER

In researching this book, we discovered many wonderful places—hotels, restaurants, shops, and more. We're sure you'll find others. Please tell us about them, so we can share the information with your fellow travelers in upcoming editions. If you were disappointed with a recommendation, we'd love to know that, too. Please write to:

Frommer's Grand Canyon National Park, 3rd Edition
Hungry Minds, Inc. • 909 Third Avenue • New York, NY 10022

AN ADDITIONAL NOTE

Please be advised that travel information is subject to change at any time—and this is especially true of prices. We therefore suggest that you write or call ahead for confirmation when making your travel plans. The authors, editors, and publisher cannot be held responsible for the experiences of readers while traveling. Your safety is important to us, however, so we encourage you to stay alert and be aware of your surroundings. Keep a close eye on cameras, purses, and wallets, all favorite targets of thieves and pickpockets.

WHAT THE SYMBOLS MEAN

The following abbreviations are used for credit cards:

AE	American Express	DISC	Discover	V	Visa
DC	Diners Club	MC	MasterCard		

FROMMERS.COM

Now that you have the guidebook to a great trip, visit our website at **www.frommers.com** for travel information on nearly 2,000 destinations. With features updated regularly, we give you instant access to the most current trip-planning information available. At Frommers.com, you'll also find the best prices on airfares, accommodations, and car rentals—and you can even book travel online through our travel-booking partners. At Frommers.com, you'll also find the following:

- Daily Newsletter highlighting the best travel deals
- Hot Spot of the Month/Vacation Sweepstakes & Travel Photo Contest
- More than 200 Travel Message Boards
- Outspoken Newsletters and Feature Articles on travel bargains, vacation ideas, tips & resources, and more!

Here's what critics say about Frommer's:

"Amazingly easy to use. Very portable, very complete."

—*Booklist*

"The only mainstream guide to list specific prices. The Walter Cronkite of guidebooks—with all that implies."

—*Travel & Leisure*

"Complete, concise, and filled with useful information."

—*New York Daily News*

"Hotel information is close to encyclopedic."

—*Des Moines Sunday Register*

"Detailed, accurate, and easy-to-read information for all price ranges."

—*Glamour Magazine*

Welcome to the Grand Canyon

Years ago, upon completing a hike in the Grand Canyon, I stood at the rim, gazing one last time at the colors below, and vowed right then to inform everyone how lucky they were to be alive. My good intentions lasted for only a day, but it was an unforgettable one, and when it was over I realized that the canyon had moved me the way religion moves fervent believers. At the time I wasn't sure why. Only after I began work on this book did I begin to understand all those things that, for me, make the canyon not just a beautiful place, but a sacred one as well.

When I returned to the canyon, I was awed by the terraced buttes and mesas, rising thousands of feet from the canyon floor and dividing the many side canyons. Early cartographers and geologists noticed similarities between these pinnacles and some of the greatest works of human hands. Clarence Edward Dutton, who scouted the canyon for the U.S. Geological Survey in 1880–81, referred to them as temples and named them after eastern deities such as Brahma, Vishnu, and Shiva. François Matthes, who drew up a topographical map of the canyon in 1902, continued the tradition by naming Wotans Throne and Krishna Temple, among other landmarks.

The temples not only inspire reverence but tell the grandest of stories. Half the earth's history is represented in the canyon's rocks. The oldest and deepest rock layer, the Vishnu Formation, began forming 2 billion years ago, before aerobic life-forms even existed. The different layers of sedimentary rock that piled up atop the Vishnu tell of landscapes that changed like dreams. They speak of mountains that really did move, eroding away into nothingness; of oceans that poured forth across the land before receding; of deserts, swamps, and rivers the size of the Mississippi—all where the canyon now lies. The fossils in these layers illustrate the very evolution of life.

Many of the latest products of evolution—over 1,500 plant and 400 animal species—still survive at the canyon today. If you include the upper reaches of the Kaibab Plateau (on the canyon's North

Grand Canyon Overview

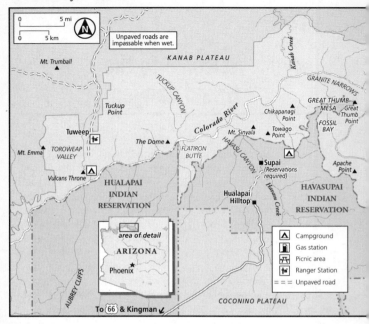

Rim), this small area of northern Arizona includes zones of biological life comparable to ones found as far south as Mexico and as far north as Alaska. The species come in every shape, size, and temperament, ranging from tiny ant lions dwelling on the canyon floor to 1,000-pound elk roaming the rims. And for every species, there is a story within the story. Take the Douglas fir, for example. Once part of a forest that covered both rims and much of the canyon, this tree has endured since the last Ice Age on shady, north-facing slopes beneath the South Rim—long after the sun-baked rim itself became too hot and inhospitable.

As much as I like the stories, I also enjoy the mysteries that can't be explained. The web of ecological cause-and-effect among the canyon's species is too complicated for any mortal to untangle. It leaves endless questions to ponder, such as why the agave blooms only once every 20-odd years. Similarly, the canyon's rocks withhold as much as they tell. More than a billion years passed between the time the Vishnu Schist formed and the Tapeats Sandstone was deposited atop it—a gap in the geological record commonly referred

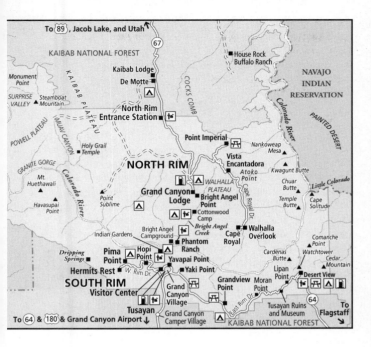

to as The Great Unconformity. Other gaps—or unconformities—exist between other layers. And river gravels that would have explained how the canyon was cut have long since washed away.

The more time I spend inside the canyon, the better I hope to understand the first people who dwelt here. A number of different tribes have lived in or around the canyon, and the Navajo, Havasupai, Kaibab Paiute, Hopi, Zuni, and Hualapai tribes still live in the area. Before the white man arrived, they awakened to the colors of the canyon, made their clothes from its plants and animals, smelled it, touched it, tasted it, and felt it underfoot. The Hopi still regard the canyon as their place of emergence and the place to which their dead return. Native Americans have left behind more than 3,000 archaeological sites and artifacts that may be as old as 10,000 years. All this runs through my mind when I walk the canyon floor.

I also contemplate some of the first white people who came to this mystical place. The canyon moved them to do extraordinary, if not always productive, things. I think about the prospectors who clambered through the canyon in search of precious minerals, and then wonder about the ones who stayed here even after their mines proved unprofitable. I wish I could have met icons like Georgie White, who began her illustrious river-running career by *swimming* 60 miles down the Colorado River in the western canyon; and Mary Colter, the brilliant architect who obsessed over creating buildings that blended with the landscape, even going so far as to grow plants out of the stone roof at the Lookout Studio. I'd still like to meet David Brower, who, as executive director of the Sierra Club, helped nix a proposal to dam the Colorado River inside the Grand Canyon. He did so by running full-page ads in the *New York Times* that compared damming the canyon to flooding the Sistine Chapel. I admire these people, who felt blessed and inspired by the canyon.

Theodore Roosevelt would also belong in this group. During his 1903 visit, the canyon moved him to say: "Leave it as it is. You cannot improve on it. The ages have been at work on it, and man can only mar it. What you can do is to keep it for your children, your children's children . . . as the one great sight which every American . . . should see." That wasn't just talk. He backed up his words, using the Antiquities Act to declare the Grand Canyon a National Monument in 1908. Congress established Grand Canyon National Park in 1919.

Although Congress called it a "park," the canyon still has a daunting, even ominous side. Everyone, no matter how many times they enter it, must negotiate with it for survival. One look at the clenched jaw of a river guide as he or she rows into Lava Rapids will remind you that the canyon exacts a heavy price for mistakes. And the most common error is to underestimate it. Try to escape, and it becomes a prison 10 miles wide (on average), 277 (river) miles long, and with walls 4,000 feet high. The canyon's menace, for me, is part of its allure—a reminder that we're still animals who haven't completely conquered nature.

Clearly, you can suffer here, but reward is everywhere. It's in the spectrum of colors: The Colorado River, filled with runoff from the Painted Desert, runs blood red beneath slopes of orange Hakatai Shale; cactus flowers explode in pink, yellow, and red; and lichens paint rocks orange, green, and gray, creating art more striking than the works in any gallery. It's in the shapes, too—the spires, amphitheaters, temples, ramps, and cliffs—and in the shadows that bend across them before lifting like mist. It's in the myriad organisms and their individual struggles for survival. Perhaps most of all, it's in the constancy of the river, which, even as it cuts closer to a beginning, reminds us that all things break down, wash away, and return to the earth in time.

1 The Park Today

The new millennium finds Grand Canyon National Park slowly implementing an ambitious plan for altering the park. This plan, known as the **General Management Plan,** dates to the mid-'90s, the tail-end of a two-decade period during which park visitation more than doubled to 4.6 million. By the mid-'90s, the park's resources were badly strained. On a typical summer day, some 6,500 vehicles drove to the South Rim, only to find 2,400 parking places. Faced with gridlock, noise, and pollution from emissions during high season, the park planned major changes, designed to accommodate the 6.8 million annual visitors that the park, at that time, expected to receive in 2010.

Under the General Management Plan, private vehicles will eventually be barred from most areas along the South Rim, including the historic district in Grand Canyon Village, the West Rim Drive, and all but one overlook (Desert View) on the East Rim Drive. Instead of driving, visitors will travel by light rail from a new transportation staging area in Tusayan (just south of the park's south entrance) to a larger orientation center—the Canyon View Information Plaza— inside the park near Mather Point. A second light rail line will link the Canyon View Information Plaza with the Village Transit Center in Grand Canyon Village. At both the Canyon View Plaza and the Village Transit Center, visitors will be able to board shuttles that will transport them to other developed areas on the South Rim.

Private cars will not be banned altogether from this part of the park. Visitors camping or staying in lodges and campgrounds away from the rim will be allowed to drive directly to those areas. Those staying nearer the rim will be driven by van from parking areas farther out. Visitors will also be able to drive through the park on Highway 64, a through-road connecting the towns of Williams and Cameron, Arizona. However, they will not be allowed to park at the overlooks west of Desert View.

The plan also calls for an extensive "greenway" trail for cyclists (rental bicycles will eventually be available), walkers, and equestrians. Paved in places, it will cover 38 miles on the South Rim between Hermit's Rest and Desert View. Another 8-mile branch of the greenway will link Tusayan with the Canyon View Information Plaza. An additional 28 miles may eventually be constructed on the North Rim.

In time, the new transit and trails system should help the National Park Service achieve its goal of restoring the rim areas to a quieter, less polluted state. Other parts of the General Management Plan move commercial activity and housing away from the rim and, in some cases, out of the park. For starters, the rim-side Kachina and Thunderbird lodges will be razed; the area they occupy will become open space. Their guest rooms may be replaced by new ones away from the rim at Maswik Lodge and in historic buildings that now serve as employee dormitories. Visitors hoping to learn in depth about the park will be able to do so in a cluster of historic buildings in Grand Canyon Village known as the **Heritage Education Campus.**

Alas, implementing the General Management Plan has proved even more challenging than expected. The park has been able to pay for some of the changes itself, using a percentage of the fees charged for admission and other park usage. But the most ambitious elements, including light rail service, will require appropriations from Congress. The light rail plan alone would cost nearly as much as the entire construction budget for the Park Service.

Congress may have lost an impetus for funding major improvements when visitation to Grand Canyon leveled off in the late 1990s—the park now expects to receive "only" 5.36 million visitors in 2005 and does not expect to top 7 million visitors until around 2025. In Fall 2001, the National Park Service gave Congress a report on bus alternatives that might serve as a less-expensive substitute for light rail. This raised hopes that the new multi-modal transit system—the cornerstone of the General Management Plan—might be implemented in the next few years.

In the meantime, the park is slowly moving forward with other elements of the General Management Plan. One major piece, the visually stunning Canyon View Information Plaza, opened in October 2000. A 2.1-mile stretch of greenway between Yavapai and Mather points has been completed. Other small changes, including additions to the greenway, should be visible in the next two years.

At present, visitors can ride the park's existing shuttle bus system around Grand Canyon Village, to all overlooks on the West Rim drive, and to Mather, Yaki, and Yavapai overlooks. Yet automobiles still strongly affect the visitor experience in most of the park's developed areas. As long as most people still drive into the park, the Canyon View Information Plaza, which was designed as a mass transit center and lacks automobile parking, will look strangely out of place.

The park's General Management Plan is designed to let the South Rim accommodate the crowds expected in the future, and the National Park Service has no plans to limit visitation there. It may, however, limit North Rim visitation. Rather than expand North Rim facilities to accommodate larger crowds—in the process jeopardizing the peacefulness of this area—the Park Service may cap the number of day-use visitors sometime before 2010. Also, a new parking area near the North Kaibab trailhead may eventually be constructed. Visitors would park their cars in the lot and then take shuttles to Bright Angel Point, where Grand Canyon Lodge is located. During the next few years, however, few changes are in store at the North Rim.

2 The Best of the Grand Canyon

Choosing the best things at Grand Canyon is like naming the best thing about your true love. Especially when your true love—all 277 miles of it—is divine. But, since every vacation consists of smaller parts, I've done my best to isolate a few of the best places and ways to appreciate the larger beauty of Grand Canyon.

- **The Most Dramatic Rim View: Lipan Point** (on the East Rim Drive, South Rim). Located above a sweeping curve in the river and with views far downstream to the west, Lipan Point is the nicest, most easily accessible place to view the canyon and a great place to watch the sunset. The **Unkar Delta,** one of the most archaeologically rich areas in the park, is visible directly below the overlook. See "East Rim Drive" in chapter 3.

- **The Best Scenic Drive: East Rim Drive** (South Rim). You'll see more of the canyon on this drive than on the other two (The Cape Royal Rd. and the West Rim Dr.). The western-most overlooks open onto the monuments of the central canyon; the eastern ones have far-ranging views of the Marble Platform and the northeast end of the canyon. Along the way, you can stop at the 825-year-old Tusayan Pueblo, which was once occupied by the Ancestral Puebloans. The Watchtower, a historic building artfully fashioned after towers built by the Ancestral Puebloans, is a perfect place to finish the drive. See "East Rim Drive" in chapter 3.

- **The Best Historic Building: Hermit's Rest** (at the western terminus of the West Rim Dr.). On the outside, this 1913 building resembles a crude rock shelter like one built by a hermit. Inside, it has an enormous, cavelike fireplace, original furniture, and candelabras on the walls. Built as a rest stop for travelers en route to a camp inside the canyon, Hermit's Rest is still a great place to collect oneself before returning to Grand

Canyon Village. See "Historic & Man-Made Attractions" in chapter 3.

- **Best Place to Picnic: Vista Encantadora** (on the North Rim's Cape Royal Rd.). The picnic tables here afford canyon views and provide a convenient stopping point when you're visiting the overlooks on the Cape Royal Road. On the South Rim, there are few tables along the rim, so you'll need to be more creative. If the weather is calm, pack a light lunch and walk along one of the rim trails until you find a smooth rim-rock or bench on which to picnic. See "North Rim: Cape Royal Drive" in chapter 3.

- **The Best Bike Ride: The West Rim Drive in summer** (South Rim). During high season, when this road is closed to most private vehicles, motorized traffic consists mostly of the occasional shuttle bus. Between shuttles, you'll often have the gently rolling road and some of the overlooks to yourself. See "Other Sports & Activities" in chapter 4.

- **The Best Rim Walk: Greenway between Yavapai and Mather Points.** This newly completed stretch of the park's ambitious greenway project travels right along the rim, affording views straight down into the canyon. Paved and smooth, it lets walkers enjoy the scenery without worrying too much about their footing. Its 10-foot width allows groups of friends to stroll side by side. And, given its location between two of the park's busiest overlooks, it can be surprisingly quiet. On the North Rim, try the Widforss Trail. See "Exploring the Backcountry" in chapter 4.

- **The Best Day Hike Below the Rim: Plateau Point Trail** (accessible via the Bright Angel Trail). With views 1,300 feet down to the Colorado River, Plateau Point is a prime destination for fit, well-prepared day hikers. The hardest part of this 6.1-mile (each way) trip is on the Bright Angel Trail, which descends 4.6 miles and 3,060 vertical feet from Grand Canyon Village to Indian Garden. The trailhead for the Plateau Point Trail is a half-mile west of Indian Garden on the Tonto Trail. From there, it's a smooth and relatively level stroll to the overlook. See "South Rim Corridor Trails" in chapter 4.

- **The Best Corridor Trail: North Kaibab** (North Rim). For people backpacking into the canyon for the first time, this is a scenic, less-crowded alternative to the South Rim corridor trails. During its 14-mile-long, 5,850-vertical-foot descent from rim to river, the trail passes through vegetation ranging from Spruce–Fir forest to Sonoran Desert. It ends near Phantom Ranch, the only lodging inside the canyon within the park boundaries. See "North Rim Corridor Trail" in chapter 4.

- **The Best Active Vacation: Oar-powered raft trips through Grand Canyon.** Expensive and worth it, these trips negotiate thrilling rapids on the Colorado River. Between the rapids, they move slowly and quietly enough to reveal the subtle magic of the canyon. During stops hikers have access to some of the prettiest spots anywhere. See "Other Sports & Activities" in chapter 4.

- **The Best RV Park: Kaibab Camper Village** (Jacob Lake, © **928/643-7804**). For once, an RV park that doesn't look like the lot at a drive-in movie. Old growth ponderosa pines and views of Jacob Lake (the tiny pond) make this RV park, located about 45 miles from the North Rim entrance, the best by far in the Grand Canyon area. Campers can pick up a few supplies at nearby Jacob Lake (the motel, store, gas station, and restaurant). Now it even has showers. See p. 108.

- **The Best Car Campground in the Park: North Rim Campground** (© **800/365-2267** or 928/638-9389). The campsites along the rim of Transept Canyon have pleasing views and are well worth the extra $5. Ponderosa pines shade all the sites, which are far enough apart to afford privacy. For hikers, the Transept Trail begins just a few yards away. If you're on the South Rim, try **Desert View Campground** (p. 100). See p. 102.

- **The Best Historic Hotel: The El Tovar Hotel** (Grand Canyon Village, © **928/638-2631**). Made of Oregon pine, this grand 1905 hotel rises darkly above Grand Canyon Village on the canyon's South Rim. Inside, moose and elk heads, copper chandeliers, and rooms with classic American furnishings add to its almost-spooky character. By far the most luxurious in the park, this hotel is the only one with room service. See p. 111.

- **The Best Bar in the Park: Bright Angel Lounge** (inside Bright Angel Lodge in Grand Canyon Village, © **928/638-2631**). Every night, tourists from around the world perch atop the stools at this long bar, their backs to a mural by a renowned Hopi artist Fred Kabotie, their elbows resting atop a coated bar top displaying historic postcards, old horseshoes, and other canyon relics. During high season, you'll hear more languages here than at the United Nations. See "The Grand Canyon After Dark" in chapter 6.

- **Best Place to Watch the Sunset: Westernmost Deck of Grand Canyon Lodge.** While the sun disappears behind the pines along the rim, you can soak up the colors on the horizon while sitting in a comfortable chair and sipping a beverage from the nearby saloon. After the sun sets, warm up by the immense outdoor fireplace on the lodge's eastern deck. For unobstructed views, go to Lipan Point on the South Rim or Cape Royal on the North Rim. See p. 117.

- **The Best Accessible Backcountry Destination: Waterfalls of Havasu Creek.** Surrounded by the red-rock walls of Havasu Canyon, these turquoise-colored falls seem to pour forth from the heavens into the cauldron of Grand Canyon. Travertine dams the creek in places, forming many seductive swimming holes. The 10-mile hike or mule ride from Hualapai Hilltop helps ease you into this area, home to the Havasupai Indians. See "Havasu Canyon & Supai" in chapter 7.

- **The Best B&B: The Inn At 410 Bed & Breakfast** (Flagstaff, *©* **800/774-2008** or 928/774-0088). Your journey doesn't end at the door of this inn. Inside, each of the elegantly decorated rooms recalls a different setting. One room celebrates the cowboy way of life, another recalls a 19th-century French Garden, and a third is fashioned after a turn-of-the-century Mexican courtyard. The intriguing decor, together with the kindness of innkeepers Sally and Howard Krueger, helps you travel the world—while catching up on your rest. See p. 132.

- **The Best Expensive Hotel: Best Western Grand Canyon Squire Inn** (Tusayan, *©* **800/622-6966** or 928/638-2681). Located just a mile outside the park, this hotel offers many of the amenities generally associated with resorts in big cities. Here, you'll find the town's best dining (in the elegant Coronado Room), its liveliest watering hole (downstairs, in the bar that locals call "The Squire"), and its only tennis courts for guests—not to mention luxuries such as a beauty shop and concierge. Located in the main building, the deluxe rooms equal the area's best. See p. 139.

- **The Best Expensive Restaurant: Chez Marc Bistro** (Flagstaff, *©* **928/774-1343**). This delightful country French restaurant, which showcases the cooking of chef Marc Balocco, could succeed in any city. Every course, from the smoked salmon crepes to the crème brûlée, not only looks divine, but tastes divine as well. The restaurant boasts an expansive selection of wines and after-dinner drinks, and the intimate, bistro-style room will make you want to fall (or stay) in love. See p. 135.

- **The Best Moderately Priced Restaurant: Pine Country Restaurant** (Williams, ⓒ **928/635-9718**). The pie here is so good, many locals order dessert first. Others can't wait to dine on straightforward dinner entrees like baked chicken, pork chops, and fried shrimp, most of which go for under $8. Alas, certain misguided customers enjoy their dinners so much, they spoil their appetites for dessert. See p. 150.

- **The Best Inexpensive Restaurant: The Black Bean Burrito Bar and Salsa Company** (Flagstaff, ⓒ **928/779-9905**). Get a burrito as heavy as a hand weight, at a price that makes it feel like a handout. Wrapped in aluminum foil and served in plastic drive-in baskets, this may be the best food value in the whole Grand Canyon area. The food is ready within seconds after you order, making this a great place to get a quick fix after a long day. See p. 136.

- **The Best Steak House: Rod's Steak House** (Williams, ⓒ **928/ 635-2671**). Beef lovers won't want to miss this Route 66 landmark, identifiable by the cow-shaped sign out front. After 50 years, the tiny menus here are as laconic as cowboys—seems the restaurant would rather serve its giant steaks than write about them. Don't miss the mud pie, the perfect finish to a simple, yet delicious, meal. See p. 151.

- **The Best Area Museum: Museum of Northern Arizona** (Flagstaff, ⓒ **928/774-5213**). One of the most extensive collections of Native American art makes this museum unique. Both functional and striking, the artifacts are compellingly displayed, in exhibits that illuminate the close relationship between the indigenous people and the land of the Colorado Plateau. There's no better place to begin learning about the area. See p. 129.

- **Best Place to Escape the Crowds: Anywhere More Than a Half-Mile From the Nearest Parking Lot or Shuttle Bus Stop.** The vast majority of park visitors seldom venture farther than a half-mile from a parking area. If you're willing to walk a half-mile or more, whether it's on a corridor, rim, or wilderness trail, you'll begin to experience some quiet and solitude. This may be the single best way to enjoy the canyon.

2

Planning Your Trip to Grand Canyon National Park

According to Park Service studies, the average visit to Grand Canyon National Park lasts about 3 hours—and many people spend even less time than that. At the other end of the spectrum lies a handful of people who spend lifetimes exploring the canyon, logging hundreds of miles on its hiking trails or weeks at a time on its river. How much time you allow depends on how well you'd like to know the canyon.

I recommend spending at least 1 full day and night inside the park, if possible. This will give you a chance to watch a sunset or (better still) a sunrise. It will also give you enough time to find a quiet place on the rim for writing postcards or listening to the canyon. If you spend 2 full days, you can hike 1 day and take a scenic drive the next. Another day is better still. A lifetime is best.

1 Getting Started: Information & Reservations

Grand Canyon National Park distributes a free trip planner that should answer most of your questions about the park. To get a copy of the planner, you can call © **928/638-7888** or visit the park's website at **www.nps.gov/grca/grandcanyon**.

MULE RIDES
Mule trips to Phantom Ranch can fill up months ahead of time, so it's wise to make your reservations as early as possible, especially if you hope to visit during September or October. For detailed information about mule rides and how to make reservations, see "Other Sports & Activities," in chapter 4.

MAPS
The best driving map of the Four Corners area is **AAA's Guide to Indian Country** ($3.95), which shows many of the more remote roads. **Trails Illustrated** publishes an excellent large-scale (1:73,500) topographical map of the Grand Canyon ($9.95). Waterproof and

tear-proof, it shows both rims and all the canyon trails from Lee's Ferry to west of Havasu Canyon, with the eastern canyon displayed on one side and the western canyon on the other. These maps, as well as more than 200 titles about the canyon, are available through the **Grand Canyon Association,** P.O. Box 399, Grand Canyon, AZ 86023 (© **800/858-2808;** www.grandcanyon.org).

Detailed topographical maps of the canyon are helpful for those hiking the canyon's wilderness trails. You can order **U.S. Geological Survey (USGS) 7.5-minute maps** of the canyon, which roughly cover a 7-mile by 7-mile square area, by calling the USGS directly (© **888/ASK-USGS**) or by visiting the USGS website (**www.usgs. gov**). Cost for direct orders is $4 per map plus a $5 handling fee. The backcountry office can tell you which USGS maps show particular areas of the canyon. The 7.5-minute maps are also usually available at **The Canyon Village Marketplace** (© **928/638-2262**) on the South Rim. The nearest North Rim outlet is at **Willow Creek Books** in Kanab, Utah (© **435/644-8884**). However, these stores, unlike the USGS, won't always have the map you need.

If you're planning to travel through the Kaibab National Forest to a remote campsite or trailhead, a map can be a lifesaver. The Kaibab National Forest Tusayan, Williams, and Chalender Ranger Districts map ($6) covers the Forest Service land along the South Rim. To buy one, stop by the **Kaibab National Forest Tusayan Ranger District Office** (© **928/638-2443**), outside the park's south entrance. The Kaibab National Forest North Kaibab Ranger District map shows the Forest Service land along the North Rim, much of which extends to the rim itself. The **Kaibab Plateau**

Planning Tip

For every season but winter, reservations for campsites, raft trips, backcountry permits, motel rooms, and train and (South Rim) mule rides should be made in advance. Mule trips and raft trips should be booked as early as possible, since they're the most likely to fill up. However, don't assume that the canyon's lodges and activities are always booked solid. In Summer 2001, a strong dollar (which discouraged foreign visitors) and high gas prices (which may have discouraged domestic travelers) left park lodges with mid-season vacancies. There are also some periods that are surprisingly slow every year, like the weeks before and after Labor Day.

Visitor Center (© **928/643-7298**) at Jacob Lake sells these $6 maps.

USEFUL BOOKS & PUBLICATIONS

Among the hundreds of books written on the canyon, several stand out. For a general overview, leaf through *Grand Canyon: A Natural History Guide* (Houghton Mifflin Co., 1993) by Jeremy Schmidt. Schmidt reveals the larger beauty of the canyon by exploring the smaller relationships between its dwellers—human and otherwise.

If you're the type who doesn't know schist (but would like to), pick up *An Introduction to Grand Canyon Geology* (Grand Canyon Association, 1999) by L. Greer Price. The author explains the geology of Grand Canyon in terms anyone can understand.

The Man Who Walked Through Time (Vintage Books, 1967), by Colin Fletcher, provides a more personal look at the canyon. As he chronicles his own solitary 300-mile walk through the canyon, the author explores how the land moves him. If people interest you most, look for *Living at the Edge* (Grand Canyon Association, 1998) by Michael F. Anderson. This carefully researched book traces the canyon's human history from the prehistoric desert cultures through the present. All of the above titles can be ordered through the **Grand Canyon Association** (© **800/858-2808**).

2 When to Go

The **South Rim** is open year-round. But don't plan on driving on the West Rim Drive from March 1 to November 30—during that period, if you don't want to walk or ride a bicycle, you'll have to rely on the park's free shuttles to move you from lookout to lookout.

Weather permitting, the **North Rim** is open from May 15 to October 16. After this date, the park remains open (without most guest services, including gas) until the first major snowstorm. The road from Jacob Lake into the park closes during the first storm and remains closed until spring.

AVOIDING THE CROWDS

When planning your trip, remember that high season runs from April through October. If you come during high season, plan on entering the park before 10am or after 2pm, so that you can avoid the lines at the entrance gates and the parking challenges inside the park.

Although mass transit won't help you avoid the crowds, it might make those crowds more bearable. During high season, there's an

Packing Tips

A wide-brimmed hat, sunglasses, and sunscreen are standard equipment at the canyon in all seasons. If you're planning to hike in cool weather, you'll be most comfortable in a water-resistant, breathable shell and several layers of insulating clothing, preferably polypropylene, polar fleece, or other fabrics that remain warm when wet. The shell-and-layers technique works especially well in spring and fall, when extreme swings in temperature occur regularly. Even in summer, you'll still want a shell and at least one insulating layer (more on the North Rim) for cold nights or storms.

hourly commercial shuttle from Tusayan to the South Rim. A historic train goes into the park year-round from Williams. The park staff recommends that you park your vehicle outside the park and use these alternative modes of transportation.

Once at the South Rim, you can ride the park's free shuttles. Three shuttle routes together serve all of **Grand Canyon Village, Canyon View Information Plaza, Mather Point, Yavapai Point, Yaki Point,** and the **West Rim Drive.** The shuttles run year-round in Grand Canyon Village and March through Nov on the West Rim Drive. (At press time, the park had not decided the wintertime status of the loop serving Mather, Yaki and Yavapai points.) When the shuttles run, the West Rim Drive and Yaki Point (including the South Kaibab Trailhead) are closed to private vehicles.

FLOOD WARNING

In mid-July, the monsoons usually begin. As hot air rises from the canyon floor, moist air from the oceans is swept up along with it. As this moist air rises, it condenses, forming towering thunderheads that unloose short-lived but intense afternoon thunderstorms. These localized storms frequently drench the park during August, the wettest month of the year, when nearly 2.25 inches of rain falls on the South Rim.

When rain threatens, hikers should avoid slot canyons, whose steep walls make climbing to safety nearly impossible. Even in wide, dry washes, hikers should be aware of the possibility of sudden, unexpected floods and be prepared to move to higher ground. One especially dangerous, commonly visited area is Havasu Canyon, where three people drowned during a flash flood in August 2001.

> ⓘ *Tips* **Buying Park Entrance Permits Outside the Park**
>
> Vending machines located outside the Flagstaff Visitors Center, the Williams-Grand Canyon Chamber of Commerce, and the IMAX Theater in Tusayan sell entrance permits to the park. By using these machines, you can avoid waiting in line at the park entrance during peak hours.

INSECTS

Mosquitos and biting flies sometimes breed near standing water (which is, itself, a rarity) on the North and South rims; and near springs in the inner canyon. However, most canyon areas are free of mosquitos and biting flies the vast majority of the time.

CLIMATE

Month	South Rim		Inner Gorge		North Rim	
	High F/C	Low F/C	High F/C	Low F/C	High F/C	Low F/C
Jan	41 (5)	18 (–8)	56 (13)	36 (2)	37 (3)	16 (–9)
Feb	45 (7)	21 (–6)	62 (17)	42 (6)	39 (4)	18 (–8)
Mar	53 (12)	36 (2)	72 (22)	59 (15)	57 (14)	32 (0)
Apr	60 (16)	32 (0)	82 (28)	56 (13)	53 (12)	29 (–2)
May	70 (21)	39 (4)	92 (33)	63 (17)	62 (17)	34 (1)
June	81 (27)	47 (8)	101 (38)	72 (22)	73 (23)	40 (4)
July	84 (29)	54 (12)	106 (41)	78 (25)	77 (25)	46 (8)
Aug	82 (28)	53 (12)	103 (39)	75 (24)	75 (24)	45 (7)
Sept	76 (24)	47 (8)	97 (36)	69 (21)	69 (21)	39 (4)
Oct	65 (18)	36 (2)	84 (29)	58 (14)	59 (15)	31 (–1)
Nov	52 (11)	27 (–3)	68 (20)	46 (8)	46 (8)	24 (–4)
Dec	43 (6.1)	20 (–7)	57 (14)	37 (3)	40 (4)	20 (–7)

The climate at the Grand Canyon varies greatly not only from season to season but from point to point. At 8,000 feet and higher, the North Rim is by far the coldest, dampest part of the park. Its temperatures run about 30°F cooler than Phantom Ranch at the bottom of the canyon, more than 5,000 vertical feet below. The North Rim averages 25 inches of precipitation per year, compared with just 8 inches at Phantom Ranch and 16 inches on the South Rim. Phantom Ranch is more than 4,000 feet lower and up to 25°F warmer than the South Rim.

IF YOU'RE GOING IN SPRING   The North Rim doesn't open until mid-May, so in early spring your only choice is the South Rim, which is cool and breezy at this time of year. The South Rim's daily highs average 60°F and 70°F in April and May, respectively. Nights can be very cold, with lows in April around freezing. Travelers should be prepared for late-winter storms, which occasionally bring snow to the rim. Storms aside, this is an ideal time to hike the inner canyon, with highs in April averaging 82°F. It's also the most popular, so make reservations early. Many of the canyon's cacti bloom in spring, dotting the already colorful walls with lavenders, yellows, and reds and making this perhaps the prettiest time of year to visit.

IF YOU'RE GOING IN SUMMER   The South Rim seldom becomes unbearably hot, and the North Rim never does. During July, the average highs on the South and North rims are 84°F and 77°F, respectively. Although the temperatures on the rim are pleasant, the crowds there can feel stifling. Escaping into the canyon may not be an alternative—at this time of year; the canyon bottom can be torrid, with highs averaging 106°F, and considerably hotter along the dark-colored rocks near the river. However, on the North Rim especially, summer nights can still be nippy. Even during July, low temperatures there average a chilly 46°F.

IF YOU'RE GOING IN FALL   After the monsoons taper off in mid-September, fall is a great time to be anywhere in the park. The crowds fall off before the red, orange, and yellow leaves on the rim-top trees follow suit. The North Rim, with its many aspens, is brightest of all. Highs on the South Rim average 76°F in September, 65°F in October, and 52°F in November. The North Rim has highs of 69°F in September and 59°F in October. (It closes in mid-Oct.) Highs average 97°F in the Inner Gorge in September. In October, however, the days cool off by 13°F, and backpackers can sometimes enjoy perfect weather. The first winter storms can hit the North Rim as early as mid-October.

Also in the fall, for 3 weeks every September, the **Grand Canyon Music Festival** brings together world-renowned classical musicians. The offerings, consisting primarily of chamber-music concerts, are held in the intimate, acoustically superb **Shrine of the Ages Auditorium** on the canyon's South Rim. Tickets for the 7:30pm concerts cost $18 for adults and $8 for children (park admission not included) and are available at the door or in advance through Grand Canyon Music Festival (© **800/997-8285** or 928/638-9215; www.grandcanyonmusicfest.org), P.O. Box 1332, Grand Canyon, AZ 86023. Check the website for the concert schedule, and to ensure that you receive the tickets you want, order by early July.

What Things Cost at the Grand Canyon	U.S. $	U.K. £
Local fare on Fred Harvey Taxi Service (from Bright Angel Lodge to Market Plaza, 1 person)	$5	£3.41
(Each additional adult)	$2	£1.36
7-lb. bag of ice at Canyon Village Marketplace	$1.29	£0.88
"I Hiked Grand Canyon National Park" T-shirt at Yavapai Lodge gift shop	$19	£12.96
Grand Canyon Coaches shuttle from Tusayan to Grand Canyon Village (one-way fare for adults)	$4 plus $6 park entrance fee	£6.82 total
(kids 16 and under)	free	
Small cup of coffee at Yavapai Cafeteria (inexpensive)	$1.25	£0.85
Room with bed and sink only at Bright Angel Lodge (inexpensive)	$48	£32.74
Double-occupancy high-end "view suite" at El Tovar Hotel (expensive) £195.10	$286	
Double-occupancy canyon-side room at Kachina Lodge (moderate)	$126	£85.95
Double-occupancy room at Holiday Inn Express in Tusayan (moderate)	$99	£67.53
(in low season)	$69	£47.07
Double-occupancy room at Super 8 Motel in Flagstaff (inexpensive)	$64	£43.66
(in low season)	$44	£29.33
Site at Mather Campground	$15	£10.23
Water/electric hookup site at Grand Canyon Trailer Village	$24	£16.37
Mule day trip to Plateau Point	$111	£75.72
Gallon of gas in Tusayan (in Aug 2001) (30¢ more than in Flagstaff)	$1.99	£1.36
Park admission (per car)	$20	£13.64
Backcountry permit (plus $5 per person per night)	$10	£6.82
Big Mac burger at Tusayan McDonald's	$2.89	£1.97

IF YOU'RE GOING IN WINTER   If you don't mind the cold, you'll love the canyon in winter. Winter is by far the quietest and most peaceful time to visit. Backcountry permits are easy to come by, the overlooks are virtually empty, and storms sprinkle snow across the red rocks. These storms, unlike summer monsoons, are not localized disturbances. Rather, they're the same large Pacific fronts that drop snow throughout the West. Closed in winter, the North Rim sometimes receives more than 200 inches of snow in a season. Although the South Rim gets considerably less, drivers should still be prepared for icy roads and occasional closures. Though trails remain open, hikers must often walk on snow and ice, especially near the tops of trails on north-facing slopes. (Small crampons can be useful for winter hiking.) When the snow isn't falling, the South Rim warms up nicely. High temperatures average 41°F in January and 45°F in February. The inner canyon can be pleasant during the coldest months. Even in January, its highs average a balmy 56°F, although snow does occasionally reach the floor.

3 Getting There

Las Vegas and Phoenix are the major cities closest to the North and South Rims, respectively. You can save money by flying into these cities, but they're too far from the canyon to stay in during your visit. Flagstaff, AZ, Williams, AZ, Tusayan, AZ, and Kanab, UT, are better choices for lodging near the Grand Canyon.

BY PLANE

Many travelers opt to fly into either the **Phoenix Sky Harbor International Airport,** 220 miles from the South Rim, or **McCarran International Airport** in Las Vegas, 263 miles from the North Rim. Both airports are served by most major airlines.

For those who would like to fly closer to the canyon, **America West Express** (© **800/235-9292**) has daily jet service (round-trip cost $200 and up) connecting Phoenix/Sky Harbor International Airport and **Flagstaff Pulliam Airport,** roughly 80 miles from the park.

Closer still is **Grand Canyon National Park Airport** in Tusayan, 1.5 miles south of the park's south entrance. **Air Vegas** (© **800/255-7474** or 702/736-3599) and **Scenic Airlines** (© **800/634-6801** or 702/638-3300) both offer daily service between Las

Vegas and Grand Canyon National Park Airport. Air Vegas, whose round-trip fare is $278, departs from **Henderson Executive Airport;** Scenic, which charges $227 round-trip, leaves from either **Tropicana Airport** (part of McCarran International Airport) or North Las Vegas Airport.

BY CAR
RENTING A CAR
Major rental-car companies with offices in Arizona and Las Vegas include **Avis** (✆ 800/230-4898), **Budget** (✆ 800/527-0700), **Dollar** (✆ 800/800-4000), **Hertz** (✆ 800/654-3131), **National** (✆ 800/227-7366), and **Thrifty** (✆ 800/367-2277).

From April through October, **Enterprise** (✆ 928/638-2871) rents cars at Grand Canyon National Airport in Tusayan.

In Flagstaff, car rentals are available through the following companies: **Avis** (✆ 800/230-4898 or 928/774-8421), **Budget** (✆ 800/527-0700), **Enterprise** (✆ 800/325-8007 or 928/ 526-1377), **Hertz** (✆ 800/654-3131 or 928/774-4452), and **National** (✆ 800/227-7368 or 928/779-1975).

DRIVING TIP Many of the Forest Service roads to remote areas on the rims are impassable in wet weather. During monsoon season, these roads can become too muddy or slippery to negotiate. In winter, there's no snow removal on them. People using these roads should be aware that they could be stranded indefinitely by a heavy snowfall, rain, or other factors.

RENTING AN RV FOR YOUR TRIP
Cruise America (✆ **800/RV-DEPOT;** www.cruiseamerica.com) rents RVs nationwide and has offices in Phoenix, Flagstaff, and Las Vegas. During 2001, Cruise America offered a weekly rate of $1,025 for a 25-foot, C-class motor home getting 8 to 10 miles per gallon (with a 40-gal tank). Low-season weekly rates for the same vehicles dropped as low as $805. Thirty-foot motor homes went for $1,285 in high season, $995 in low season. Some campgrounds do not allow the largest RVs. When making reservations at a campground, make sure that your RV meets its regulations.

BY TRAIN
Amtrak (✆ **800/872-7245** or 928/774-8679 for station information only) regularly stops in downtown Flagstaff, where lodging, rental cars, and connecting bus service are available. You can take

NM	National Monument
NP	National Park
N PRES	National Preserve
NRA	National Recreation Area
NWR	National Wildlife Refuge

the train from Albuquerque to Flagstaff for $59 to $106 one way. The one-way fare from Los Angeles to Flagstaff ranges from $64 to $114. Amtrak also serves Williams, where connecting rail service (on the historic and lively Grand Canyon Railway) is available. Fares are the same as for Flagstaff.

BY BUS

During high season, **Nava-Hopi Bus Lines** (© **800/892-8687** or 928/774-5003) offers twice daily service from Flagstaff to Tusayan (cost $14) and Grand Canyon Village (cost $20, including $6 park entrance fee).

Driving Distances

Mileage from the South Rim of Grand Canyon National Park to:

Albuquerque, NM	407
Bryce Canyon National Park, UT	310
Cameron, AZ	57
Canyon de Chelly National Monument, AZ	243
Denver, CO	649
Flagstaff, AZ	78
Gallup, NM	273
Grand Canyon National Park Airport	9
Kanab, UT	222
Kingman, AZ	188
Las Vegas, NV	290
Los Angeles, CA	556
North Rim Grand Canyon National Park	215
Petrified Forest National Park	189
Phoenix, AZ	220
Williams, AZ	59
Zion National Park, UT	272

Mileage from the North Rim (entrance) of Grand Canyon National Park to:

Flagstaff, AZ	193
Fredonia, AZ	71
Jacob Lake, AZ	30
Kanab, UT	78
Las Vegas, NV	277
Phoenix, AZ	335
Salt Lake City, UT	438
Williams, AZ	225
Zion National Park, UT	119

Daily shuttle service between the North and South rims is available from May 15 through October 15 on the **Trans-Canyon Shuttle** (© **928/638-2820**). The fare is $65 one way, $110 round-trip, for adults. For kids 12 and under, the fare is $55 one-way, $90 round-trip. You must make a reservation to take the shuttle.

Grand Canyon Driving Times & Distances

Lightface numbers *indicate driving times*
Bold numbers *indicate distances in miles*

In this schematic we assume 100 miles will take an
average of 1 hour, 49 minutes (excluding stops)
at an average speed of 55 miles per hour

23

4 Learning Vacations & Special Programs

The Grand Canyon Field Institute, a nonprofit organization cosponsored by the Grand Canyon Association and Grand Canyon National Park, lets you experience the canyon with those who understand it best. Every year it schedules dozens of backpacking trips and outings lasting from 2 to 9 days. Some explore broad subjects such as ecology; others hone narrow skills such as orienteering or drawing. People intimately familiar with the canyon, who are experts on the topics covered, guide all of the excursions. Because the courses vary greatly, the Field Institute assigns a difficulty level to each and attempts to ensure that participants find ones suited to their skill levels and interests. If you love the canyon, there's no better way to pass a few days. To contact the Field Institute you can call (*©* **928/638-2485;** write to P.O. Box 399, Grand Canyon, AZ 86023; or check out its website at **www.grandcanyon.org/fieldinstitute/**.

5 Tips for Travelers with Disabilities

The steep, rocky trails below the rim pose problems for travelers with disabilities. People with limited vision or mobility may be able to walk the Bright Angel or North Kaibab trails, which are the least rocky in the canyon. If you need to take a service dog on trails below the South Rim, check in with the ranger office at the corner of Center Road and Village Loop Road. On the North Rim, check in at the Backcountry Office.

On the rims themselves, many attractions are accessible to everyone. On the **South Rim,** the East Rim Drive is an excellent activity. Four of its overlooks—Yaki, Grandview, Moran, and Desert View—are wheelchair accessible, as are Tusayan Museum and Pueblo. (Ask for assistance at the information desk.) At Desert View, the bookstore and grocery are accessible, but no designated seating is available in the snack bar. Along this drive, restrooms for the mobility impaired can be found at Yavapai Point, Tusayan Museum, Desert View (just east of Desert View General Store), and Desert View Campground. (The campground has no designated sites.)

The West Rim Drive poses more problems. For starters, most of the shuttles serving it are not wheelchair accessible. Advance reservations are required for accessible shuttle service (*©* **928/638-0806**). It's easier for people in wheelchairs to drive themselves. Although the drive is closed to most private cars when the shuttles are running, people with disabilities can obtain permits for their vehicles at **Canyon View Center.** On the drive itself, Hopi Point, Pima Point, and Powell Memorial are all wheelchair accessible. The road also affords a number of nice "windshield views" from pullouts where one need not leave the car to see the canyon. To reach the gift shop at Hermit's Rest, you'll have to negotiate two five-inch steps and a route that slopes gently sideways. Near Hermit's Rest is a wheelchair-accessible chemical toilet. Despite having many historic buildings, most of **Grand Canyon Village** is wheelchair accessible. The notable exceptions are Kolb Studio and Lookout Studio. Hopi House is accessible only through a 29-inch-wide door on the canyon side of the building. Also, some hallways in Yavapai Lodge are too narrow for wheelchairs. Wheelchair-accessible restrooms are found at the Canyon View Information Plaza, Canyon Village Marketplace, Yavapai Observation Station, the El Tovar Hotel, Bright Angel Lodge, Mather Campground, and Maswik Lodge. Mather Campground has six sites for people with disabilities.

The South Rim's new visitor center, the Canyon View Center, has been tailored to people with disabilities. Walkways and doorways are gradual and open. People with disabilities can drive to nearby Mather Point, which is wheelchair accessible, and reach the plaza via a paved walkway. (*Note:* If, as planned, the National Park Service closes Mather Point to private vehicles, people with disabilities will need to obtain permits to park at Mather Point. These permits will be available at the park entrances.)

Those who have difficulty walking can usually negotiate the 1.5-mile-long rim trail between Bright Angel Lodge and Yavapai Point (except when icy). If they desire, they can continue an additional 0.5 miles to Mather Point on a stretch of the Park's new greenway. Wide and smooth, the greenway has moderate grades and offers stunning canyon views.

On the North Rim, the gas station and grocery pose problems for people in wheelchairs, but most other buildings are wheelchair accessible. The two most popular North Rim overlooks—Point Imperial and Cape Royal—are each accessible, although neither has a designated parking space. Grand Canyon Lodge is accessible via both a lift and a ramp, and the North Rim Campground has two accessible sites. Wheelchair-accessible restrooms are located at the Backcountry Office (assistance required), Grand Canyon Lodge (assistance may be required), the North Rim Campground, and behind the visitor center.

The canyon's mule-trip concessionaires accommodate people with certain disabilities, as do many river companies. Also, **Fred Harvey**

(📞 **303/297-2757** or 928/638-2631) can sometimes arrange for buses with lifts for its bus tours if it's informed in advance. For details about the accessibility of park buildings and facilities, pick up the park's free *Accessibility Guide* at the park's information centers.

As for raft companies, **Western River Expeditions** (📞 800/453-7450), **Arizona Raft Adventures** (📞 800/786-RAFT), **Grand Canyon Expeditions** (📞 800/544-2691), and **Canyon Explorations, Inc.** (📞 800/654-0723) are all good choices for people with certain disabilities.

6 Tips for Travelers with Pets

Hot weather and crowds make the canyon a bad place for pets. If you do bring your dog to the South Rim, you can take it on a leash on rim trails inside the park's developed areas, but not in the backcountry, below the rim, on buses, or inside public buildings. Rather than leave your dog in the car, use the **Grand Canyon Kennel** (📞 928/638-0534), near Maswik Lodge in Grand Canyon Village. Open daily 7:30am to 5pm, it will care for your pet during the day and overnight. Cost for day care is $9 for dogs, $6 for cats. Overnights cost $13.50 for dogs over 50 pounds, $10 for dogs under 50 pounds, and $7.50 for cats. Payment is by cash only. Be sure to call ahead for reservations, as this kennel frequently sells out. Upon arriving, you'll be asked to show proof that your pet's shots are up to date. There's no kennel on the North Rim, and the Park Service discourages people from bringing pets there. On the North Rim, the only trail open to pets is the bridle path linking the lodge with the trailhead for the North Kaibab Trail.

7 Tips for Travelers with Children

The park's **Junior Ranger** program can help engage your kids during your stay. Pick up a Junior Ranger guide at these locations: Canyon View Information Plaza, Yavapai Observation Station, Desert View Information Center, Tusayan Museum, or the North Rim Visitor Center. The guide outlines steps to become a Junior Ranger. These include attending a walk or talk by a ranger, completing the educational games and puzzles in the guide, and picking up litter or recyclables inside the park (or simply listing reasons for protecting the area). The activities are tailored to three age groups, together spanning ages 4 to 14. After completing the steps, your youngster will receive a certificate and be eligible to purchase (for $1.50) a Junior Ranger patch. The park also has a Junior Ranger program in which participants use a field guide and binoculars to identify species, and another with a special focus on geology.

During summer, the park offers additional programs aimed at children, including daily nature walks. Parents must accompany their children on these activities. For a complete listing of kids' activities, consult the park's free newspaper, *The Guide*.

The canyon may not be as huggable as Barney (far from it) or as mesmerizing as a GameBoy, but its size, beauty, and danger (especially danger) still impress many kids. In addition to the Junior Ranger program described above, kids may also enjoy the following activities:

- **Look for deer.** At sunset, take a quiet walk in the grass along the train tracks by Grand Canyon Village, or watch a meadow along the entrance road on the North Rim. See how many deer you can count. But please don't feed or approach them.

- **Hike a rim trail.** If your kids are too small to make the steep descent into the canyon, take them walking on the canyon rim. This gets them away from the car and into less crowded areas. On the South Rim, the greenway from Grand Canyon Village to Mather Point is a nice option. On the North Rim, the Transept or Cliff Springs trails are both fun for kids.

- **Go birding.** During the daytime, sit on the rim and watch raptors and ravens ride the thermals. See if you can identify eagles, hawks, or vultures—and perhaps even California condors. Watch swifts and swallows dart around the rim. Use chapter 8, "A Nature Guide to Grand Canyon National Park," to help identify many of the different animals and plants.

- **Watch the wranglers prepare the mules for the trip into the canyon.** At 8am daily (9am in winter), the wranglers bring the mules to the corral on the South Rim just west of Bright Angel Lodge. While the mules entertain the kids, the wranglers will entertain the adults with their humorous lecture on mule-ride protocol. One word of caution: Certain tourist-weary mules have copped an attitude and will bite when petted.

- **See the canyon on the big, big screen.** When the canyon fails to entertain your young ones in person, show it to them on the 82-foot-high screen at the IMAX Theater outside the park in Tusayan.

8 Protecting Your Health & Safety

In 2001, two Arizona writers published a disconcertingly thick book detailing every known fatal accident within the canyon. *Over the Edge: Death in Grand Canyon* (Puma Press, Flagstaff, 2001) not only tells captivating stories but serves as a handy reminder of what *not* to do in the park. (For starters, don't remove your hiking boots and run barefoot toward the river.) Below is a list of guidelines that will keep you from becoming a subject of *Over the Edge: Volume II*.

- **Choose reasonable destinations for day hikes.** Although most park visitors quickly recognize the danger of falling into the canyon, they don't always perceive the danger of walking into it. Every year, the canyon's backcountry rangers respond to hundreds of emergency calls, most of them on the corridor trails (Bright Angel, North Kaibab, and South Kaibab). Day hikers are lured deep into the canyon by the ease of the descent, the sight of other hikers continuing downward, and (sometimes) the goal of reaching the river. As they drop into the canyon's hotter climes in late morning, temperatures climb doubly fast. By the time they turn around, it's already too late. They are hot, fatigued, and literally in "too deep." When hiking in the canyon, particularly during the summer months, pick a reasonable destination, and don't hesitate to turn back early.

- **Don't hike at midday during hot weather.** When hiking at temperatures over 100°F, you'll sweat fluids faster than your body can absorb them, no matter how much you drink. For this reason, hiking in extreme heat is inherently dangerous.

- **Drink and eat regularly.** During a full day of hiking, plan to drink more than a gallon of fluids—on the hottest days, make it more than two. Consume both water and electrolyte-replacement drinks such as Gatorade. Also, remember that eating carbohydrate-rich, salty foods is as important as drinking. If you consume large amounts of water without food, you can quickly develop an electrolyte imbalance, which can result in unconsciousness or even death.

- **Wear sunscreen and protective clothing.** Even during winter, the Arizona sun can singe unsuspecting tourists. To protect your skin and cool your body, wear long-sleeved white shirts, wide-brimmed hats, sunglasses, and high-SPF sunscreen.

- **Move away from rim overlooks during thunderstorms.** On the rim, you may be the highest point—and best lightning rod—for miles around.

- **Exercise caution on the rims.** Every year a handful of people fall to their death in the canyon. To minimize risk, don't blaze trails along the rim, where loose rock makes footing precarious. Use caution when taking photographs and when looking through the viewfinder of your camcorder (unless, by chance, you want your final footage to wind up on the FOX Network). Be prepared for gusts of wind, and keep an eye on your children.
- **Yield to mules when hiking.** If you encounter mules, step off the trail on the uphill side and wait for instructions from the wranglers. This protects both you and the riders.

3

Exploring the Grand Canyon

At the edge of the Grand Canyon, even the breezes seem to take a deep breath. Sometimes the best thing to do at the canyon is to take one yourself. Find a quiet place on the rim or off a trail and sit for an hour or so. Feel the warm air rise, watch the shadows and light play across the monuments, and listen to the timeless hush. No matter how fast you drive, and no matter how many angles you see the canyon from, you'll never completely "do" the canyon. So relax.

1 Essentials

ACCESS/ENTRY POINTS

The park has three gated entrances—two on the **South Rim** and one on the **North Rim.** The one that's most convenient to travelers from Flagstaff, Williams, and Phoenix is the park's **South Entrance Gate,** 1 mile north of Tusayan on Highway 64. Traffic occasionally backs up here during peak hours in high season. Many travelers from Flagstaff, as well as those from points east, prefer entering the South Rim area through its **East Entrance Gate,** near Desert View, 28.5 miles west of Cameron, Arizona, on Highway 64. From Flagstaff, the drive to the East Entrance Gate is about 8 miles longer than to the South Entrance.

The gate to the **North Rim** (separated from the South Rim by 210 highway miles) isn't convenient to anywhere, except perhaps the small store, motel, and gas station at Jacob Lake, Arizona, 30 miles north on Highway 67. (The North Rim itself is 14 miles south of the gate.) The closest real town is **Fredonia, AZ,** 71 miles to the north on Highway 89A. Parts of the park can also be accessed via Forest Service dirt roads.

INFORMATION CENTERS

CANYON VIEW INFORMATION PLAZA Completed in Fall 2000 near Mather Point, the Canyon View Information Plaza was designed to orient visitors arriving at the park via a new light-rail system. Though the rail system has not yet been built, the Information Plaza has the streamlined appearance of a modern mass

Tips Exploring the Park Without a Car

From mid-March through late October, **Grand Canyon Coaches** (© 928/638-0821) offers a regular shuttle service linking six Tusayan stops to Grand Canyon Village. To avoid parking problems inside the park, leave your car at **Grand Canyon National Park Airport** (or at your hotel) in Tusayan and take the shuttle into the park. Other Tusayan stops include **Best Western Grand Canyon Squire Inn, IMAX Theater, Tusayan General Store, The Grand Hotel,** and **Moqui Lodge.** The adult one-way fare is $4 (16 and under free) plus a $6 park entrance fee. The shuttle schedule is posted at each stop. An all-day pass costs $7.

The best time to be car-less inside the park is from March 1 to Nov. 30, when all of the park's free shuttle routes are operating. Departing regularly from before dawn until after sunset, the shuttle buses serve all of **Grand Canyon Village, Canyon View Information Plaza, Mather Point, Yavapai Point, Yaki Point,** and the **West Rim Drive.** Because the buses run every 15 to 30 minutes (depending on the time of day and the route), you seldom have to wait too long at a stop. The shuttles operate seasonally on the West Rim Drive, and year-round in Grand Canyon Village. Consult the park's free publication, *The Guide,* for detailed information on shuttle stops and schedules.

When the shuttles aren't running, you may need to take advantage of **Fred Harvey's 24-hour taxi service** (© 928/638-2822). These taxis do not have meters. Their fares vary according to distance and the number of passengers. For example, a trip between Bright Angel Lodge and Market Plaza costs $5 for the first person, $2 for each additional adult. The trip from Grand Canyon Village to Tusayan costs $10 for one or two adult passengers, plus $5 for each additional adult.

transit hub, with ample room for crowds and no automobile parking lots. Outdoors in the landscaped plaza, kiosks provide basic information on tours, trails, canyon overlooks, cycling, and other topics. The main South Rim visitor center is located inside the long, glass-fronted building known as the **Canyon View Center.** Here, you'll find additional displays on the canyon and the Colorado Plateau, an area for Ranger presentations, and an information desk. To get here, you'll need to take a free shuttle, walk, or park at nearby Mather Point.

YAVAPAI OBSERVATION STATION   Located 0.5 miles west of Canyon View Center on Yavapai Point, this historic station has an observation room where you can identify many of the monuments in the central canyon. Rangers frequently lead interpretive programs here. (For more information, see the section on the East Rim Drive, below.)

DESERT VIEW CONTACT STATION   Staffed by volunteers, this small station 26 miles east of Grand Canyon Village sells books and has information on the canyon. This station is just inside the park's East Entrance, 28.5 miles west of Cameron on Highway 64.

TUSAYAN MUSEUM   Located three miles west of Desert View, Tusayan Museum has an information desk staffed by rangers in addition to displays on the area's indigenous peoples.

KOLB STUDIO   Located on the rim at the west end of Grand Canyon Village, Kolb Studio houses a small bookstore and an art gallery with free exhibits.

NORTH RIM VISITOR CENTER   This visitor center near Grand Canyon Lodge has a small bookstore and information desk.

ENTRANCE FEES

Admission to Grand Canyon National Park costs $20 per private vehicle (includes all occupants) and $10 for adults (ages 17 and over) on foot, bicycle, or motorcycle. The receipt is good for a week and includes both rims. Adults who enter the park in organized groups or on commercial tours usually pay about $8 each, though the rates vary some.

SPECIAL DISCOUNTS & PASSES

A number of special passes are available at the park's entrance stations. **Golden Eagle Passports** entitle holders to unlimited use of all National Park Service sites, including Grand Canyon, for 1 year from the date they make this $50 purchase. A **Grand Canyon Passport** ($40) entitles the holder to free admission to Grand Canyon for one calendar year. For $10, U.S. residents aged 62 and older can purchase a **Golden Age Passport,** which admits the holder, free of charge, for life at all National Park Service sites. Another card, the **Golden Access Passport,** entitles U.S. residents with permanent mental or physical disabilities to the same privileges afforded by the Golden Age Passport. This card is free, but the applicant must apply in person at Canyon View Center, Desert View Information Center, Tusayan Museum, or the North Rim Visitor Center.

CAMPING FEES

Camping at **Mather Campground,** the largest on the South Rim, costs $15 per site during high season. **Desert View Campground,** open from mid-May to mid-October, costs $10 per site. And the **North Rim Campground,** also open from mid-May to mid-October, costs $15 per site. At all three campgrounds, no more than two vehicles and six people can share a site. **Trailer Village,** an RV park on the South Rim, charges $24 per hookup for two people, plus $1.75 for each additional adult. For more information, see chapter 5.

PARK RULES & REGULATIONS

The following list includes a set of rules established to protect both the park and its visitors:

- Bicycles must stay on roads. That means no mountain biking on the trails or on the park's new stretch of greenway.
- It's illegal to remove any resources from the park. This can be anything from flowers to potsherds. Even seemingly useless articles such as bits of metal from the canyon's old mining operations have historical value to the park's users and are protected by law.
- Dogs must be leashed at all times. They're allowed on certain rim trails in developed areas of the park, but are banned from trails below the rim, buses, or in park lodging. The only exceptions are certified service dogs.
- Fires are strictly prohibited except in the fire pits at North Rim, Desert View, and Mather campgrounds. In the backcountry, you can use a small campstove for cooking.
- Weapons including guns, bows and arrows, crossbows, slingshots, and air pistols are all prohibited, as are fireworks. If, by chance, you have a hang glider and are considering jumping into the canyon, forget it. It's illegal, and you'll be fined.

🌀 *FAST FACTS:* The Grand Canyon

ATM The lone ATM in the park is on the South Rim at Bank One, located in Market Plaza next to the Canyon Village Marketplace.

Fuel There is only one gas station inside the park on the South Rim. **Desert View Chevron,** on Highway 64, 25 miles east of Grand Canyon Village, is open daily from late April through September. Hours vary seasonally. If you're entering the park from the south and are running low on fuel, make sure to gas up in **Tusayan,** 1 mile south of the park's south entrance. On the North Rim, the **Chevron Service Station** is open daily 8am to 5pm (7am to 7pm in summer), also seasonally. You can also get gas at the general store across from Kaibab Lodge, 18 miles north of the North Rim on Highway 67.

Garages A garage with 24-hour emergency towing service (📞 928/638-2631) currently operates inside the park on the South Rim, though it may be removed in the near future. The garage itself is open from 8am to noon and 1pm to 5pm daily. The nearest automotive service to the North Rim is at **Judd Auto** (📞 928/643-7107) in Fredonia. Judd Auto has 24-hour towing and a reputation for being honest.

Health Services If you have a medical emergency on either rim, dial 📞 911 (or 9911 from motel rooms) to obtain assistance from Park Rangers. On the South Rim, a **health clinic** (📞 928/638-2551) is located on Clinic Road, off Center Road between Grand Canyon Village and the South Rim entrance road. The clinic is open on weekdays from 9am to 6pm, Saturday noon to 6pm. The nearest pharmacies are in Williams, AZ. Health services have been nonexistent on the **North Rim** ever since the small clinic there closed in 2000. In non-emergency situations, you'll need to drive all the way to the hospital in Kanab, UT.

Laundry Laundromats can be found inside the park on both rims. Open 6am to 11pm daily, the **South Rim's Laundromat** is in the Camper Services building near Mather Campground. Open 7am to 9pm daily, the **North Rim's Laundromat** is near the North Rim Campground.

Lost & Found For items lost in or near the park's South Rim lodges, call 📞 **928/638-2631,** ext. 6503. For those lost elsewhere on the South Rim, call 📞 **928/638-7798** Tuesday to

Friday 8am to 5pm. Found items can be returned to the Canyon View Information Plaza. On the North Rim, report lost and found items in person at the visitor center or at the Grand Canyon Lodge front desk (*C* **928/638-2611**).

Outfitters On the South Rim, **Canyon Village Marketplace** (*C* **928/638-2262,** open daily 8am to 8pm in summer, 8am to 7pm in winter) in Grand Canyon Village rents and sells camping and backpacking equipment. There is no equipment for rent on the North Rim, but the **North Rim General Store** (*C* **928/638-2611,** ext. 270), usually open from 7am to 9pm, sells a very limited supply of camping equipment.

Police For emergencies dial *C* **911** (9911 from motel rooms).

Post Offices On the **South Rim,** the post office (*C* **928/ 638-2512**) in Market Plaza has window hours from 9am to 4:30pm on weekdays and from 11am to 3pm Saturdays. On the **North Rim,** a tiny post office at Grand Canyon Lodge is open Monday to Friday 8 to 11am and 11:30am to 4pm and Saturday 8am to 1pm.

Supplies There are three grocery stores inside the park. The largest, **The Canyon Village Marketplace** (*C* **928/638-2262**), is in Market Plaza in Grand Canyon Village. Its hours are usually 8am to 8pm in summer, 8am to 7pm the rest of the year. **Desert View General Store** (*C* **928/638-2393**), at Desert View (25 miles east of Grand Canyon Village on Hwy. 64), is open daily 8am to 7pm in summer, 9am to 5pm the rest of the year. On the North Rim, the only provisions are at the **North Rim General Store** (*C* **928/638-2611,** ext. 270), adjacent to North Rim Campground. It's usually open daily 7am to 9pm.

Weather Updates Recorded weather information, updated every morning, is available by calling *C* **928/638-7888.** Forecasts are also posted at the main visitor centers.

2 How to See the Park in Several Days

The itineraries below list some captivating activities for your visit. These same activities are described in detail later in the book. And remember, the rims are 210 highway miles apart.

IF YOU HAVE 1 OR 2 DAYS

ON THE SOUTH RIM   After stopping at the visitor center, hike a short distance down the **Bright Angel Trail** in the morning. (If

How Grand Is the Grand Canyon?

Size: 1,904 square miles (more than 1½ times the size of Rhode Island)

Length of River in Canyon: 277 miles

Vertical Drop of River in Canyon: 2,215 feet

Average Width of Canyon: 10 miles

Widest Point: 18 miles

Narrowest Point: 600 feet (in Marble Canyon)

Average Depth: 1 mile

Lowest Point: 1,200 feet (at Lake Mead)

Highest Point on South Rim: 7,400 feet

Highest Point on North Rim: 8,801 feet

Colorado River Facts (as it flows through the canyon)

Length: 277 miles

Average Width: 300 feet

Average Depth: 40 feet

Average Gradient: 8 feet per mile

the weather is hot or if your condition is not top-notch, walk a portion of the **greenway** between Grand Canyon Village and Mather Point.) During midday, attend a Ranger presentation, for which times and locations are posted at the visitor centers. Later in the day, take the shuttle on the **West Rim Drive.** From any of the stops on the drive, you can walk a short distance along the **West Rim Trail** to quiet spots where you can savor the canyon. If possible, watch the sunset from **Hopi Point.**

The next morning, get an early start and watch the sunrise from **Desert View** on the South Rim. (Be sure to go up into The Watchtower.) On your way back to Grand Canyon Village, stop at the viewpoints on the **East Rim Drive.** Most of these viewpoints are open to cars year-round and have expansive views of the central and northeastern canyon. Upon returning to Grand Canyon Village, take a walking tour of the historic buildings. Relax over an iced tea on the veranda of the lounge at the El Tovar Hotel.

ON THE NORTH RIM   In the morning after checking in at the visitor center, hike down the top of the **North Kaibab trail.** A less-strenuous option is the short walk from Grand Canyon Lodge to Bright Angel Point. In the afternoon, drive down the **Cape Royal**

Road. After returning to Grand Canyon Lodge, buy a cold beverage at the saloon, then sip it while sitting on the lodge's enormous, canyon-facing deck. After sunset on calm evenings, warm yourself by the fireplace on the deck of Grand Canyon Lodge.

If you're an early riser, head to **Point Imperial** before dawn the next day to watch the sun rise. Then take a walk on one of the rim trails—**the Transept Trail, the Uncle Jim Trail** (to Uncle Jim Point), or, my favorite, **the Widforss Trail** (to Widforss Point).

IF YOU HAVE 3 OR 4 DAYS

With 3 or 4 days at the canyon, 3-day hikes may be in order.

ON THE SOUTH RIM   Choose from the Bright Angel, South Kaibab, Grandview, Hermit, and West Rim trails.

ON THE NORTH RIM   Try the North Kaibab Trail and two rim trails. There are fewer diversions on the North Rim, so be prepared for deep relaxation on the third and fourth days.

ON BOTH RIMS   Consider riding a mule into the canyon, accompanying a Ranger on a guided walk, or sitting and reading on the porch of one of the canyon's lodges.

3 Driving Tours

The South Rim is easily accessible by car off Highway 64, which connects Williams and Cameron. Inside the park's southern gate, the South Entrance Road diverges from Highway 64 and leads to **Grand Canyon Village.** A National Historic District, the village feels like a small town, with hotels, restaurants, shops, and a train depot. The loop road can be confusing, so take your time, watch carefully for signs, and use the village map included in the park newspaper, *The Guide.*

Scenic drives hug the canyon rim on either side of the village. The **West Rim Drive** heads west for 8 miles to its terminus at Hermit's Rest. The **East Rim Drive** covers 25 miles between Grand Canyon Village and the Desert View overlook on the southeastern edge of the park. Two of the 25 miles are on the park's entrance road, 23 are on Highway 64. The two scenic drives have numerous pull-offs that open onto the canyon, some with views of the river.

Some 210 highway miles and 4 hours of driving separate the North Rim from the South Rim. On the way, Highway 89A crosses the Colorado River near the canyon's northeastern tip, where the river begins cutting down into the rocks of the Marble Platform and the Grand Canyon begins. As you drive west from Lee's Ferry, you'll

West Rim Drive & South Rim Trails

see where rocks make a single fold along a fault line and rise more than 4,000 vertical feet from the Marble Platform to the level of the Kaibab Plateau—the canyon's North Rim.

The **North Rim** is more than 1,000 feet above the busier South Rim. Highway 67 travels south 44 miles from Highway 89A at Jacob Lake to where it dead-ends at Bright Angel Point, site of the Grand Canyon Lodge. A 23-mile-long paved scenic drive travels from Highway 67 southeast to the tip of the Walhalla Plateau, a peninsula east of Bright Angel Point. This drive, which ends at Cape Royal, has overlooks of the eastern Grand Canyon. On this curvy road, signs appear quickly. Pay attention, as there are few places to turn around. The 3-mile-long spur road to Point Imperial, the highest point on the North Rim, forks to the northeast off this road.

The rims at the **western end of the canyon** are lower, rockier, and more remote than those in the central canyon. Only a few roads cross these lands. The canyon ends abruptly at the Grand Wash cliffs, where the Colorado River flows out of Grand Canyon and into Lake Mead. To drive from rim to rim around the western end of the canyon, you'd have to cross the Colorado River at the Hoover Dam, near Las Vegas.

WEST RIM DRIVE

Start:	Grand Canyon Village.
Finish:	Hermit's Rest.
Time:	About 3 hours.
Highlights:	Closed to private cars (except for those carrying people with physical disabilities) during high season, the overlooks are quieter than those on the East Rim drive and afford excellent river views.
Drawbacks:	Occasional long waits for buses. The 8-mile-long road from Grand Canyon Village to Hermit's Rest is open to private cars when the shuttles aren't running. (The shuttles run Mar 1–Nov 30.)

Stop1
Trailview 1 & 2

These viewpoints en route to Maricopa Point are a great place to look back at Grand Canyon Village. Below the village, the switchbacks of the Bright Angel Trail descend along a natural break in the cliffs. This break was created by erosion along the Bright Angel Fault, one of many fault lines that crisscross the main canyon.

Looking north across the canyon, you can see how the fault created two side canyons in a straight line, on opposite sides of the river. Runoff seeps into the cracks along fault lines, beginning the process of forming side canyons such as these. Below, Indian Garden, where Havasupai Indians farmed for generations, is identifiable by the lush vegetation that grows around the spring there. Past Indian Garden a trail travels straight out to the edge of the Tonto platform, where it dead-ends. This is not the Bright Angel Trail, which descends another side canyon to reach the Inner Gorge, but a spur known as the Plateau Point Trail.

Stop 2
Maricopa Point

The Orphan Mine southwest of this point produced some of the richest uranium ore in the Southwest during the 1950s and 1960s. Below and to the west, you can see some of the metal framework of the tramway that moved ore to the rim from 1956 to 1959. Later, a 1,500-foot-high elevator replaced the tramway. A metal headframe from that elevator remains visible on the rim, directly above the old shaft. Mining continued here, sometimes at night, through 1966.

Stop 3
Powell Memorial

Here you'll find a large memorial to John Wesley Powell, the one-armed Civil War veteran who is widely believed to have been the first person to float through the canyon. Funded in part by the Smithsonian Institute, Powell first drifted into the canyon on August 5, 1869. He and his crew of eight portaged around rapids when the walls were gradual enough to allow it. In parts of the canyon's Inner Gorge, however, the walls became too steep to climb, and the men were forced to float blindly, in wooden boats, through some of the world's most dangerous waters.

Parts of the Inner Gorge are visible below this point, but only a tiny stretch of the river can be seen. Where Powell saw the Inner Gorge's dark, steep rocks lining the water, he thought not of their beauty but of the peril they represented. He called the gorge "our granite prison" and described his men "ever watching, ever peering ahead, for the narrow canyon is winding and the river is closed in . . . and what there may be below, we know not."

When the men stopped above what appeared to be another set of dangerous rapids after 3 weeks in the canyon, three of them left the expedition by walking out into what is now known as Separation Canyon, but were never seen again. The irony here was that the expedition had already passed most of the worst rapids. The remaining crew negotiated the last white water and soon arrived at a small Mormon outpost bearing the first records of the inner canyon's rocks, geography, and life-forms. Powell later fleshed out these records and notes in a lengthy diary, "The Exploration of the Colorado River and its Canyons." The names of the three crewmembers who left at Separation Canyon do not appear on the monument.

Stop 4
Hopi Point 🚌

Because it projects far into the canyon, the tip of Hopi Point is the best place on the West Rim Drive to watch the sunset. As the sun drops, its light will play across four of the canyon's loveliest temples. The flat mesa almost due north of the point is Shiva Temple. The temple southwest of it is Osiris; the one southeast of it is Isis. East of Isis is Buddha Temple.

Named for a destructive yet popular Hindu god, Shiva Temple was the site of a much-ballyhooed 1937 mission by a team of scientists from the American Museum of Natural History. Believing that the canyon isolated the forest atop Shiva Temple the same way oceans isolated the Galapagos Islands, the team set out to find species that had evolved differently from those on the rim. The East Coast press drummed up sensationalistic stories about the trip, even going so far as to hail it as a search for living dinosaurs. Alas, the search didn't turn up any new species, let alone dinosaurs. Rather, the team learned that cliffs and desert didn't bar the movements of most Grand Canyon species. (The Colorado River poses a more significant barrier.) The most noteworthy discovery: an empty Kodak film box and soup cans deliberately left behind by canyon local Emery Kolb, who was upset when the expedition declined his offer to help. Kolb easily made the ascent himself, proving that the cliffs were hardly a barrier.

Stop 5
Mohave Point ⍫

This is a great place to observe some of the Colorado River's most furious rapids. Farthest downstream (to your left) is Hermit Rapids. Above it, you can make out the top of the dangerous Granite Rapids, one of the steepest navigable rapids in the world. Just above Granite Rapids, the bottom of Salt Creek Rapids is visible. As you look at Hermit Creek Canyon and the rapids below it, you can easily visualize how flash floods washed rocks from the side canyon into the Colorado River, forming the natural dam that creates the rapids.

Stop 6
The Abyss

The walls in this side canyon steeply fall 2,600 feet to the base of the Redwall Limestone. The best way to experience the steepness is to follow the rim trail a few hundred yards west of the overlook, where the cliffs are most sheer.

Stop 7
Pima Point ⍫

Three thousand feet below Pima Point you can see some of the foundations and walls from the old Hermit Camp, a tourist destination built in 1912 by the Santa Fe Railroad. Situated alongside Hermit Creek, the camp featured heavy-duty tents, each with stoves, Indian rugs, and windows. An aerial tramway connected this point with the camp below. Used to lower supplies, it made the 3,000-foot descent in roughly a half hour.

To get to Hermit Camp, tourists traveled 51 miles by train from Williams to Grand Canyon Village, 9 miles by stagecoach from the village to the top of the Hermit Trail trailhead, and 8 miles by mule to the camp. After the Park Service wrested control of the Bright Angel Trail from Ralph Cameron in the 1920s, Phantom Ranch became a more popular tourist destination, and Hermit Camp closed its doors in 1930.

The Hermit Trail, however, remains popular. North of the overlook, below the fin of rock known as Cope Butte, you can see it zigzagging down the blue-green Bright Angel Shale.

Stop 8
Hermit's Rest 🍴
Before descending to Hermit Camp, tourists rested at this Mary Colter–designed building, built in 1914. Here, Colter celebrated the "hermit" theme, making the building look as if an isolated mountain man had constructed it. It resembles a crude rock shelter, with stones heaped highest around the chimney. A large fireplace dominates the interior. Colter covered the ceiling above it with soot, so that the room had the look of a cave warmed by fire—much like the nearby Dripping Springs overhang where "The Hermit of Hermit Canyon," Louis Boucher, once passed time. Colter had a knack for finding the perfect details. Note the anthropomorphic rock above the fireplace, the candelabras, and the hanging lanterns. Some of the original hand-carved furniture is still here.

A snack bar sells candy, ice cream, chips, soda, and ham or turkey sandwiches. Two heavily used restrooms are behind the main building. Before leaving, take one last look at the canyon. The three-pronged temple across the canyon to the north is the Tower of Ra, named for the always-victorious Egyptian sun god. Seen from above, each prong points to a different set of rapids: the near arm to Hermit Creek, the middle to Boucher, and the far one to Crystal—waters that have triumphed over more than a few river guides.

EAST RIM DRIVE

Start:	Yavapai Point, about a mile east of Grand Canyon Village.
Finish:	Desert View overlook, near the park's east entrance.
Time:	About 4 hours.
Highlights:	Spectacular views of both the central and northeastern canyon.
Drawbacks:	Packed parking lots in summer.

East Rim Drive travels 2 miles on the South Entrance Road, which links Tusayan and Grand Canyon Village. The remaining 23 miles are on the stretch of Highway 64 linking the South Entrance Road and the Desert View overlook. The Yavapai and Mather overlooks are on the South Entrance Road; the remaining seven stops, including six canyon overlooks, are accessible from Highway 64.

Stop 1
Yavapai Observation Station

Yavapai Point features some of the most expansive views both up and down the canyon. A historic observation station here has huge plate glass windows overlooking the central canyon, along with interpretive panels identifying virtually all the major landmarks.

From here you can spot at least four hiking trails. To the west, the Bright Angel trail can be seen descending to the lush Indian Garden area. The straight white line leaving from this general area and eventually dead-ending, is the Plateau Point Trail. Directly below the overlook and to the north, the Tonto Trail wends its way across the blue-green Tonto Platform. Across the Colorado River, find the verdant area at the mouth of Bright Angel Canyon. The North Kaibab Trail passes through this area yards before ending at the river, just below Phantom Ranch. Turning to face east, find the saddle just south of O'Neill Butte. The South Kaibab Trail crosses this saddle.

Stop 2
Mather Point

If there's such a thing as a bad overlook, this is it. Visitors who see the canyon only once, seem to do it from here. People entering the park from the south generally catch their first glimpse of the canyon in this area. Many of them immediately steer off the highway, sometimes onto the dirt alongside the road, and rush to the overlook. It's a clamorous place, epitomizing the "industrial tourism" that the late author Edward Abbey so dreaded.

Grand Canyon National Park, perhaps sensing that this was a natural stopping point, built a large, new visitor center a short walk from this overlook. The only automobile parking near the visitor center is at Mather Point, so visitors now park at Mather Point and walk to the new plaza, making the overlook even more crowded.

Stop 3
Yaki Point ☀

Accessible by car when the shuttles aren't running, this overlook is one of the best places to see some of the canyon's most notable monuments, including Vishnu Temple, Zoroaster Temple, and Wotans Throne. As erosion and runoff cut side drainages into the land around the larger canyon, pinnacles such as these are sometimes isolated between the drainages. In time, these monuments will erode away altogether, as will more of the rims. The South Kaibab trailhead is located nearby.

Stop 4
Grandview Point ☀

At 7,406 feet, this is one of the highest spots on the South Rim. In the 1890s, it was also one of its busiest. In 1890, one of the canyon's early prospectors, Pete Berry, filed a mining claim on a rich vein of copper on Horseshoe Mesa, visible to the north of the overlook. To remove ore from the mine, Berry built—and in some cases hung— a trail to it from Grandview Point. He erected cabins and a dining hall on the mesa, then, as visitors began coming, added a hotel a short distance away from Grandview Point. Built of ponderosa pine logs, the Grand View Hotel flourished in the prerailroad days. To reach the hotel, which for a brief period was considered the best lodging at the canyon, tourists took a grueling all-day stagecoach ride from Flagstaff.

In 1901, however, the Santa Fe Railroad linked Grand Canyon Village and Williams, putting an end, almost immediately, to the Flagstaff-to-Grandview stagecoach run. Once at Grand Canyon Village, few tourists wandered 11 miles east to Grandview Point, and the hotel went out of business in 1908. The mine fared no better. Plagued by high overhead, it shut down shortly after the price of copper crashed in 1907. Only a trace of the foundation remains of the Grand View Hotel, but the historic Grandview Trail is still used by thousands of hikers annually (see chapter 4 for details), and debris from the old mine camp still litters Horseshoe Mesa.

Stop 5
Moran Point ⨷

This point is named for landscape painter Thomas Moran, whose sketches and oil paintings introduced America to the beauty of the canyon in the years before landscape photography. After accompanying Maj. John Wesley Powell on a surveying expedition in 1873, Moran illustrated Powell's book, *The Exploration of the Colorado River and its Canyons.* Moran's painting, *The Grand Chasm of the Colorado,* later adorned one wall of the nation's capitol. These and other works helped lure some of the first tourists to the canyon in the 19th century.

Moran Point is the best place from which to view the tilting block of rock known as **The Sinking Ship.** Standing at the end of the point, look southwest at the rocks level with the rim. The Sinking Ship can be seen beyond the horizontal layers of Coronado Butte (in the foreground). It's part of the Grandview Monocline, a place where rocks have bent in a single fold around a fault line. Looking down the drainage below Coronado Butte, you'll see the red splotches of Hakatai Shale that give Red Canyon its name.

The first white people to see the canyon probably saw it from somewhere on the rim between here and Desert View. In 1540, Spanish explorer Francisco Vásquez de Coronado was scouring the Southwest for the mythical Seven Cities of Cíbola, with its equally mythical fortune in gold. After hearing of a great river and settlements north of the Hopi pueblo of Tusayan, he sent a small force led by Garcia Lopez de Cardenas to explore the area. Hopi guides led Cardenas and his men, who began the journey in armor, to the South Rim somewhere near here. Upon seeing the Colorado River, the Spaniards initially estimated it to be 6 feet wide. (It's closer to 200 in this area.) When Cardenas asked how to reach it, the Hopi, who had made pilgrimages to the bottom of the canyon for generations, professed not to know. For 3 days Cardenas's men tried unsuccessfully to descend to the river. In the process they learned what many canyon hikers would later discover: "What appeared to be easy from above was not so, but instead very hard and difficult." They gave up, and no white people returned to the canyon for 200 years.

Stop 6
Tusayan Pueblo ☝

By studying the tree rings in the wood at these dwellings, archaeologists determined that parts of this 14-room stone-walled structure were built in 1185 by the Ancestral Pueblo People. Among the pueblos that have been excavated near Grand Canyon, Tusayan Pueblo was the most recently occupied. By 1185 most of the Ancestral Puebloans had already left the canyon. For unknown reasons, however, the dwellers of this pueblo stayed on, despite a prolonged drought (also known from tree rings) and despite the nearest year-round water source being up to 7 miles away.

A self-guided tour takes you through this small collapsed pueblo, which includes the stone foundations of two kivas, living areas, and storage rooms, all connected in a U-shaped structure.

This dwelling, like many Ancestral Pueblo abodes in present-day northern Arizona, has a clear view of the San Francisco peaks, including Mt. Humphreys, which at 12,643 feet is the highest point in Arizona. These peaks formed when volcanoes boiled up through weak spots in the earth's crust between 1.8 million and 400,000 years ago. The descendants of the Puebloans, the modern Hopi, believe these peaks are home to the spirit beings known as Kachinas.

Built in 1932, **Tusayan Museum** celebrates the traditions of the area's indigenous people. Displays in this dimly lit historic building include traditional jewelry, attire, and tools, as well as historic photos. It's worth coming here just to see the 3,000-year-old split-twig figurines, made by members of a hunter-gatherer clan known as the **Desert Culture.** These mysterious figurines of deer or sheep were found under cairns (piles of stones) in caves inside the canyon.

Note: There are bathrooms at Tusayan Pueblo.

Stop 7
Lipan Point ☝☝

With views far down the canyon to the west, Lipan Point is a supreme place to catch the sunset. It also overlooks the Colorado River where the river makes two sweeping curves. Between those curves, on the opposite bank, Unkar Creek has deposited a large alluvial fan. From A.D. 800 to 1150, the Ancestral Pueblo People grew beans and corn in this rich soil. Archaeologists have found many granaries and dwellings in the area—not to mention evidence of the use of astronomy. At least some of the Puebloans migrated to the rim during summer, to hunt the abundant game and farm there.

Stop 8
Navajo Point

Like Lipan Point, this one offers fine views of the Grand Canyon Supergroup, a formation of igneous and sedimentary Precambrian rocks that has eroded altogether in many other parts of the canyon. The long, thin streaks of maroon, gray, and black, which tilt at an angle of about 20 degrees, are layers of this formation. They're visible above the river, directly across the canyon. As you look at these rocks, note how the level, brown Tapeats Sandstone, which in other canyon locations sits directly atop the black Vishnu Formation, now rests atop the Supergroup—hundreds of feet above the schist. Where the Supergroup had not yet eroded away, the Tapeats Sandstone was often deposited atop it, protecting what remained. In still other locations, the Supergroup rocks formed islands in the ancient Tapeats Sea, and no sand—the raw material for Tapeats Sandstone—was deposited atop them.

Stop 9
Desert View 🕭

Here you'll find **The Watchtower,** a 70-foot-high stone building designed by Mary Colter. Colter modeled it after towers found at ancient pueblos such as Mesa Verde and Hovenweep. To get an idea for the shape she wanted, she made a clay model of the building, atop an exact replica of the land at Desert View. Her model seems to have worked. Like Colter's other buildings, this one seems to emerge from the earth, the rough stones at its base blending seamlessly with the rim rock.

The Watchtower is connected to a circular observation room fashioned after a Hopi kiva—a ceremonial room that often adjoined the real pueblo towers. To climb the Watchtower, you'll first have to pass through this room, currently being used as a gift shop. Admission to the Watchtower costs 25¢. The walls inside the watchtower are decorated with traditional Native American art. Some of the finest work is by Hopi artist Fred Kabotie, whose depiction of the Snake Legend, the story of the first person to have floated down the Colorado River, graces the Watchtower's Hopi Room. At the top is an enclosed observation deck, which at 7,522 feet is the highest point on the South Rim.

The rim at Desert View offers spectacular views of the northeast end of the canyon. To the northeast you'll see the cliffs known as the Palisades of the Desert, which form the southeastern wall of Grand Canyon proper. If you follow those cliffs north to a significant rock outcropping, you're looking at **Comanche Point.** Beyond Comanche Point, you can barely see the gorge carved by the Little Colorado River. In 1956, at the point where that gorge intersects the Grand Canyon, two planes collided and crashed, killing 128 people. Most of the debris was removed from the area around the confluence of the rivers, but a few parts, including a wheel from one of the planes, remain. (None are visible from the rim.)

The flat, mesalike hill to the east is **Cedar Mountain.** This is one of the few places where the story told by the rocks at Grand Canyon *doesn't* end with the Kaibab Limestone. Cedar Mountain and Red Butte (a hill just south of Tusayan along Hwy. 64) were both deposited during the Mesozoic Era (245–65 million years ago). They linger, isolated, atop the Kaibab Limestone, remnants of the more than 4,000 feet of Mesozoic deposits that once accumulated in this area. (Sedimentary rock like this is usually deposited when the land is near or below sea level, as the land in this area was for long periods in the past. It erodes when elevated, the way the Grand Canyon is now.) Though nearly all of these layers have eroded off Grand Canyon, they can be seen nearby in the Painted Desert, the Vermilion Cliffs, and at Zion National Park.

This is the last overlook on the East Rim Drive. Past Desert View, Highway 64 continues east, roughly paralleling the gorge cut by the Little Colorado River. It leaves the Grand Canyon, which follows a more northerly course upstream of Desert View. About 10 miles above the confluence, the canyon narrows and the walls begin to drop, eventually disappearing below river level at Lee's Ferry (68 miles upstream of where the river passes Desert View), where the canyon begins.

NORTH RIM: CAPE ROYAL DRIVE

Start:	Grand Canyon Lodge
Finish:	Point Imperial, at the northeastern end of the park.
Time:	About 4 hours—more if you do any hiking.
Highlights:	Sparse crowds and lovely views of the eastern canyon.

Drawbacks: Has only one viewpoint (Cape Royal) from which to see the central canyon. The Colorado River is not visible from as many points on this drive as on the South Rim drives. From the Grand Canyon Lodge, I recommend driving 23 miles directly to Cape Royal, on the Walhalla Plateau. Make your stops on the way back to the Grand Canyon Lodge. That way, you can do the short hikes near Cape Royal while your legs are fresh, then stop at the picnic areas, closer to the lodge, on your way back.

Stop 1
Cape Royal 🥭🥭

Lined by cliff rose and piñon pine, a gentle, paved 0.3-mile (each way) trail opens onto some of the most stunning views in the park. It first approaches a natural bridge, Angel's Window, carved into a rock peninsula along the rim. Through the square opening under the bridge, a part of the lower canyon, including a slice of the Colorado River, can be seen from the trail. This opening in the Kaibab Limestone was formed when water seeped down through cracks and then across planes between rock beds, eventually eroding the rock from underneath.

The left fork of the trail travels about 150 yards, ending at the tip of the peninsula above **Angel's Window.** With sheer drops on three sides, Angel's Window is a thrilling place to stand.

The right fork of the trail goes to the tip of Cape Royal. From here, Wotans Throne, a broad mesa visible in the distance from many South Rim overlooks, looms only 1.5 miles to the south. Also to the south, and nearly as close, is Vishnu Temple. Closer still is Freya Castle, a pinnacle shaped like a breaking wave. Across the canyon, the tiny nub on the rim is the 70-foot-high Watchtower at Desert View.

> **OPTIONAL STOP**
> The **Cliff Springs Trail** (3 miles north of Cape Royal, in a small pull-out). This half-mile walk ends at a small spring in a side canyon. (See "Trails on the North Rim," in chapter 4.)

Stop 2
Walhalla Overlook and Walhalla Glades 🥭

Ancestral Puebloans no doubt enjoyed the views from here. Follow the tan line of Unkar Creek as it snakes down toward Unkar Delta. Enriched by the river deposits of the creek, the soil and abundant water at the delta made for excellent farming. Many Ancestral

Puebloans lived there, growing corn, beans, and squash on terraces that caught runoff and left deposits of rich soil.

When the canyon heated up, they also spent time on the North Rim, at dwellings such as the ones across the street from this overlook. A flat dirt path leads to Walhalla Ruin, which includes the foundations of two small pueblos. In this area, the Ancestral Puebloans could farm, taking advantage of the extra moisture and a growing season that was lengthened by the warm breezes blowing out of the canyon. In addition to farming, the Puebloans also gathered food and hunted the abundant game on the rim.

> **OPTIONAL STOP**
> **Cape Final Trail** (4.9 miles south of Roosevelt Point). This gentle, 1.5-mile-long (one-way) hike follows an old Jeep trail to an overlook at Cape Final. (See "Trails on the North Rim," in chapter 4.)

Stop 3
Roosevelt Point
This is one of the best places in the canyon to see the confluence of the gorge of the Little Colorado River and the Grand Canyon. They meet at nearly a right angle, unusual in that most tributaries enter at close to the same direction as the larger rivers. Geologists have used this observation to buttress arguments that the ancestral Colorado River exited the canyon via the Little Colorado gorge, but little evidence supports this theory. The cliffs south of this junction, which form the southeast wall of Grand Canyon proper, are known as the Palisades of the Desert. Those north of the confluence are called the Desert Facade.

Stop 4
Vista Encantadora
By starting your driving tour of the Walhalla Plateau early in the day, you can reach Vista Encantadora in time for a late picnic lunch. You'll find several tables near the rim. While you picnic, you can look down an upper drainage of Nankoweap Creek and at the rock pinnacle known as Brady Peak.

Stop 5
Point Imperial 🔎🔎
A 3-mile spur road leads from the Cape Royal Road to Point Imperial, which at 8,803 feet is the highest point on the North Rim and the best place on either rim to view the northeastern end of the park. To

Cape Royal Drive & North Rim Area

To Jacob Lake & Kanab, Utah

0   1 mi
0   1 km

(67) **KAIBAB PLATEAU**

**North Rim
Entrance Station**

Point Imperial

▲ *Mt. Hayden*
(2552 m/ 8372 ft)

Nankoweap Creek

**Vista
Encantadora**

Ken Patrick Trail

Uncle Jim
Trail

**Uncle Jim
Point**

**North Rim
Store**

**Roosevelt
Point**

**WALHALLA
PLATEAU**

▲ *Atoko
Point*

N. Kaibab Trail

Old Bright Angel Trail

Transept Trail

Widforss Trail

*Roaring
Springs*

**Grand Canyon
Lodge**

start drive here

**Bright Angel
Point**

Cape Royal Drive

**Widforss
Point**

*Oza
Butte*

▲ *Manu
Temple*

**Cottonwood
Campground**

North Kaibab Trail

BRIGHT ANGEL CANYON

OTTOMAN AMPHITHEATER

**Walhalla
Overlook**   Walhalla
Ruins

Cliff Spring Trail

finish drive here

Cape Royal   Angels
Window

Cape Royal Trail

**Bright Angel
Campground**

**Phantom
Ranch**

Colorado River

Campground	▲
Gas station	🏠
Jeep Trail	▪▪▪
Picnic Area	🞧
Ranger Station	🏠
Restrooms	🚻

the northeast, 3,000 feet below the overlook, you'll see the brownish-green plane known as the Marble Platform. The Colorado River cleaves this platform between Lee's Ferry and where Grand Canyon proper yawns open just east of here. Because the Marble Platform has the same rock layers as Grand Canyon, **Marble Canyon** is considered by geologists to be the uppermost section of Grand Canyon.

Bordering the Marble Platform on the north are the **Vermilion Cliffs.** Located along the Utah-Arizona border, these cliffs are also the next steps up in the Grand Staircase, a geological formation in which progressively younger rock formations rise like steps from Marble Canyon to Bryce Canyon in southern Utah. The Vermilion Cliffs run southwest to northeast. Where this formation turns toward the south near Lee's Ferry, the cliffs are known as the **Echo Cliffs.**

Looking southeast, you can see where the gorge of the Little Colorado River intersects the Grand Canyon. Past that confluence, the landforms of the Painted Desert stain the horizon a rich red. This desert, made up of badlands and other erosional features carved from the soft clays of the Chinle Formation, surrounds the Little Colorado River and one of its tributaries, the Puerte River. Like the Vermilion Cliffs, the Painted Desert is made up of "younger" rocks than are found in Grand Canyon.

Fun Fact **Wild Things**

If you watch carefully, you'll see wildlife everywhere during your stay. Even during the day, **raptors** soar above the canyon, **lizards** sun themselves on rocks, and **squirrels** scurry across the rim. The best time to view larger animals is at dawn or dusk, when they become more active. To see large animals such as elk, drive into the **Kaibab National Forest** near Grandview Point. **Deer,** which often graze alongside the train tracks near Grand Canyon Village, are hard to miss—especially when you're driving. On the North Rim, the meadows alongside the entrance road on the North Rim are frequented by **wild turkey, deer,** and (less often) **coyotes.** If you're serious about wildlife watching, bring binoculars. Sit a few hundred yards downwind of one of the small water holes (in this arid country, they're called "lakes") in these meadows and wait quietly for the animals. To learn more about the species in this area, turn to the "The Fauna" section of chapter 8.

4 Ranger Programs & Organized Tours

On both rims, the park offers a host of Ranger programs whose schedule changes seasonally. A typical schedule includes guided hikes and walks, kids' programs, and discussions of geology, native plant and animal species, and natural and cultural history. Evening programs are offered nightly, all year-round. All the programs are free and open to everyone. You just need to show up at the meeting places, which are scattered around the park (overlooks, trailheads, archaeological sites, and so on). For an up-to-date schedule, consult the park newspaper, *The Guide.*

BUS TOURS

Of the many private companies that offer bus tours, **Fred Harvey** has the most extensive schedule. Among the choices are East Rim (Desert View) and West Rim (Hermit's Rest) tours ($27 and $15, respectively, for adults; under 16 free), sunset tours to Hopi or Mojave Point ($11.50), sunrise tours ($11.50) to one of several rim stops, and all-day outings ($32) that combine two of the shorter tours. Unlike the drivers on the free shuttles, Fred Harvey drivers narrate the tours. Don't believe everything they say. Though they mean well and offer some valuable information, they were not hired for their command of natural science and history. (Just be glad you don't have distracted professors driving the bus.) For advance reservations, call ✆ **303/297-2757.** Once at the canyon, visit the Fred Harvey desks at Yavapai, Maswik, or Bright Angel lodges, or call ✆ **928/638-2631,** ext. 6015.

 Nava-Hopi Tours (✆ **928/774-5003**) offers 1-day guided canyon tours that depart from Flagstaff at 8:30am and return by 5:30pm. The cost for adults is $42 plus an $8 park admission fee. For kids ages 5 to 15, the tour costs $21, and no admission fee is charged.

5 Historic & Man-Made Attractions

Please refer to the map "Grand Canyon Village" on p. 113 in chapter 6 to find the exact locations of the historic buildings in the South Rim.

SOUTH RIM

Most of the historic buildings on the South Rim are concentrated in Grand Canyon Village, a National Historic District. Outside of the village, **Hermit's Rest** on the West Rim Drive and **The Watchtower** on the East Rim Drive are also of historical significance. For information on these two sites, refer to the West Rim (p. 39) and East Rim (p. 42) driving tours. Strange and beautiful, these historic buildings—like the canyon itself—take time to appreciate.

Mary Colter, a Minneapolis schoolteacher who in 1902 began decorating the shops that sold Indian art on the Santa Fe Railroad line, designed more than a half dozen of these historic buildings. As both a decorator and self-trained architect, Colter later designed these Grand Canyon landmarks: Hopi House (1905), the Lookout (1914), Hermit's Rest (1914), Phantom Ranch (1922), Watchtower (1932), and Bright Angel Lodge (1935). Colter's work drew heavily on the architectural styles of Native Americans and Spanish settlers in the Southwest, long before these styles became fashionable among Anglos. The most noteworthy historic buildings in Grand Canyon Village are detailed below.

THE BRIGHT ANGEL LODGE ⚐   In the 1930s, the Santa Fe Railroad asked Mary Colter to design moderately priced accommodations for the many new tourists who had begun driving to the canyon. Colter laid out a number of cabins, as well as this rustic log-and-stone lodge, which would house a lounge, restaurant, and curio shop. Completed in 1935, the lodge, located near the west end of Grand Canyon Village, looks low from outside but has a spacious lobby with wood walls, flagstone floors, and a high ceiling with an exposed log framework. A remarkable hearth is found in what was once the lounge and is currently the site of the Fred Harvey Museum. Known as "the geologic fireplace," it features the rock layers found in the canyon, stacked in the same order in which they occur there. Rounded, smooth river stones lie at the bottom of this bell-shaped hearth and Kaibab Limestone, the rim rock, is on top.

The museum tells the story of Harvey Girls—young women who came west during the years from 1883 through the 1950s to staff the Fred Harvey restaurants and hotels along the rail lines.

BUCKEY O'NEILL CABIN   This is the second-oldest structure in Grand Canyon Village (the oldest being Red House Station, which was moved to the rim in 1890). It was the home of Buckey O'Neill, who in the 1890s worked at a number of jobs, including sheriff, judge, reporter, and prospector, in the area. After discovering what he believed to be a rich copper vein in Anita, 14 miles south of the canyon, he pushed for the construction of a railroad line connecting Williams with Grand Canyon—via Anita, naturally. A Chicago mining company bought out O'Neill, but the project collapsed when the mine turned out to be less than rich. In 1901, the Santa Fe Railroad, perhaps realizing that Canyon tourism would pay far greater dividends than copper, bought the line and laid the remaining track. When Mary Colter designed cabins for Bright Angel Lodge, she fought for the preservation of the O'Neill Cabin, eventually building her own ones around it. Today, this cabin, a few feet west of Bright Angel Lodge, is the most luxurious guest suite in the park.

THE EL TOVAR HOTEL 🐾🐾   A year after the Santa Fe Railroad linked the South Rim with Williams, Fred Harvey commissioned Charles Whittlesey, an architect who had worked alongside Mary Colter on the Alvarado Hotel in Albuquerque, to build a large luxury hotel on the rim. Whittlesey fashioned the El Tovar after the northern European lodges of that period. Built of Oregon pine, this 100-room hotel offered first-class luxury accommodations at the canyon, attracting luminaries such as George Bernard Shaw and Theodore Roosevelt. To find it, walk 200 yards east along the rim from Bright Angel Lodge. (For more on the El Tovar, see chapter 6.)

GRAND CANYON DEPOT   Built in 1909, this is one of three remaining log train depots in the United States. It closed after the last train from Grand Canyon departed in 1968, then reopened in 1990, roughly a year after the railway resumed service. Located about 100 yards south of the El Tovar, this two-story depot is built of logs that are flat on three sides, making for smooth interior walls and a rounded, rustic exterior. Once home to the station agent and his family, the upstairs of the depot now houses Park Service offices.

HOPI HOUSE 🐾🐾   Aware that travelers were captivated by the idea of meeting Native Americans, Fred Harvey brought a group of Hopi artisans to Grand Canyon Village. At the same time that it was erecting the El Tovar Hotel on the rim, the company commissioned Mary Colter to design a structure 100 feet east of the hotel that could serve as both a dwelling for the Hopi and a place to market their wares.

Colter fashioned Hopi House after the pueblos in Oraibi, Arizona. Completed in 1905, this faux adobe structure rises in tiers, with each level connected by exterior wood ladders (and interior stairways). The roof of each level serves as the porch for the one above. Inside, low doorways and nooks in the walls recall the snug quarters found in real pueblos. The concrete floors are made to look like dirt, the plaster walls to look like adobe. Log beams support thatched ceilings.

Through 1968, the Hopi artisans lived on the top floor of this building while they created and sold their pottery, rugs, and jewelry on the lower floors. They chanted and danced nightly on a platform behind the building. Today, Hopi House still sells Native American art on the lower two floors, and Native American dancers have recently begun performing again. Once used for religious purposes, the kiva on the second floor remains off-limits to non–Native Americans.

KOLB STUDIO ☞ In 1902, two brothers, Emery and Ellsworth Kolb, began photographing tourists descending the Bright Angel Trail on mules. After snapping the photos, they ran to Indian Gardens, where they had water to develop their plates, then raced back to the rim in time to sell the photos. Flush with profits from the business, they built this home and studio alongside the trailhead of the Bright Angel Trail, along the rim at the westernmost edge of Grand Canyon Village, in 1904. Several years later the brothers launched a more ambitious project: a motion picture of a raft trip through Grand Canyon. Completed in 1912, the film earned them international fame and drew throngs of people to the studio's viewing room.

After clashing regularly throughout the years, the two brothers eventually flipped a coin to see which one would have the privilege of remaining at their beloved Grand Canyon. Emery won two out of three tosses. So while Ellsworth moved to Los Angeles, Emery continued to live and work at Kolb Studio, introducing the brothers' film to audiences each day until his death at age 95 in 1976, after which the Park Service took over the building. Today, Kolb Studio houses a bookstore and gallery (located in the former viewing room), which features exhibits year-round. Photos and clips from the Kolbs' films are shown in an interactive CD-ROM video (a must-see) inside the store.

LOOKOUT STUDIO ☞ Seeing the crowds drawn to Kolb Studio, The Fred Harvey Company decided to launch a similar business, only closer to the railroad terminus. Mary Colter was hired to design the building, which she eventually named The Lookout. Unlike some of her buildings, which were fashioned after occupied pueblos or well-preserved ruins, this one, on the canyon rim about 100 yards east of Kolb Studio, resembled a collapsed ruin. Its original chimney and low-slung roof looked like a pile of rocks and seemed barely higher than the canyon rim. To add to the effect,

Colter planted indigenous plants on the roof. After its completion in 1914, tourists came here to buy souvenirs or to photograph the canyon from the deck, where a high-power telescope was placed. Today, Lookout Studio still serves much the same purpose.

VERKAMP'S CURIOS   A true visionary, John G. Verkamp may have been the first to sell curios at the Grand Canyon. In 1898, before the railroad even reached Grand Canyon Village, Verkamp was hawking souvenirs out of a tent on the grounds of the Bright Angel Lodge. Although his first attempt at the business failed, Verkamp returned in 1905, after the trains began running, and opened a curio shop in a wood-shingled, Craftsman-style building 200 feet east of Hopi House. This time he succeeded. His descendants still run the store, making it one of the last privately held businesses in the park.

NORTH RIM

GRAND CANYON LODGE & CABINS ☆   This lodge sits quietly on the North Rim, gracefully blending into its surroundings. Built in 1928 by the Pacific Railroad, the lodge burned down in 1932 and was rebuilt in 1937. Inside, an expansive 50-foot-high lobby opens onto an octagonal sunroom with three enormous windows offering picturesque views of the canyon. You can also enjoy the views in a chair on one of two long decks outside the sunroom. For a cool treat, descend the lodge's back steps and look directly below the sunroom. There, you'll find the much darker "Moon Room." For more information see chapter 6.

4

Hikes & Other Outdoor Pursuits in the Grand Canyon

There's no better way to enjoy the canyon than by walking right down into it and seeing all the rock layers and the plant and animal life up close. You can day-hike part of the way into the canyon on a number of trails.

Although hiking below the rims is the most stimulating way to experience the canyon, it can also be dangerous, especially at midday during summer. If it's hot out or you aren't up to climbing, consider walking on one of the rim trails or on the new greenway being constructed on the South Rim. The rim trails are especially nice in the forests on the North Rim.

On the South Rim, the wide, lush **Bright Angel Trail** is the least difficult canyon trail for day hikers. It is well maintained, has shade and drinking water, and is less steep than other canyon trails. A few well-prepared hikers will be comfortable traveling 6 miles one way to the end of the **Plateau Point Trail** 🐾, which departs from the Tonto Trail just north of where the Tonto crosses the Bright Angel Trail. If you go any farther on a day hike, there's a good chance that you'll run out of energy and/or daylight while climbing back to the rim.

Other popular day hikes on the South Rim include the **South Kaibab Trail** to Cedar Ridge, the **Hermit Trail** to either Dripping Springs (via the Dripping Springs Trail) or Santa Maria Spring, and the **Grandview Trail** to Horseshoe Mesa. Because it is steeper and has no water and little shade, the South Kaibab Trail is considered more strenuous than the Bright Angel Trail, but it offers panoramic views. The Hermit and Grandview trails, which are unmaintained and very steep in places, are more rugged than the South Kaibab.

On the North Rim the **North Kaibab Trail,** which has seasonal water and abundant shade, is the best option for day hikers descending into the canyon. Day hikers, as a rule, shouldn't go farther than Roaring Springs, 4.7 miles and 3,000 vertical feet below the trailhead. Even strong hikers may have problems returning to the rim before sunset, if they go past Roaring Springs on a day hike.

The trail descriptions later in this chapter cover many canyon paths, including turn-around points for day hikers. However, because of remote locations and/or rugged conditions, the **South Bass, North Bass, Nankoweap, Tanner, New Hance, Boucher, Thunder River, Bill Hall** and **Deer Creek** trails are not covered in this book. You can ask questions about these trails and obtain free trail descriptions at the Backcountry Information Center (*©* **928/ 638-7875**). More detailed descriptions can be found in guidebooks and individual trail guides sold through the Grand Canyon Association (*©* **800/858-2808**).

Wherever you hike, carry plenty of water and know where the next water sources are. Eat and drink regularly. If you hike into the canyon, allow yourself twice as much time for the trip out as for the descent.

BACKPACKING FOR BEGINNERS

By camping inside the canyon, you can give yourself time to explore the lower elevations of the park. However, the extreme changes in temperature and elevation can make the Grand Canyon a nightmare for inexperienced or unprepared backpackers. The jarring descent strains your knees; the climb out tests your heart. Extreme heat often precludes hiking during the middle of the day, and water is scarce. Because of these hazards, a first-time backpacker should consider hiking on gentler terrain before venturing into the canyon.

1 Preparing for Your Backcountry Trip

PACKING TIPS FOR BACKPACKERS

What you carry (or don't) in your pack is just as important as your choice of trails. Warm temperatures and dry weather make the canyon an ideal place for traveling light. Lighten your load by carrying dry food such as instant beans and ramen noodles. In summer, you can go lighter still by leaving the stove at home and preparing cold meals. Some foods that are usually heated, like ramen noodles or couscous, will soften in cold water—even inside a water bottle— over time. During early summer, carry a tent's rain fly or bivy sack instead of a tent. At this time of year, you're more likely to die of problems related to heat—and heavy packs—than from the cold. Just be sure you know how to rig your shelter, in case rain does fall.

Also, make sure you have enough water containers. I usually carry 6 to 8 quarts in summer and sometimes, for long, waterless walks, bring even more. Drink all the time—start before you get thirsty—and refill your bottles whenever you have the chance.

Recommended Hiking Distances

The following is a list of trails recommended for day hikers, and the farthest point that day hikers should try to go on them.

For Less-Experienced Hikers:

South Rim Trail	2.1 miles one-way
West Rim Trail	8 miles one-way
Bright Angel Point Trail	0.25 miles one way
Transept Trail	1.5 miles one-way
Widforss Trail	5 miles one-way
Bright Angel Trail to Mile-and-a-Half-House	1.5 miles one-way
North Kaibab Trail to Supai Tunnel	2.7 miles one-way

For Fit, Well-Prepared Hikers:

South Kaibab Trail to Cedar Ridge	1.5 miles one-way
North Kaibab Trail to Roaring Springs	4.7 miles one-way
Bright Angel Trail to Indian Garden or to Plateau Point	4.6 miles one-way / 6.1 miles one-way
Grandview Trail to Horseshoe Mesa	3.0 miles one-way
Hermit Trail to Santa Maria Spring	2.5 miles one-way
Hermit and Dripping Springs Trails to Dripping Springs	3.0 miles one-way

Eating carbohydrate-rich, salty food is just as important. If you guzzle too much water without eating, you run the risk of developing an electrolyte imbalance that can result in unconsciousness or death. Loss of appetite is common during a hike. Try to eat every time you take a drink, even if you don't feel hungry. Also, carry powdered Gatorade or another electrolyte replacement drink. See "Equipment Checklist," below.

GETTING PERMITS

Permits are required for all overnight camping in the backcountry that falls within the park's boundaries. This includes all overnight stays below the rims (except in the cabins and dorms at Phantom Ranch) and on park land outside of designated campgrounds. Good for up to 11 people, each permit costs $10 plus an additional $5 per person per night.

Regular hikers can purchase a **Frequent Hiker Membership,** which costs $25 but waives the $10 permit fee for a year from the date of purchase.

Permits for the month desired go on sale on the first of the month, more than 4 months earlier. For example, permits for all of May go on sale on January 1; permits for June go on sale February 1, and so on. If you're not purchasing a permit in person, you'll need to complete a **Backcountry Permit Request Form,** included in the free Backcountry Trip Planner mailed out by the park. The Backcountry Trip Planners also suggest itineraries for first-time Canyon hikers and offer advice on safe, low-impact hiking. To receive one, call the park's main extension at ✆ **928-638-7888** and choose the "backcountry information" option. Or, write to Grand Canyon National Park, P.O. Box 129, Grand Canyon, AZ 86023, and request a **Backcountry Trip Planner** (not to be confused with one of the park's regular trip planners). You can also download a Permit Request Form and instructions by surfing to **www.nps.gov/grca**. To increase your odds of receiving a permit, be as flexible as possible when filling out the form. It helps to request three alternative hikes, in order of preference, and more than one starting date. Keeping your group small also helps.

Once you fill out your Permit Request Form, you can take it in person to the Backcountry Information Center on either rim; fax it to ✆ 928/638-2125 no earlier than the date the permits become available, or mail it postmarked no earlier than that date. No requests are taken by phone. Allow one to three weeks for processing, after the Backcountry Information Center receives your form.

If you have questions about a trail or about the process itself, the Backcountry Information Center, at ✆ **928/638-7875,** takes calls weekdays between 1 and 5pm Mountain Standard Time. You can visit the office in person from 8am to noon and 1 to 5pm daily. The **North Rim Backcountry Office,** which keeps the same hours as the main (South Rim) office but closes seasonally, can be reached at ✆ **928/638-7868.**

Permits can sometimes be obtained in person outside the park's developed areas (and in some cases, outside the park) at the **Kaibab Plateau Visitor Center** (✆ 928/643-7298) in Jacob Lake, AZ; at **Pipe Spring National Monument** (✆ 928/643-7105) near Fredonia, AZ; and at Ranger stations at **Tuweep, Meadview,** and **Lee's Ferry.** The Kaibab Plateau location is particularly convenient for backpackers hoping to hike the Nankoweap, North Bass, Bill

⟋ Equipment Checklist

- Tent or light shelter
- Ground cloth
- Sleeping bag (very lightweight in summer)
- Sleeping bag stuff sack (can be used to hang food)
- Sleeping pad
- Patch kit (if pad is inflatable)
- Backpack (external frame is better)
- Signal mirror
- Compass
- Headlamp with batteries
- Spare batteries and bulbs
- First-aid kit (adhesive tape, supportive elastic wrap, mole-skin, mole foam, iodine, gauze pads, bandages, aspirin, antihistamine, diarrhea medication, tweezers)
- Water-purifying tablets (pumps often clog)
- Two 1-quart unbreakable plastic water bottles plus one or two 4-liter nylon water bags
- Small plastic or collapsible metal shovel for burying human waste
- Waterproof matches
- Lightweight campstove and fuel (optional)
- Stove repair kit and spare parts (if carrying stove)
- Topo maps
- Trail descriptions published by the Backcountry Information Center
- Swiss army knife
- Eating utensil
- Lightweight cooking pot
- Hiking boots
- Two long-sleeved T-shirts
- One pair shorts

Hall, or Thunder River Trails, all of which are accessed via roads through the Kaibab National Forest. At the Pipe Spring, Tuweep, Meadview, and Lee's Ferry locations, you may not always find personnel capable of processing your request.

- Thick socks
- Breathable water-resistant shell
- Polypropylene underwear (top and bottom)
- Polar fleece leggings and uppers (seasonal)
- Winter cap and gloves (seasonal)
- Wide-brimmed hat
- 100% UV protection sunglasses
- High SPF sunscreen and lip balm
- Extra plastic freezer bags
- Toilet paper
- Garbage bag
- Notebook and pen (optional)
- Lightweight camera and film (optional)
- ¼-inch nylon rope (if necessary for hike)
- Trail mix
- Ramen noodles
- Dehydrated beans
- Dried foods
- Granola bars
- Turkey or beef jerky
- Energy bars
- Dried milk
- Cold cereal
- Raisins
- Crackers
- Very hard cheese
- Salted peanut butter (in plastic jar)
- Bagels

Note: Dried or freeze-dried food is fine only if you have access to water. If not, take food that doesn't require water during preparation.

2 Exploring the Backcountry

For the purposes of this book, I've divided the park trails into three categories: corridor, wilderness, and rim. In the Grand Canyon, most of the rim trails and all of the corridor and wilderness trails are considered part of the backcountry.

Backcountry Permit Waiting List

If you show up at the park without a permit and find the backcountry booked, you may be able to obtain one by putting your name on the waiting list. If you want to hike the corridor trails during the spring, summer, and fall, you should expect to spend at least one day on the waiting list before obtaining a permit. To place your name on the waiting list, show up in person at the Backcountry Information Center. The ranger will give you a number at that time. To stay on the waiting list, you'll have to show up at the Backcountry Information Center at 8am every morning until you receive an opening. Usually permits are for the next night, but occasionally, permits for that night are issued. Even though cancellations don't always happen, the center sometimes sets aside a spot or two at the Bright Angel Campground or Cottonwood Campground for people on the list.

CORRIDOR TRAILS   When descending into the canyon for the first time, even experienced backpackers should consider one of the three **corridor trails,** North Kaibab, South Kaibab, or Bright Angel, discussed in detail below. Well maintained and easy to follow, these are regularly patrolled by park rangers. Each has at least one emergency phone and pit toilet. Drinking water is available at several sources along both the Bright Angel and the North Kaibab trails, but not on the South Kaibab. (Some of these sources are seasonal.) Check at the Backcountry Information Center for current water availability before starting your hike. While hiking the corridor trails, you can spend your nights at **Bright Angel, Cottonwood, or Indian Garden** campgrounds, each of which has a ranger station, running water (seasonal at Cottonwood), and toilets.

WILDERNESS TRAILS   By hiking on corridor trails, you can acclimate yourself to the conditions in the canyon without having to negotiate the boulder-strewn and sometimes confusing **wilderness trails,** which also go into the canyon. Rangers are seldom encountered on these trails, which are not maintained by the park. These trails have washed away in some places; in others, they descend steeply through cliffs. They can also be difficult to discern. On the less-traveled wilderness trails, help can be very far away if something goes wrong.

The corridor trails provide access to backcountry campgrounds, but most wilderness trails accommodate only **at-large camping,** meaning that it's up to each hiker to find his or her own campsite. Unlike the campgrounds, the campsites along wilderness trails do not have purified water or ranger stations nearby, and only a few have pit toilets. On the busiest wilderness trails, campers may be limited to **designated sites.**

RIM TRAILS   As the name implies, rim trails travel on the rim of the canyon and do not descend into the canyon's interior. Some rim trails stay inside the park's developed areas. These are usually paved, with relatively gradual inclines. These trails can be very busy, but they sometimes afford nice views. Other rim trails go farther away from developed areas and into the nearby piñon-juniper, ponderosa pine, and spruce-fir forests. These trails have a few rugged, steeply rolling stretches, but most are quite manageable. Often uncrowded, many of these trails lead to scenic canyon overlooks.

3 Trails on the South Rim

Visitors to the South Rim have two rim trails from which to choose: the **West Rim Trail** and the **South Rim Trail.** Both start in Grand Canyon Village and travel in opposite directions along the rim, with the West Rim Trail traveling 8 miles west to Hermit's Rest and the South Rim Trail extending 2.1 miles northeast to Mather Point. Both can be very busy, especially near Grand Canyon Village. And both offer stunning canyon views while passing through rim-top scenery that is less than pristine. The South Rim Trail is paved, wide, and easy to walk on; the West Rim Trail is longer, more rugged, and has a few lonesome stretches. Unfortunately, much of it lies close to the West Rim Drive.

Tips Locations of Ranger Stations

Backcountry ranger stations are found at **Indian Garden, Phantom Ranch,** and **Cottonwood Campground** (in summer only). Emergency phones, connected to the park's 24-hour dispatch, are at the rest houses along the Bright Angel Trail and near the intersection of the South Kaibab and Tonto trails. On the **North Kaibab Trail,** an emergency phone can be found near Roaring Springs.

> ## A Note About Difficulty of Trails
>
> Because of the huge elevation changes on the canyon trails, none should be called easy. (More people are rescued off the Bright Angel Trail, generally considered the "easiest" trail into the canyon, than off any other trail.) In general, please note that rating a trail easy, moderate, or difficult oversimplifies the situation. For example, the **Hermit Trail** is easy to follow and relatively gradual between the rim and just above Santa Maria Spring, but it's considerably more rugged after that; the **Tonto Trail** is easy to walk on in places, but has almost no water and very little shade. The following is a very subjective ranking of some of the most popular trails that go from the rim into the canyon from **least to most difficult.**
>
> | South Rim | North Rim |
> |-----------|-----------|
> | Bright Angel | North Kaibab |
> | South Kaibab | Thunder River |
> | Grandview | Bill Hall/Thunder River |
> | Hermit | Nankoweap |
> | Hermit/Dripping Spring/Boucher | North Bass |

West Rim Trail   **Highlights:** Beats riding the bus to all the overlooks. **Drawbacks:** Seeing and hearing the buses, and the crowds at the overlooks. **Difficulty:** One steep climb; tricky footing in isolated locations.

Don't let the name of this trail confuse you. The West Rim Trail meanders along the *South Rim* of the canyon, from Grand Canyon Village all the way to Hermit's Rest. (If you go looking for a west rim of the canyon, you may end up in Lake Mead.) In doing so, it travels near the West Rim Drive and passes through all the same scenic overlooks, described in the driving tour (see chapter 3). Walking instead of driving along this stretch of road is a great way to see the canyon while putting some elbow room between yourself and the crowds at the overlooks. The 1.25-mile stretch from the village to Maricopa Point is paved, with one 200-vertical-foot climb. Past Maricopa Point, the trail planes off somewhat and the pavement ends. For the rest of the way to Hermit's Rest, the trail becomes a series of footpaths that meander through piñon-juniper woodland along the rim (when not crossing overlooks). Sagebrush roots and loose rocks make for tricky footing, but the scenery is lovely, and the crowds thin as you move farther west. The nicest stretch is between the Abyss and Pima Point. Here, the trail detours away from the West Rim Drive, going towards the canyon and away from the road. This is one of the few places on the trail where you won't hear an occasional bus.

As 16 miles might be too much hiking for 1 day, I recommend hiking out on this trail from Grand Canyon Village and taking the shuttle back (mid-Mar through mid-Oct). By hiking out, you can avoid revisiting the same overlooks on the shuttle ride back—the shuttles stop at every turnout while en route to Hermit's Rest, but only stop at Mohave Point and Hopi Point on their way back to Grand Canyon Village.

If you don't want to walk the whole 8 miles, here's a list of distances, which will help determine how far you've gone and whether you want to continue to the next lookout.

Trailhead to Trailview I:	0.6 miles
Trailview I to Maricopa Point:	0.7 miles
Maricopa Point to Powell Point:	0.5 miles
Powell Point to Hopi Point:	0.3 miles
Hopi Point to Mohave Point:	0.8 miles
Mohave Point to the Abyss:	1.1 miles
The Abyss to Pima Point:	2.9 miles
Pima Point to Hermit's Rest:	1.1 miles

8 miles to Hermit's Rest. Access: Rim-side sidewalk at the west end of Grand Canyon Village. Water sources at Grand Canyon Village, Hermit's Rest, Park Headquarters, and Yavapai Point. Maps: Trails Illustrated Topo Map or Village Area Map (included in *The Guide*).

South Rim Trail   **Highlights:** Paved, easy to walk on, and close to the edge. **Drawbacks:** More crowded than the West Rim Trail. **Difficulty:** A boulevard. The sidewalk is so wide, it's more like a road than a trail.

This smooth, paved trail connects Grand Canyon Village and Mather Point. Around the lodges, the path is a flat sidewalk teeming with people. The crowds dissipate somewhat between the east edge of the village and Yavapai Point. Near Yavapai Point, you'll find many smooth flat rocks along the rim—great places from which to contemplate the canyon. Located 1.5 miles northeast of the Historic District in Grand Canyon Village, **Yavapai Point** has a historic (1928) observation station with large windows overlooking the canyon. From here, you can walk another 0.6 miles to Mather Point on a portion of the park's new greenway (and even farther in the

Note About Trail Descriptions

The trail descriptions in this chapter are not intended for use in route finding. It's up to each hiker to hike smart, be physically fit, and have the skills and equipment needed to stay on the trail. Also, more detailed trail descriptions are available. The Grand Canyon Association (*©* **800/858-2808**) publishes a number of guides to the most popular trails.

near future). This 10-foot-wide, paved walkway usually travels within a few feet of the rim. It takes you away from the crowds and provides ever-changing canyon views. If you grow fatigued during your walk, you can catch shuttles at Mather or Yavapai Points.

2.1 miles to Mather Point. Access: Grand Canyon Village, along the rim behind the El Tovar Hotel. Water sources at Grand Canyon Village, Hermit's Rest, Park Headquarters, and Yavapai Point. **Maps:** Trails Illustrated Topo Map or Village Area Map (included in *The Guide*).

4 Trails on the North Rim

The rim trails on the North Rim rank among the park's treasures. Start with either the **Transept Trail** or the **Bright Angel Point Trail,** which are different sections of the same pathway. At the bottom of the stairs behind Grand Canyon Lodge, the Bright Angel Point Trail goes to the left, while the Transept Trail goes right. The Bright Angel Point Trail is a short (quarter-mile) paved path to a stunning overlook on a tiny peninsula between Transept and Bright Angel Canyons. It's nearly always crowded, but well worth seeing. The Transept Trail is longer, more thickly forested, and far less crowded, but it has less panoramic views.

Bright Angel Point Trail *✿* **Highlights:** Stunning views of Transept and Bright Angel Canyons. **Drawbacks:** Crowds at Bright Angel Point Overlook. **Difficulty:** Safe and easy, unless there's lightning.

This paved trail travels a quarter mile along a narrow peninsula dividing Roaring Springs and Transept canyons. On the way, it passes a number of craggy outcroppings of Kaibab Limestone, around which the roots of wind-whipped juniper trees cling like arthritic hands. Although the trail stays at about the same level as the rim, junipers supplant ponderosa pines here because of the warm winds that blow out of the canyon. The trail ends at 8,148-foot-high Bright Angel Point. From this overlook you can

⛺	Campground
⛽	Gas Station
☎	Phone
🏕	Picnic Area
▲	Primitive Campsite
🏠	Ranger Station
🚻	Restrooms

0   2 mi

0   2 km

Point Imperial

Mt. Hayden

Nankoweap Creek

67

Ken Patrick Trail

Bright Angel Spring

Uncle Jim Trail

North Rim Store

Uncle Jim Point

Vista Encantadora

Widforss Trail

North Kaibab Trail

Transept Trail

Roaring Springs

WALHALLA PLATEAU

Grand Canyon Lodge

Bright Angel Point

THE TRANSEPT

Cape Royal Rd.

Widforss Point

Manu Temple

Cottonwood

Buddha Temple

Deva Temple

Bright Angel Creek

Hillers Butte

BRIGHT ANGEL CANYON

Scheilbach Butte

Brahma Temple

Cape Final

Walhalla Overlook

Zoroaster Temple

OTTOMAN AMPHITHEATER

Cliff Spring Trail

Angels Window

Phantom Creek

Cape Royal

Clear Creek Trail

Cape Royal Trail

follow Bright Angel Canyon (with your eyes) to its intersection with the larger gorge of the Colorado River. On a quiet day, you can hear Roaring Springs, a tributary of Bright Angel Creek and the water source for both the North and the South rims of the canyon.

0.25 mile each way. Access: By descending the back steps off the patios at Grand Canyon Lodge. Water source at Grand Canyon Lodge. Map: *The Guide.*

The Transept Trail ✿ **Highlights:** Ponderosa pine forest and views of Transept Canyon. **Drawbacks:** May be busy, especially near Grand Canyon Lodge. **Difficulty:** Generally easy. Its undulations provide interval training.

Traveling 1.5 miles northeast along the rim of Transept Canyon, this trail connects the lodge and the North Rim Campground. Passing through old-growth ponderosa pine and quaking aspen, it descends into, then climbs out of, three shallow side drainages, with ascents steep enough to take the breath away from people unaccustomed to the 8,000-foot altitude. A small Indian ruin sits alongside the dirt.

1.5 miles each way. Access: Behind North Rim General Store (near the campground), or by descending the back steps off the patios at Grand Canyon Lodge. Map: *The Guide.*

Ken Patrick Trail ⋒ **Highlights:** A stretch skirts the rim; nice views of Nankoweap Creek drainages. **Drawbacks:** Mule-trampled near North Kaibab Trailhead parking lot, faint in other spots, and steeply rolling near Point Imperial. **Difficulty:** The longest, faintest, most scratchy—and all around toughest—rim trail.

This long, steeply rolling trail travels through ponderosa pine and spruce-fir forest between the head of Roaring Springs Canyon and Point Imperial. Along the way, it poses a number of challenges. Starting at the North Kaibab end, the first mile of the trail has been pounded into a dustlike flour (where not watered down into something resembling cake batter) by mules. Where the mules turn around after a mile, the trail becomes faint. It becomes even less distinct about 4 miles in, after passing the trailhead for the old Bright Angel Trail.

After crossing the Cape Royal Road (the only road that you encounter, about two-thirds of the way to Point Imperial), the trail descends into, then climbs out of, a very steep drainage overgrown with thorn-covered New Mexican locust. While challenging, the 3-mile stretch between the road and Point Imperial is also the prettiest on the trail, skirting the rim of the canyon above upper drainages of Nankoweap Creek. In these areas you'll see plenty of scarlet bugler, identifiable by tubular red flowers with flared lower petals, as well as a number of Douglas firs interspersed among the ubiquitous ponderosa pines.

10 miles each way. Access: From the south side of the parking area for Point Imperial or from the parking area for the North Kaibab Trail (on the North Rim entrance rd., 2 miles north of Grand Canyon Lodge). No water sources. Maps: Trails Illustrated Topo Map.

Uncle Jim Trail **Highlights:** Views of Bright Angel and Roaring Springs canyons, and easy access make this a great place for a picnic. **Drawbacks:** Mule traffic. **Difficulty:** Has some hills, but is suitable for families.

Shooting the Canyon: Tips for Photographers

It's not easy to capture the canyon's spirit on film. Here are some tips to help you take the best possible photos:

A **polarizing filter** is a great investment if you have the kind of camera that will accept lens filters. It reduces haze, lessens the contrast between shadowy areas and light areas, and deepens the color of the sky.

The best times to photograph the canyon are at **sunrise** and **sunset,** when filtered and sharply angled sunlight paints the canyon walls in beautiful shades of lavender and pink. At these times the shadows are also at their most dramatic. To capture these ephemeral moments, it's best to use a tripod and a long exposure. The worst time to photograph the canyon is at noon when there are almost no shadows, and thus little texture or contrast. *The Guide,* the park's official visitor newspaper, includes a table with sunrise and sunset times.

Keep in mind that the Grand Canyon is immense. A wide-angle lens may leave the canyon looking on paper like a distant plane of dirt. Try zooming in on narrower sections of the canyon to emphasize a single dramatic landscape element. Or, if you're shooting with a wide-angle lens, try to include something in the foreground (people or a tree branch) to give the photo perspective and scale.

When shooting portraits against a sunrise or sunset, use a flash to illuminate your subjects; otherwise your camera meter may expose for the bright light in the background and leave your subjects in shadow.

—*by Karl Samson*

A lasso-shaped loop accessible via the Ken Patrick Trail, the Uncle Jim Trail circles Uncle Jim Point, which divides Roaring Springs and Bright Angel canyons. By taking the right branch of the lasso, you'll soon reach an overlook near the tip of Uncle Jim Point, named for a former game warden, Jim Owens, who slaughtered hundreds of mountain lions on the North Rim in the early 1900s. (Owens's handiwork, part of a misguided predator-control program, may have contributed to an explosion in the deer population and an ensuing famine.) From here, you'll have views across Roaring Springs Canyon to Bright Angel Point and up Roaring Springs Canyon, to where the upper switchbacks of the North Kaibab Trail are visible. This overlook is a scenic, easily accessible spot for a picnic lunch. After passing it, the trail skirts the edge of Bright Angel Canyon before looping back.

5 miles round-trip (including Ken Patrick Trail). Access: 1 miles down Ken Patrick Trail from North Kaibab trailhead parking area. No water sources. Maps: Trails Illustrated Topo Map.

Cape Final Trail   Highlights: An uncrowded, flat, boulder-free walk to a canyon overlook. **Drawbacks:** Parking area is easy to miss. **Difficulty:** Nice and easy.

Because this trail is relatively flat and boulder free, it's a good choice for a first hike in the backcountry. It meanders through ponderosa pine forest on an old Jeep trail, ending at Cape Final, where you'll have views of the northern canyon and Juno Temple.

2 miles each way. Access: An unmarked dirt parking area off the Cape Royal Rd., 4.9 miles south of Roosevelt Point. No water sources. Map: Trails Illustrated Topo Map.

Cliff Springs Trail ⚐   Highlights: Passes springs and an Ancestral Pueblo granary. **Drawbacks:** A few rocky stretches. **Difficulty:** Craggy spots pose challenges for people lacking agility.

Both scenic and fairly short, this is a nice hike for most families. Although this dirt trail seems at first to head into forest *away* from the canyon, it quickly descends into a narrow, rocky canyon that drains into the larger one—a reminder that the Walhalla Plateau is a peninsula in Grand Canyon. Spruce and fir trees dominate the northern exposures in this side canyon, while ponderosa pines and even piñon and juniper trees grow in the sunnier spots. Roughly a quarter mile from the trailhead, the trail passes a small Ancestral Pueblo granary. After crossing a small drainage, it hugs the north wall of the side canyon, passing under limestone overhangs, in light colored green by the canopies of box elder trees (identifiable by their leaflets in groups of three and by their double-winged fruit). The springs drip from one of these overhangs, where mosses carpet the fissures in the rock. A waist-high boulder marks the end of the trail.

5 miles each way. Access: A small pullout 0.3 mile north of Cape Royal on the Cape Royal Rd. Water sources at Cliff Springs (purify before drinking). Map: Trails Illustrated Topo Map.

Widforss Trail ⚐⚐   Highlights: A nice escape into ponderosa pine forest, culminating with canyon views from Widforss Point.

Drawbacks: Much of the trail is away from the rim, with the canyon out of sight. **Difficulty:** Distance and rolling terrain combine to make this a challenge.

This trail, named for Gunnar Widforss, a landscape painter, may be the nicest rim hike in the park. It curves around the head of Transept Canyon before venturing south to Widforss Point. A brochure, sometimes available at the trailhead, explains points of interest in the first 2 miles, during which the trail undulates through ponderosa pine and Spruce–Fir forest.

At the head of Transept Canyon, about halfway to Widforss Point, you'll pass several nice overlooks that make for good resting spots. You'll also see a balancing rock, formed when water seeping across planes in the rock eroded beds of Kaibab Limestone from underneath the ones above.

Past the head of Transept Canyon, the trail heads south through old-growth ponderosa pine, and the canyon passes out of view. Under the red-orange-trunked trees, lupine blankets the forest floor with blue flowers. You'll also note a number of badly singed pines. In the late '90s the National Park Service conducted prescribed burns in this area, eliminating excess deadfall and undergrowth from the forest floor. Burns like these are designed to bring the forest closer to its natural state. Before humans began suppressing blazes, natural fires swept through the ponderosa pine forest an average of every 7 to 10 years. (For more on prescribed burns, see chapter 8.)

The trail, remaining hilly most of the way, reaches the rim again at Widforss Point. There, you'll have a nice view of five temples. The three to the southeast are Zoroaster (farthest south), Brahma (north of Zoroaster), and Deva (farthest north); to the southwest, Buddha Temple sits like a sphinx with two long legs. Out of one of those legs rises Manu Temple. Near the rim are a picnic table and several good campsites.

5 miles each way. Access: A dirt road 0.25 mile south of the Cape Royal Rd. Follow this road 0.7 mile to the parking area, which is well marked. No water sources. Map: Trails Illustrated Topo Map.

5 South Rim Corridor Trails

Bright Angel Trail ✿ **Highlights:** Long stretches near lush, cool creekbeds. **Drawbacks:** During high season, you'll pass hundreds of hikers and a few mules. **Difficulty:** Water sources, ample shade, and a wide, well-maintained surface; the most accommodating trail into the canyon from the South Rim.

Both Native Americans and early settlers recognized this as a choice location for a trail into the canyon. First, there's an enormous fault line, along which so much erosion has taken place that even the usually sheer Redwall Limestone holds vegetation. Then there's the water—more of it than in any other place on the South Rim. The springs at Indian Garden supplied Grand Canyon Village as late as 1970.

For centuries, the Havasupai used this trail to descend from the rim, where they hunted in winter, to Indian Garden, where they farmed year-round. This went on until the 1920s when the Park Service expelled the remaining tribe members. Although most of the Havasupai now live on a reservation in the central canyon, a few of their pictographs (rock paintings made with mineral dyes) remain along the trail. Some are high on the rocks just past the first tunnel; others can be seen on a sandstone overhang above Two-Mile Corner, the first switchback below Mile-and-a-Half Rest House.

When Pete Berry, Niles Cameron, and Ralph Cameron prospected for minerals here in the late 1800s, they improved the trail to the point where most people could hike it. As more visitors came to the canyon, Ralph Cameron realized that the trail might be more lucrative than gold. He bought out his partners, then used mining law to take control of the land near and below Grand Canyon Village. Although the Santa Fe Railroad challenged his authority in the early 1900s, it wasn't until the 1920s that Cameron lost the trail. By then he had charged countless hikers a $1 fee to descend it.

If Cameron earned a dollar for every hiker on this trail today, he'd be doing just fine. More than 500,000 people hike on the Grand Canyon's three corridor trails (South and North Kaibab, and Bright Angel) every year, and the Bright Angel is the most popular. It's a freeway: wide, dusty, relatively gradual, with some occasional mule manure thrown in.

On a day hike, walk down to **Mile-and-a-Half House** or **Three-Mile House,** each of which has shade, an emergency phone, and seasonal drinking water. Or continue down to the picnic area near the spring at Indian Garden, where lush vegetation will surround you and large cottonwood trees provide shade.

Watch the layers on this trail as you descend. As you move from the Kaibab Formation to the Toroweap Formation, the wall on your left will gradually turn from cream-colored to pinkish-white. After the second tunnel you'll start down through the steep buff-colored cliffs that form the Coconino Sandstone. As you do, compare the elevations of the cliffs on either side of the fault. The ones to the

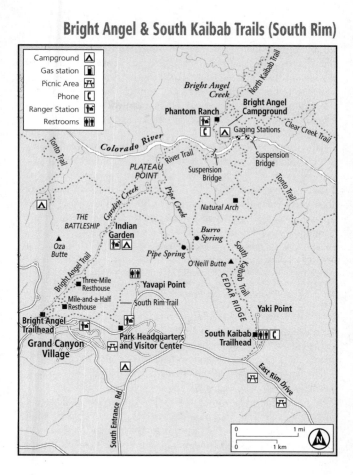

Map legend:
- Campground △
- Gas station
- Picnic Area
- Phone
- Ranger Station
- Restrooms

Map labels: Bright Angel Creek, North Kaibab Trail, Phantom Ranch, Bright Angel Campground, Gaging Stations, Clear Creek Trail, Tonto Trail, Colorado River, River Trail, Suspension Bridge, Suspension Bridge, PLATEAU POINT, Pipe Creek, Natural Arch, Tonto Trail, Garden Creek, THE BATTLESHIP, Indian Garden, Burro Spring, Oza Butte, Pipe Spring, O'Neill Butte, South Kaibab Trail, Bright Angel Trail, Three-Mile Resthouse, Yavapai Point, CEDAR RIDGE, Mile-and-a-Half Resthouse, South Rim Trail, Yaki Point, Bright Angel Trailhead, Grand Canyon Village, Park Headquarters and Visitor Center, South Kaibab Trailhead, South Entrance Rd., East Rim Drive

Scale: 0 — 1 mi / 0 — 1 km N

west have been offset and are 189 feet higher. At the bottom of the
Coconino Sandstone, the Hermit Shale, deep red in color, is visibly
eroding out from under the harder cliffs above it. This weakens the
cliffs, which then break off along joints.

After dropping through the Supai Group and Redwall layers, the
trail begins its long, direct descent to Indian Garden. As you near
Indian Garden, you'll begin to see species found near water, including willow, mesquite, catclaw acacia, and even Arizona grape, a
native species that grows tart but edible grapes. In spring, the purple
blooms on the redbud are bright enough to be seen from the rim.
Fit, well-prepared day hikers may wish to hike an additional

1.5 miles past Indian Garden on the Tonto and Plateau Point trails. The Plateau Point Trail eventually crosses the Tonto Platform to an overlook of the Colorado River, 1,300 feet below.

Below Indian Garden, the Bright Angel Trail follows Garden Creek down a narrow canyon in the Tapeats Sandstone. After leaving the Garden Creek drainage, the trail descends through much of the Vishnu Formation in a series of switchbacks known as the Devil's Corkscrew. It then follows Pipe Creek to the Colorado River and the junction with the River Trail. There you'll find a small rest house with an emergency phone and pit toilet—but no pretreated drinking water. After skirting the river for 1.7 miles on the River Trail, you'll reach the Silver Suspension Bridge. When you cross it, you'll be near **Bright Angel Campground.** See "Backcountry Campgrounds," later in this chapter.

4.6 miles to Indian Garden; 7.8 miles to Colorado River; 9.3 miles to Bright Angel Campground. Access: Trailhead is just west of Kolb Studio, near Grand Canyon Village. Water sources at Mile-and-a-Half Rest House (seasonal), Three-Mile Rest House (seasonal), Indian Garden, Colorado River, Bright Angel Campground. Maps: Grand Canyon (7.5 min.), Phantom Ranch (7.5 min.).

South Kaibab Trail 🏃🏃   Highlights: Panoramic views for much of the distance from the rim to the river. **Drawbacks:** Mule traffic and its byproducts. **Difficulty:** You won't find water, abundant shade, or shelter; more dangerous than the Bright Angel—and steeper.

The South Kaibab Trail was the Park Service's way of bypassing Ralph Cameron, who controlled the Bright Angel Trail in the early 1900s. Cameron used mining law to lay claim to the land around the Bright Angel Trail and charged $1 to every person descending it. Later, as a senator, he pushed to deny funding for the Park Service. In 1924, exasperated by Cameron's maneuverings, the Park Service began to build the South Kaibab Trail, which, like the Bright Angel Trail, linked Grand Canyon Village with the Colorado River and Phantom Ranch. Unlike the Bright Angel Trail, which follows natural routes into the canyon, this one was built using dynamite and hard labor.

The South Kaibab Trail begins by making a series of switchbacks through the upper rock layers. As you descend the Kaibab Formation, note the Douglas firs, remnants of the last Ice Age. After that Ice Age ended 10,000 years ago, the firs retreated off the South Rim, clinging only to a few due-north slopes where they received almost no direct sunlight. As the trail descends the Coconino Sandstone, watch for evidence of cross-bedding—diagonal lines formed by windblown sand in an ancient desert.

Below the Coconino, the trail descends onto Cedar Ridge, a platform that has pit toilets and a hitching post for mules. This is an excellent place for day hikers to picnic and rest before hiking the 1.5 miles back out. Continuing northward down the ridge, it then reaches a saddle underneath O'Neill Butte, with views 1,000 feet down to the Tonto Platform on either side. The trail then rounds the east flank of the butte, eventually reaching another saddle. It descends in steep switchbacks through the Redwall, then slices downhill across the Tonto Platform toward the Inner Gorge. From the Tonto Platform, make sure to glance back at the natural rock bridge in the cliffs. At the tip-off, where the trail begins its drop into the Inner Gorge, an emergency telephone and toilet are available.

As you begin your descent of the Tapeats Sandstone, you'll see the Colorado River between the dark, sheer walls of the Inner Gorge. The pink in the otherwise black walls is Zoroaster Granite, formed 1.2 billion years ago when molten rock was squeezed into fissures in the Vishnu Schist. From here it's an hour's walk to the Kaibab Suspension Bridge and Bright Angel Campground.

Note: From March through November, you cannot drive to the South Kaibab trailhead. The park's free shuttle service begins ferrying hikers to the trailhead at least one hour before sunrise every morning.

6.3 miles to Colorado River; 7.3 miles to Bright Angel Campground. Access: Trailhead at Yaki Point (Hwy. 64, E. Rim Dr., 5 miles east of Grand Canyon Village). Water sources at Colorado River and Bright Angel Campground. Maps: Phantom Ranch (7.5 min.) quadrangle.

6 North Rim Corridor Trail

North Kaibab Trail ⋆⋆ **Highlights:** Less crowded than the Bright Angel Trail. Great for a first backpack trip into the canyon. **Drawbacks:** At 14.4 miles and with a vertical drop of 5,850 feet, it's much longer, and drops farther, than the South Rim corridor trails. **Difficulty:** Descends gradually from rim to river. Ample water and shade. Tests endurance more than agility.

Forget the myth about corridor trails being easy. The North Kaibab Trail will test any hiker who attempts to go from rim to river (or vice versa) in a day. By comparison, the South Rim corridor trails, the Bright Angel and South Kaibab, travel 9.2 and 6.7 miles, respectively, and fall about 4,800 vertical feet from rim to river. Despite the length and the big vertical drop, the North Kaibab Trail may be the nicest place for backpackers to first experience the canyon. The scenery is lovely, the grades on the trail manageable.

The North Kaibab has beautiful views down two side canyons—Roaring Springs and Bright Angel—but unlike the South Rim trails, you see less of the gorge cut by the Colorado River. It's also less crowded than the South Rim corridor trails.

The trail begins with a long series of switchbacks down the head of Roaring Springs Canyon. At over 8,000 feet, the first switchbacks are in thickly forested terrain that could just as easily be found in the Rocky Mountains. Aspen, Douglas fir, and Gambel oak shade the trail and hide many of the rocks in the Kaibab and Toroweap layers. The Coconino Sandstone, whose sheer cliffs hold too little soil for these trees, stands out against the greenery, its white rocks streaked tan and black by mineral deposits.

The next major landmark is **Supai Tunnel.** At 2.7 miles from the trailhead, and with seasonal water, shade, and rest rooms available, this is an excellent turnaround point for day hikers. Beyond the tunnel, the canyon warms up, and heat-tolerant plants such as squaw-bush, pale hoptree, piñon pine, and juniper appear. The trail descends in relatively gradual switchbacks through the Supai Group, then crosses a bridge over a creek bed. Past the bridge, the creek plummets. The trail travels along the south wall of Roaring Springs Canyon, on ledges above Redwall cliffs. A spire of Redwall Limestone known as **"The Needle"** marks the point where the trail begins its descent of the Redwall.

Roaring Springs, the water source for both rims, becomes audible just above the confluence of Bright Angel and Roaring Springs canyons. A 0.2-mile-long spur trail descends to the springs, where water pours from an opening in the Muav Limestone and cascades downhill, pooling at the bottom of the creek bed. Around those pools grow Arizona grape, scouring rushes, and box elder and

---

Tips Bright Angel or South Kaibab—Which to Choose?

The South Kaibab trail is steeper and shorter than the Bright Angel Trail. And while the Bright Angel offers ample shade and water, the South Kaibab has no water and little shade. Strong backpackers planning to do a loop hike to Phantom Ranch should descend the South Kaibab Trail and climb out on the easier Bright Angel Trail. To break up the hike, spend one night at Bright Angel Campground and one at Indian Garden.

cottonwood trees. You'll find drinking water, shade, and picnic tables here. This is the farthest a day hiker should go.

Below the springs are a pump house, a heliport, and a residence for the pump house operator. In this area, the trail begins a long, gradual descent to the Colorado River, traveling on or near the floor of Bright Angel Canyon for most of the way. The rocks along this stretch can be difficult to sort out. In addition to the layers seen everywhere in the canyon, you'll find members of the Grand Canyon Supergroup, including the reddish-brown Dox Sandstone, purplish Shinumo Quartzite, orange-red Hakatai Shale, and numerous dikes and sills—places where lava filled cracks in the earth.

Two miles past Roaring Springs is Cottonwood Campground. By camping at Cottonwood Campground on the way to and from the river, backpackers can extend their trips while hiking reasonable distances.

About a mile past Cottonwood Campground, a spur trail leads to **Ribbon Falls,** the centerpiece of a large natural amphitheater. The waterfall is usually a short detour off the North Kaibab trail. But when the water level is high, you'll need to backtrack to the bridge after seeing the falls, instead of fording the river farther downstream. Even so, don't pass up a chance to hike to the base of these falls, which roll off a high sandstone ledge and arc gracefully to earth, skimming an apron of travertine on the way. This apron formed when calcium carbonate precipitated out of the water as rock. You may see small, brown birds known as dippers (the name alone describes them) fishing in the pools around these falls.

About 2.5 miles past the falls, the trail enters a long stretch of narrows known as **"The Box"** and remains there, winding alongside Bright Angel Creek, until just above Phantom Ranch. To keep hikers dry in these narrows, the Civilian Conservation Corps (CCC) in the 1930s built three bridges over the creek and blasted ledges in the cliffs of the Vishnu Formation. An immense flash flood swept away most of the originals—steel and all—in 1966. A more recent flood, in July 1999, damaged the trail so badly that it was closed for more than 2 months.

2.7 miles to Supai Tunnel; 4.7 miles to Roaring Springs; 6.8 miles to Cottonwood Campground; 14.4 miles to the Colorado River. Access: On North Rim entrance rd., 2 miles north of Grand Canyon Lodge. Water sources at Roaring Springs (seasonal), Bright Angel Creek, Cottonwood Campground (seasonal), Phantom Ranch, Bright Angel Campground. Maps: Bright Angel Point (7.5 min.) and Phantom Ranch (7.5 min.) quadrangles.

7 South Rim Wilderness Trails

Hermit Trail 𝒶𝒶   **Highlights:** Late-afternoon sun feels good on cold days. **Drawbacks:** Less panoramic than other trails from the South Rim to the river. **Difficulty:** Steep in places; washouts and rock fall complicate route finding. Cobblestone portions near the top are broken and rugged.

In 1912, the Santa Fe Railroad sought to establish a route into the canyon that Ralph Cameron, the "owner" of the Bright Angel Trail, couldn't control. So it built the Hermit Trail 8 miles west of Grand Canyon Village. Paved with sandstone slabs and with low walls on the outside, the Hermit Trail was generally regarded as the nicest in

Hermit Trail/Dripping Springs/Boucher Trails (South Rim)

the canyon in the 1910s. The vine-covered shelter at Santa Maria Spring was built at about the same time, as was Mary Colter's new building known as Hermit's Rest.

Today, the Hermit Trail remains wide at the top, with long, gradual switchbacks descending to the bottom of the Coconino Sandstone and onto the expanse of Waldron Basin. However, the old sandstone slabs have broken or slid in places, making the trail far more rugged than it was in the 1920s. Because the upper trail is on west-facing cliffs, it's cool in the morning and hot in the afternoon. Below the Coconino Sandstone, the trail, passing a few low-lying piñon and juniper trees, intersects both the Waldron and the Dripping Springs trails. Go right both times. Near the head of the brick-red Hermit Gorge, the trail makes a few switchbacks down into the Supai Group, eventually reaching a delicious water source, Santa Maria Spring. At 2.5 miles down, this spring is a nice turnaround point for day hikers. To be safe, treat the water before drinking.

Past the spring, the trail heads toward the tip of Pima Point, remaining fairly level—except when negotiating areas covered by rockfall or when making short descents, via switchbacks, lower into the Supai Group rocks. Finally, reaching a break in the Redwall, it careens downhill in tight switchbacks known as the Cathedral Stairs. Below the Redwall, the trail slices downhill, then makes a series of long switchbacks onto the Tonto Platform.

At the junction with the Tonto Trail, the Hermit Trail continues west (left) toward Hermit Creek. Later you'll reach another junction. The trail forking to the right from here descends to Hermit Creek between the Hermit Creek campsites and the Colorado River. Hikers camping at Hermit Rapids should take this shortcut. Others, including those using the Hermit Creek sites, should continue straight, passing this turnoff. In this area, you'll also find remnants of the old Hermit Camp. Guests here in the 1920s were shuttled around the camp in a Model T that had been transported to the camp in pieces and reassembled on site—a luxury you may pine for by this point.

If you do walk the 1.5 miles down the creek to the beach at Hermit Rapids, you'll pass several nice pour-overs and small pools. Along the walls, watch for sacred datura, identifiable by its large, teardrop-shaped leaves and white, lilylike flowers. You may have company at the beach—river trips frequently stop here to scout the rapids below the confluence.

Note: Backpackers planning overnight trips on the Hermit Trail can receive special permits to drive on the West Rim Drive, at the Backcountry Information Center.

2.5 miles to Santa Maria Spring; 7.8 miles to Hermit Creek; 9.3 miles to Colorado River. Access: Parking area west of Hermit's Rest. Water sources at Santa Maria Spring, Hermit Creek, and Colorado River. Maps: Grand Canyon (7.5 min.) quadrangle.

Dripping Springs Trail ᐟ **Highlights:** Uncrowded; ascends to springs in a deep alcove. **Drawbacks:** Does not afford expansive views. **Difficulty:** Relatively easy, but with a few steep inclines and some genuinely scary exposures.

Although this trail doesn't have expansive views of the inner canyon, it offers the peace and solitude needed to appreciate the desert's sounds, smells, and lighting. The most physically demanding part is the 1,340-vertical-foot descent from the Hermit Trail trailhead to the junction with the Dripping Springs Trail. On the Dripping Springs Trail, it's a gradual westward climb to the springs themselves. (There are however, a few sections of trail near the head of Hermit Gorge that roll steeply and are narrow and exposed.) The trail eventually curves into an upper drainage of Hermit Basin, rounding the base of Eremita Mesa. The springs are partway up this drainage.

The 30-foot-deep rock overhang at Dripping Springs looks like a great place for a hermit to live. Perhaps this is why everyone assumed that Louis Boucher, the prospector who lived in this area in the early 1900s, *was* a hermit. It even looks a bit like the oversized fireplace of Hermit's Rest, the building Mary Colter designed as her own tribute to a loner's way of life. Not much remains of Boucher's camp. But the springs still trickle out of the overhanging rock, through moss and maidenhair fern, and drip into a pool below. If you fill up, purify the water.

Note: Dripping Springs is also accessible via a short, steep trail from the rim directly above it. To purists, this is the real Dripping Springs Trail. Because the road to the original Dripping Springs Trail is now closed a mile or so from the trailhead, the above route is preferable for most hikers.

3 miles from Hermit trailhead to Dripping Springs. Access: Located off of the Hermit Trail at the head of Hermit Gorge. Water sources at Dripping Springs (purify before drinking). Map: Grand Canyon (7.5 min.) quadrangle.

Grandview Trail 🏃🏃   **Highlights:** An historic trail, which provides views down into two side canyons. **Drawbacks:** Cobblestone ramps become slippery when wet or icy. In winter, crampons may be required. **Difficulty:** Suitable for most fit hikers; steep and exposed in a few locations near the top.

Hiking the Grandview Trail is a great way to take in human history along with the canyon scenery. Strong day hikers can descend the 2,600 vertical feet over 3 miles to Horseshoe Mesa, look over the remnants of Pete Barry's turn-of-the-century copper mine, and still make it back to the rim for dinner. Backpackers can use it to begin or close out loop hikes. However, because the cobblestone ramps below Grandview Point become especially slick in wet weather, I'd avoid this trail during storms.

The trail itself is part of the history. All but the top 430 feet of it was built in the 1890s. (The current upper section was completed around 1910.) In some places, the trail builders used dynamite to blast away rock from sheer cliffs, forming ledges where none had been. In others they pinned a trail against the walls. To do this, they drilled holes into the rocks, pounded metal rods into the holes, then laid logs lengthwise above the rods. They then crammed rocks and dirt into openings and, as a finishing touch, paved the trail with a layer of cobblestones. Be sure to look at the trail from below to admire its structure.

For day hikers who are agile but not particularly strong, a smart place to turn around is at the saddle between upper Hance and Grapevine canyons. Known as the Coconino Saddle, it's about three-quarters of a mile from the rim. Here, you'll find shade, flat spots for resting, and views of both canyons. At the bottom of the Coconino Sandstone, the trail traverses east, then turns north, descending through the Hermit Shale and the Supai Group and onto Horseshoe Mesa. On the mesa, it intersects the Horseshoe Mesa Trail.

Whether you go right, left, or straight at this junction, you'll eventually intersect the Tonto Trail. By going right, you'll descend 700 feet through the Redwall Limestone on the southeast side of the mesa. Steep and rocky, this precarious route is the quickest path to water. Below the Redwall, a short spur trail leads to the perennial Miner's Spring. (Purify it for safety.) You'll also find several mines here, including the New Tunnel (new in 1906), with a boiler and a compressor outside. In addition to being unstable, the mines have high levels of radon, so it's best to stay out of them.

By going left, you'll descend the west side of the mesa to the ephemeral Cottonwood Creek, past where the first miners lived. By going straight, you'll travel out onto the northwest "arm" of the mesa, where you'll see the foundations of buildings from the mine camp, as well as old bottles, cans, and pieces of metal stoves. Also present, but less conspicuous, is evidence of past Indian activity: bits of chert (quartz rocks from which arrowheads were made) and old agave roasting pits. A pit toilet is available for campers in this area, who must camp in designated, posted sites.

3 miles from Grandview Trail trailhead to Horseshoe Mesa; 6.8 miles to Tonto Trail (via the East Horseshoe Mesa Trail). Access: From Grandview Point (on Hwy. 64, 12 miles east of Grand Canyon Village). No water sources on Horseshoe Mesa. Water source at Miner's Spring (off the east Horseshoe Mesa Trail, well below the rim of Horseshoe Mesa). Maps: Grandview Point (7.5 min.) and Cape Royal (7.5 min.) quadrangles.

Tonto Trail 🐾🐾   **Highlights:** Links many of the South Rim trails, creating some of the nicest loop hikes in the park. **Drawbacks:** Long, shadeless, dry stretches make knowledge of water sources imperative. **Difficulty:** Smooth and relatively level when not dipping into rocky, rugged drainages.

This 95-mile trail traverses much of the lower canyon atop the Tonto Platform. Rather than hike all of it, most people include parts in shorter loop hikes linking trails from the South Rim. Hiking here is often more strenuous than expected. Distances that look short on the map sometimes take long periods to cover, as the trail contours around numerous drainages that cut partway into the Tonto Platform. Because the platform has little to no shade, and because many of its water sources are seasonal, long hikes here during summer are ill advised. Especially dangerous are the stretches between the Grandview and South Kaibab trails and between Slate Canyon and the South Bass Trail, both of which lack reliable water.

95 miles from Red Canyon (east) to Garnet Canyon (west). Access: The Hance, Grandview, South Kaibab, Bright Angel, Hermit, Boucher, and South Bass trails all intersect the Tonto Trail. Water sources at Hance, Cottonwood (usually), Grapevine, Pipe, Monument, Hermit, and Boucher creeks, Indian Garden Spring, the Colorado River in several locations. Ask at the Backcountry Information Center about water sources before starting hike. Map: Topo map for section hiked.

8 North Rim Wilderness Trail

Clear Creek Trail 🐾   **Highlights:** A scenic, relatively flat spur off the North Kaibab Trail, with views of Zoroaster Temple, Clear Creek, and the Colorado River. **Drawbacks:** Dangerously hot and dry in summer. **Difficulty:** Like the Tonto, smooth and relatively level when not dipping into craggy drainages.

After leaving the North Kaibab Trail, the Clear Creek Trail climbs in steep switchbacks east of Bright Angel Creek, eventually reaching an overlook of the Colorado River, sandwiched between the dark walls of the Granite Gorge. The trail then travels east above the river, gradually ascending to the Tonto Platform.

Before it reaches that level, however, watch for the interface between the black, 2-billion-year-old Vishnu Formation and the flat brown facade of the Tapeats Sandstone. You can touch the point of contact between these layers. This is as close as you'll get to "touching" the Great Unconformity, the gap of 1.2 billion years in the geological record caused by past erosion.

After reaching the Tonto Platform, the trail continues to the east (and then southeast), veering around the tops of numerous drainages, all beneath the imposing presence of Zoroaster Temple to the north. This long, shadeless stretch, where blackbrush and agave are among the tallest plants, makes the Clear Creek Trail a risky place for summer hiking. Eventually the trail crests a small rise, revealing a view of the confluence of the Colorado River Gorge and the drainage cut by Clear Creek. Turning northeast, the trail crosses Zoroaster Canyon and then traverses above Clear Creek before finally descending to the creek bed itself.

There are a number of nice campsites in the area just west of Clear Creek, all within easy walking distance of a pit toilet. From these campsites you can strike out on a number of excellent day hikes. Follow the creek 4 miles north to Cheyava Falls, a seasonal waterfall that, at 800 feet, is tallest in the canyon. Or, walk (and down-climb) 6 miles south to the Colorado River. The narrows en route to the Colorado are subject to flash floods and should be avoided during wet weather and spring runoff.

8.7 miles from Phantom Ranch to Clear Creek Drainage. Access: 0.3 mile north of Phantom Ranch on the North Kaibab Trail. Water source at Clear Creek. Maps: Phantom Ranch (7.5 min.) quadrangle.

9 Backcountry Campgrounds

The park's three backcountry campgrounds—**Bright Angel, Cotton-wood,** and **Indian Garden**—are located deep inside the canyon and are accessible only via hiking trails. To stay at these campgrounds, you must be willing to hike long distances into the canyon carrying the necessary clothes, shelter, food, and water, and then hike back out with all of the same belongings (including your trash). You will also need a permit from the park's Backcountry Information Center. If you lack either the necessary incentive or the necessary permit (or both), try camping at one of the car campgrounds in the park's developed areas. At these campgrounds, you can sleep under the stars, a few feet away from your loaded vehicle. For more information, see chapter 5, "Camping with a Car in the Grand Canyon Area."

Bright Angel Campground 🐾🐾🐾   The **River Trail** (which begins at the foot of the Bright Angel Trail), the **South Kaibab Trail,** and the **North Kaibab Trail** all converge below Bright Angel Campground, which lies on the north shore of the Colorado River. The River Trail crosses the Colorado River on the Silver Suspension Bridge just west of the campground; the South Kaibab Trail crosses on the Kaibab Suspension Bridge just east of the campground. The lowest section of the North Kaibab Trail parallels the campground on the opposite side of Bright Angel Creek. Bright Angel Campground is 14.4 miles from the North Kaibab trailhead; 9.3 miles from the Bright Angel trailhead; and 7.3 miles from the South Kaibab trailhead.

This long, narrow campground lies in a purgatory between the cool waters of Bright Angel Creek and black cliffs of the Vishnu Formation, which are hot as grills in the summer. A few hundred yards away, the Colorado River rumbles past, eddying against a beach that is a popular stopping point for raft trips. A walkway divides the campground, which is open all year. Roughly half of the 31 campsites are on the cliff side; the other, nicer half are on the creek side. Most are shaded by cottonwood trees, a few of which were planted in the 1930s by CCC workers whose camp was here. (Most of the trees planted by the CCC washed away in a 1966 flash flood.) Phantom Ranch is a half mile to the north. Though all three of the campgrounds inside the canyon offer lovely surroundings, the proximity of Bright Angel Campground to the Colorado River makes it especially stunning.

Cottonwood Campground ★★ As you hike up the North Kaibab Trail from the Colorado River, the walls of Bright Angel Canyon part like the Red Sea below this campground. Between them rests a valley floor soft enough and damp enough to support a few cottonwood trees, most of which grow by the ranger station. Most of the 14 campsites are surrounded by shrub oak, whose low-slung branches barely shade the sites and picnic tables. Bright Angel Creek flows past the west side of the campground. On a hot summer day, it's the only cool place around.

Halfway between the North Rim and the Colorado, Cottonwood Campground is a great place to camp while en route to (or from) the river. For a nice 4-day hike from the North Rim, schedule 2 nights here around a night at Bright Angel Campground. But

---

Tips Camping Tip

Permits to camp at **Bright Angel Campground, Cottonwood Campground,** and **Indian Garden Campground** are available through the park's Backcountry Information Center at P.O. Box 129, Grand Canyon, AZ 86023. All three campgrounds have pit toilets, drinking water, and picnic tables.

Camping Etiquette & Special Regulations

First, the standard camping etiquette: Pack out all your garbage, including uneaten food and used toilet paper. You are *not* doing anyone a favor by leaving uneaten food in the ammo cans at the campgrounds. Stay on designated trails. Don't disturb plants, wildlife, or archaeological resources. Camp in obvious campsites—stay off the vegetation and cryptogamic soils. If pit toilets are not available, bury human waste in holes 4 to 6 inches deep, 6 inches across, and at least 200 feet from water and creek beds. When doing dishes, take water and dishes at least 200 feet from the water source, and scatter the waste water. When bathing, take water away from the water source. Use only biodegradable soap (or, better yet, none at all) for both dishes and bathing. Hang food and trash out of reach of wildlife.

There are also a few canyon-specific regulations. No campfires are allowed (only camp stoves). Also, be sure to camp inside the use areas specified on your permit. These are shown on the Trails Illustrated topographical map of the canyon. Finally, pay attention to trail-specific rules provided by the Backcountry Information Center. If you have any questions about the hike—especially water sources—ask a ranger. The Backcountry Information Center can't always determine whether a hike suits you. It's up to you to ask the necessary questions about trail conditions, water sources, and the location of campsites.

don't underestimate how hard it is to get here: The walk from the North Kaibab trailhead to Cottonwood Campground covers 6.8 miles and drops 3,170 feet—that's nearly a half mile longer than the entire length of the South Kaibab Trail, with nearly three-quarters of the vertical drop.

Indian Garden Campground ⚶⚶ You can use this campground, 4.6 miles from the Bright Angel trailhead and 3,100 vertical feet below the rim, to break up hikes from the South Rim to the Colorado River. The 14 sites are surrounded by lush riparian vegetation that taps into Indian Garden Spring, just a short walk down the canyon. For a nice 4-day hike from the South Rim, schedule 2 nights here around one at Bright Angel Campground.

10 Other Sports & Activities

CONDOR VIEWING

In recent years, many Grand Canyon visitors have spotted the largest land bird in North America. Members of the vulture family, California condors will cruise up to 100 miles a day, at speeds approaching 50 mph. When mature, condors are grayish-black except on their heads, which are orange and featherless. Under each wing, a triangular white patch is sometimes visible.

In December 1996, six of these birds, whose wings can span nearly 10 feet, were released on the Vermilion Cliffs along Highway 89A near Lee's Ferry. Twenty-two more have been set free in northern Arizona since then. Of the 55 California Condors in the wild, 22 now live in the Grand Canyon area. The releases were part of a larger project aimed at reintroducing the birds to the wild after they nearly went extinct in the 1980s.

In August 2001, the birds soared, often alongside turkey vultures, above South Rim overlooks near Maricopa Point. Because condors have poor olfactory senses, they sometimes follow turkey vultures and other raptors to carrion. Other than size, the easiest way to tell the two species apart is the way they soar: vultures hold their wings in a "V"; condors keep theirs in a plane. Unless the condors change their habits, they will probably reappear above the South Rim in the years to come.

North of the canyon, you might spot the birds by driving 14 miles east of Jacob Lake on Highway 89A to House Rock Valley Road (the first road to your left after you leave the National Forest). Turn left (north) and go 2 miles to a small ramada. Scientists leave food for the youngest birds in the cliffs above the ramada. If the condors are in the area, you'll probably meet workers who are tracking them. They carry a spotting scope and binoculars and will help you sight the birds.

Wherever you spot them, please don't approach, feed, or otherwise disturb the condors. If you see one who appears to be hurt or endangered, notify the **Peregrine Fund Condor Project** (© **928/ 355-2270**). Be prepared to identify the time and location of the sighting and, if possible, the wing-tag number of the bird.

CROSS-COUNTRY SKIING

The crisp air, deep snow, and absolute silence make the **North Rim** a delightful place to ski. The closest skiing to the park starts south of Jacob Lake, at the gate that closes Highway 67; you can park your car here, and then ski south on the snow-covered highway. Snowmobiles are banned from the highway and the land east of the highway. If you'd like to ski into the park (44 miles and several days' travel from the gate) and spend a night on the North Rim, you'll need to obtain a backcountry permit from the **Backcountry Information Center** (✆ 928/638-7875).

When snow sticks on the **South Rim,** you can cross-country ski at the Grandview Nordic Center in the Kaibab National Forest near Grandview Point. To get there, drive east toward Desert View on Highway 64. About 1.7 miles past the Grandview Point turnoff, turn right on the road to the Arizona Trail. Park where the snow begins, then ski or walk down the road roughly a quarter mile to a bulletin board with instructions for the trails. The Forest Service has marked three loops in this area, each meandering through meadows and ponderosa pine forest: the intermediate 7.5-mile-long Twin Lakes Loop; the easy 1.1-mile Grandview Lookout Loop; and the easy 3.7-mile Boundary Loop. There's no charge. For more information call the **Kaibab National Forest Tusayan Ranger District Office** at ✆ **928/638-2443.** The **Canyon Village Marketplace** (✆ **928/638-2262**) in Market Plaza in Grand Canyon Village rents cross-country skis, boots, and poles for under $20.

FISHING

You're welcome to fish in the Colorado River, provided you have an Arizona Fishing Permit and trout stamp. One-day nonresident permits are available for $12.50 (or 5 days for $26) at the **Canyon Village Marketplace** (✆ **928/638-2262**) in Grand Canyon Village; at **Marble Canyon Lodge** (✆ **800/726-1789** or 928/ 355-2225), a quarter mile west of the Navajo Bridge on Highway 89A; and at **Lee's Ferry Anglers Guides and Fly Shop** (✆ **800/ 962-9755** or 928/355-2261), at Cliff Dwellers Lodge, 9 miles west of Navajo Bridge on Highway 89A. **The Marble Canyon/ Vermilion Cliffs** area is about 45 miles southwest of Page and 2½ hours north of Flagstaff.

Once you get your fishing permit, the next challenge is getting to the best fishing spots. To fish inside park boundaries, you either have to hike to the Colorado River or be on a river trip and fish during breaks from rafting (for information on river trips, see "River Rafting Trips," later in this chapter).

The best trout fishing inside the park is at the eastern end of the canyon—upstream of Phantom Ranch. The river is clear and cold (48°F) year-round directly below the dam, making this a great trout hatchery (and a chilling place for the native species, which evolved to live in muddy water and extreme variations in temperature). Downstream, the river gradually warms and gathers sediment from its tributaries, causing the trout population to dwindle and enabling the bottom-feeders to survive. The five most abundant fish species in the park are carp, speckled dace, flannel-mouth sucker, rainbow trout, and blue-head sucker.

Some of the best trout fishing in the Southwest is just upstream of the park's easternmost boundary, between Glen Canyon Dam and Lee's Ferry. Most of the hot spots in this 16-mile-long stretch of river can be reached only by boat, but anyone can walk up a mile of shoreline from the parking area at Lee's Ferry. If you don't have your rod and waders with you, you can rent them, and boats too, from **Lee's Ferry Anglers Guides and Fly Shop** (© 800/962-9755 or 928/355-2261; www.leesferry.com). This shop, the best in the area, offers a complete guide service and carries a full line of fishing gear and tackle.

HORSEBACK RIDING
SOUTH RIM HORSEBACK RIDING

For horseback riding near the South Rim, go to **Apache Stables** (© 928/638-2891; www.apachestables.com), which operates from April through October at Moqui Lodge, just outside the park's south entrance. Most of the horses at the stables are "dog-friendly," as our guide put it. They're retired ranch horses that average 15 years in age. Because they're gentle and know the trails around the stables, you need only kick your steed periodically to make sure it keeps going. The rest of the time, you can relax and enjoy your horse's swaying and the ponderosa pine forest.

The friendly horses make this a great, albeit expensive, family activity. Children as young as 8 (and 48 in. tall) are allowed on the 1-hour trail rides, which, like the 2-hour ones, loop through the Kaibab National Forest near the stables. Apache Stables also offers a 4-hour, 12-mile round-trip ride east through the forest to near Grandview Point. There, riders dismount and cross Highway 64 on foot to admire the canyon. You must be 10 or over to go on the 2-hour ride, 14 to go on the 4-hour ride. Weight limits are 235 lbs., 225 lbs., and 200 lbs. for the 1-, 2-, and 4-hour rides, respectively.

Other options are an evening trail ride and a wagon ride, both going to a campfire where participants roast marshmallows and other food they bring. (No grill is available.) When the marshmallows have all been consumed (either by people or flames), everyone returns together on the wagon.

Prices are $95.50 (plus tax) for the 4-hour East Rim ride, $55.50 for the 2-hour ride, $30.50 for the 1-hour ride, $40.50 for the campfire trail ride, and $12.50 for the campfire wagon ride. Participants should wear long pants and closed-toed footwear, and bring plenty of water. Backpacks are not allowed, but fanny packs are okay.

NORTH RIM HORSEBACK RIDING

On the North Rim, **Allen's Guided Tours** (© **435/644-8150**) offers horseback rides from 8am to 6pm Monday to Saturday from May 15 through Sept. 15. Departing from a corral a quarter mile south of Jacob Lake on Highway 67, the tours travel on gentle terrain in the Kaibab National Forest. 1- and 2-hour rides cost $20 and $35, respectively. Half-day rides, which follow a stretch of the Arizona Trail, cost $55. Full-day rides, which cost $85, travel to and from an overlook of the eastern canyon and include a bag lunch. The full-day ride must be booked a day in advance and requires a minimum group of four. There is no weight or age limit.

CYCLING

Inside the park, cyclists are required to stay on roads, many of them narrow and crowded. Routes such as Highway 64 and the Cape Royal Road are inherently risky for cyclists. But at least two good rides exist. From March through November, the West Rim Drive is closed to most private cars, making it a haven for cyclists. You'll still have to yield to tour buses, shuttles and a handful of private vehicles, and watch out for people on foot, many of whom will be oblivious to your approach. On the North Rim, the entrance road is wide enough to accommodate experienced cyclists.

MOUNTAIN BIKING

To mountain bike near Grand Canyon, you'll need to cross out of Grand Canyon National Park into the Kaibab National Forest, which borders the park on both rims. On the North Rim, avid cyclists are flocking to the new **Rainbow Rim Trail**—an 18-mile stretch of expert-level single track that provides access to five remote canyon overlooks. Old logging roads, jeep trails, and footpaths crisscross other areas of the North Rim, providing a variety of cycling options. Visit the **Kaibab Plateau Visitor Center** in Jacob Lake (© **928/643-7298**) for directions, maps, road conditions, and trail descriptions.

On the South Rim, you'll find enjoyable mountain biking on a stretch of the **Arizona Trail** that starts at Grandview Lookout Tower. To reach the lookout, take Highway 64 east from Grand

Canyon Village. About 1.7 miles east of the Grandview Point turnoff, turn right (south) onto the road for the Arizona Trail. Leaving the park, follow this dirt road 1.3 miles to Grandview Lookout and the trailhead. Beginning here, you can ride more than 20 miles of intermediate-level single-track (with a few short, technically demanding stretches thrown in), much of it along the Coconino Rim.

Another trail system, with loops of 3.7, 10.2, and 11.2 miles, is located near Tusayan. These loops follow old Jeep trails through rolling hills in the ponderosa pine forest. The trails have a few steep, rocky areas, but most of the terrain is only moderately difficult. To reach them, find the marked parking area 0.3 miles north of Tusayan on the west side of Highway 64. A single trail heads north from there, eventually crossing under the highway through a concrete tunnel and providing access to the loops. (*Note:* this is also a great place to run when you're staying in Tusayan.) For information on these trails and maps of the Tusayan Ranger District (© 928/638-2443), visit the **Forest Service Office** a half mile south of the park entrance on Highway 64.

BIKE RENTALS
SOUTH RIM   On the South Rim, you can rent mountain bikes at the Best Western Grand Canyon Squire Inn (© **800/622-6966**), 1½ miles south of the park entrance on Highway 64. The hotel charges $10 for up to two hours, $15 for two to four hours, and $25 for four to eight hours. Higher-end bicycles can be rented in Flagstaff at **Absolute Bikes** (© **928/779-5969**), 18 N. San Francisco St.

NORTH RIM   No bike rentals are available on the North Rim. However, **Kaibab Adventure Outfitters** (© **800/451-1133** or 435/259-7423; www.kaibabtours.com) of Moab, UT, offers van-supported 5-day mountain-bike tours (cost: $850) of the North Rim.

MULE TRIPS
SOUTH RIM MULE TRIPS
Wearing floppy hats and clutching rain slickers, the day's mule riders gather at 8am (9am in winter) every morning at a corral west of Bright Angel Lodge to prepare for their rides. You can almost hear the jangling nerves as they contemplate the prospect of descending narrow trails above steep cliffs on animals hardly famous for their intelligence. Although the mules walk close to the edges and have

been known to *back* off the trails, accidents are rare, especially among riders who follow the wrangler's instructions. In fact, Fred Harvey has been guiding mule trips into the canyon for more than 90 years without a single fatality from a fall.

The rides, while usually safe, can nonetheless be grueling. Most people's legs aren't used to bending around a mule, and the saddles aren't soft. In addition to the pounding, the canyon can be scorching, and chances for breaks are few. Because the rides are strenuous for both riders and mules, the wranglers strictly adhere to the following requirements: You must weigh less than 200 pounds, be at least 4 feet 7 inches tall, and speak fluent English. If the wranglers think you weigh too much, they won't hesitate to put you on the scale. Acrophobes and pregnant women are also discouraged from taking the rides.

The least expensive ride—the one-day trip to Plateau Point—may also be the most grueling, since it involves a whopping six hours in the saddle. It travels down the Bright Angel Trail to Indian Garden, then follows the Plateau Point Trail across the Tonto Platform to an overlook (Plateau Point) of the Colorado River. Having descended 3,200 vertical feet, the riders return on the same trails. This 12-mile round-trip ride, which breaks for lunch at Indian Garden, doesn't reach the rim until mid- to late afternoon. Cost: $118.76.

The other rides are part of 1- or 2-night packages that include lodging and meals at Phantom Ranch. Going down, they follow the Bright Angel Trail to the river, then travel east on the River Trail before finally crossing the river via the Kaibab Suspension Bridge. Coming back they use the South Kaibab Trail. The 10.5-mile descent takes 5½ hours; the 8-mile-long climb out is an hour shorter. The Phantom Ranch overnight costs $335.95 for one person, $601.68 for two, and $276.90 for each additional person. The Phantom Ranch 2-night trip, which is offered only from mid-November through March 31, costs $428.75 for one, $727.50 for two, and $319.75 for each additional person. A livery service is also available. One-way transportation of a 30-pound duffel (or less) costs $53.20.

NORTH RIM MULE TRIPS

Mule rides on the North Rim are through a small, family run outfit called **Canyon Trail Rides** (see "Reserving a Mule Trip," below). Four types of rides are offered. Open to ages 6 and up, the easiest ride goes 1 mile along the rim on the Ken Patrick Trail before turning back. This 1-hour ride costs $20 per person. Two half-day rides, each costing $45 per person, are offered. One stays on the

> ### *Tips*   Reserving a Mule Trip
>
> Mule trips to Phantom Ranch can fill up months in advance, so make your reservations early. Reservations for the next 23 months can be made beginning on the first of the month. For example, all dates in December 2002 would first go on sale January 1, 2000. For **advance reservations** call ✆ **303/297-2757.** The **Bright Angel Transportation Desk** at ✆ **928-638-2631,** ext. 6015, can tell you about openings the next day. If you arrive without reservations, you can put your name on a waiting list by going to the desk in person. Reservations for South Rim mule rides are easier to obtain in winter, a time when temperatures in the lower canyon are often very pleasant.
>
> The mule rides on the North Rim tend to fill up much later than those on the South Rim—if at all. To sign up, visit the **Canyon Trail Rides** desk (open daily 7am–6pm) at Grand Canyon Lodge, or call ✆ **928/638-9875.** The off-season number is ✆ **435/679-8665,** and the Web address is **www.canyonrides.com.**

rim, following the Ken Patrick and Uncle Jim trails to a canyon viewpoint; the other descends 2 miles into the canyon on the North Kaibab Trail, turning back at Supai Tunnel. The all-day ride, which includes lunch, travels 5 miles on the North Kaibab Trail to Roaring Springs before turning back. Cost for the all-day ride is $95. Riders must be at least 12 to go on the all-day ride. No one over 200 pounds is allowed on the canyon rides; for the rim rides, the limit is 220. All riders must speak English.

OVERFLIGHTS

Six companies at Grand Canyon National Park Airport in Tusayan currently offer scenic airplane or helicopter rides over the canyon. With more than 600,000 people taking air tours over the canyon every year, the flights, which generate a great deal of noise in parts of the park, have become a politically charged issue.

They also raise safety concerns. A total of 41 people, more than half of them sightseers, have died in seven plane and helicopter crashes in and around Grand Canyon since 1991. This includes six people who died in a helicopter crash in August, 2001.

For many vacationers, however, the question is not whether to fly, but whether to take an airplane or a helicopter. The airplane flights, by and large, last longer and cost less. Most airplane tours remain airborne (ideally) for 40 to 50 minutes, at costs ranging from $75 to $89 per person; most helicopter tours fly (one hopes) for 30 minutes, at costs of $99 to $105. The planes also cover more ground, crossing the canyon near Hermit's Rest and returning along the East Rim, near Desert View. The helicopter tours, meanwhile, usually fly out and back in the same corridor near Hermit's Rest. (Some do go for the full loop.) The helicopters cruise lower—just above the rim. And while they're not immune to an occasional bump, they tend to be smoother. (*Tip:* Whether you take an airplane or helicopter, your flight will be smoother if you go early in the day.)

During my helicopter ride, cinematic scores played over headphones, setting an epic tone that didn't quite jibe with the canyon. The flight afforded stunning aerial views of the topography, but precluded smelling or touching it. It was also a bit stomach-churning. It didn't help that I was pinned in the helicopter's middle seat between two large, sweaty strangers. The IMAX movie often achieves similar effects—without disturbing the wilderness.

The following companies offer air tours originating from Tusayan: **Papillon Grand Canyon Helicopters** (© **800/528-2418** or 928/638-2419; www.papillon.com); **Air Grand Canyon/Sky Eye Air Tours** (© **800/247-4726** or 928/638-2686; www.airgrand canyon.com); **AirStar Helicopters** (© **800/962-3869** or 928/638-2622; www.airstar.com); **Grand Canyon Airlines** (© **800/528-2413** or 928/638-2407; www.grandcanyonairlines.com); **Kenai Helicopters** (© **800/541-4537** or 928/638-2764; www.flykenai.com).

RIVER RAFTING

White-water raft trips inside the park generally last from 3 to 14 days and must be booked well ahead of time. However, several companies offer shorter trips on the Colorado River near or inside Grand Canyon.

Aramark-Wilderness River Adventures, 50 S. Lake Powell Blvd., Page, AZ (© **800/528-6154** or 928/645-3279), offers half-day and full-day smooth-water raft trips from the base of Glen Canyon Dam to Lee's Ferry, where the companies floating into Grand Canyon *begin* their trips. You'll complete the motorized half-day trip, which travels below the sandstone walls of the Vermilion and Echo cliffs, in about 5 hours. On the full-day trip, the boat drifts, engines off, for more of the time, and a lunch is served on the beach. Cost for the half-day trip is $59 for adults, $39 for 11 and under. The full-day trip, which takes seven hours, costs $79 for adults, $69 for 11 and under.

Grand Canyon Airlines offers the half-day trip, plus round-trip bus transportation (totaling 290 miles) from Grand Canyon National Park Airport in Tusayan. Cost for this 12-hour tour is $101 ($53 for 11 and under). For reservations call ✆ **800/528-2413** or 928/638-2463.

One-day trips through the westernmost part of Grand Canyon are available through **Hualapai River Runners** (✆ **800/622-4406** or 928/769-2210), P.O. Box 246, Peach Springs, AZ 86434. These motorized trips, which cost $250 per person, begin with rapids in the lower Granite Gorge of Grand Canyon and end on Lake Mead. Trip participants meet at 6am at Hualapai Lodge, on the Hualapai Indian Reservation, and do not return until between 6 and 8pm that night. The reservation is more than two hours drive from Grand Canyon Village.

RIVER RAFTING TRIPS

MOTORIZED   Motorized trips are fastest, often covering the 277 miles from Lee's Ferry (above the canyon) to Pierce Ferry (in Lake Mead) in 6 days, compared to as many as 19 for nonmotorized trips. The motorized trips use wide pontoon boats that almost never capsize, making them slightly safer. Also, it's easier to move about on these solid-framed boats than on oar or paddle boats, a plus for people who lack mobility. Because of the speed of the trips, however, there's less time for hiking or resting in camp. If motorized trips are for you, consider using the companies **Aramark-Wilderness Adventures** (✆ **800/992-8022** or 928/645-3296) or **Western River Expeditions** (✆ **800/453-7450** or 801/942-6669).

NONMOTORIZED   For mobile people who want to bask in the canyon's beauty, I strongly recommend nonmotorized trips, even if it means seeing half the canyon instead of all of it. A motorless raft glides at close to the water's pace, giving passengers time to observe subtle, enticing patterns—swirls of water in eddies; the play of shadows and light as the sun moves across rock layers; the opening, unfolding, and gradual closing of each side canyon. Without motors running, the sound of the river provides a dreamlike backdrop to the journey.

There are two types of nonmotorized boats: paddle boats and oar boats. **Oar boats** are wooden dories or rubber rafts, each of which holds six passengers and a guide who does most or all of the rowing.

Exploring the Backcountry on a Raft

Taking a raft trip through the canyon allows you to see the canyon from a new perspective and gives hikers access to some of the prettiest spots anywhere.

All the companies operating in the Grand Canyon are experienced and run excellent trips, subject to the whims of the Colorado River and the storms that move through the canyon. For about $225 per day, all provide food, portable toilets, and some camping equipment, as well as access to parts of the inner canyon that are difficult, if not impossible, to reach on foot. Among them are some of the most beautiful places on earth.

While most trips begin at Lee's Ferry, the end points vary. Trips last anywhere from 3 to 15 days. Some companies allow for partial trips by picking up or dropping off passengers at various points in the canyon (most often at Phantom Ranch). The companies also differ on what makes a trip special. For example, some allow for plenty of day hiking; others don't. Because the trips do vary greatly, it's important to consider all factors described in the "River Rafting Trips" section of this chapter before planning yours.

If the guides are highly skilled, the passengers on an oar-powered trip have an excellent chance of floating the entire river without taking a life-threatening swim in the rapids. (The latest statistics on river-related deaths show commercial river trips to be as dangerous as golf. Far more people get hurt in camp than on the river.)

In a **paddle boat,** six passengers paddle, assisted by a guide who instructs them and helps steer. This experience is ideal for fit people who want to be involved at all times. However, because of the inexperience of the participants, paddle boats are probably more likely to capsize than oar boats or motorized rigs. And paddling can become burdensome during the long, slow-water stretches, especially when a head wind blows. **Canyon Explorations/Expeditions** (© **800/654-0723** or 928/774-4559) and **Outdoors Unlimited** (© **800/637-7238** or 928/526-2852) both have excellent reputations for paddle trips.

If an oar-powered company appeals to you, I recommend the company known as **O.A.R.S.** (© **800/346-6277** or 209/

736-2924, see listing below), which has some of the most experienced guides on the river. On my trip with O.A.R.S., the three guides had a combined 52 years on the Colorado. They were responsible, informative, and fun, sharing the joy they found in the canyon. During the busiest months, O.A.R.S. assures quality service by sending six crewmembers out with each group of 16 passengers—providing one of the best crew-to-client ratios on the river.

Another factor to consider before scheduling your trip is the season. In **April,** the cacti bloom in the lower canyon, splashing bright colors across the hillsides, and the river is relatively uncrowded. However, cold weather—even snow—can occasionally make these trips a test of the spirit. In **May** the weather is usually splendid, but the river is at its most crowded. **June and July** can be oppressively hot. In **late July and August,** monsoons break the heat and generate waterfalls all along the river, but they also soak rafters. From **September 15 to the end of October,** no motorized rigs cruise the river, so the canyon is quiet, although cold weather can once again be a problem.

RIVER RAFTING COMPANIES

Aramark-Wilderness River Adventures   Aramark-Wilderness offers both motorized and oar-powered trips with trip lengths varying from 4 to 12 days; with 8-day motorized trips and 12-day oar trips. P.O. Box 717, Page, AZ 86040. ☏ **800/992-8022** or 928/645-3296. www.riveradventures.com.

Canyon Explorations   Canyon Explorations offers oar-powered and paddle trips with lengths varying from 6 to 18 days, including one trip with a string quartet, and two trips that set aside extra time for hiking. P.O. Box 310, Flagstaff, AZ 86002. ☏ **800/654-0723** or 928/774-4559. www.canyonexplorations.com.

O.A.R.S.   O.A.R.S. offers both oar-powered trips and paddle trips with trip lengths varying from 5 to 16 days. P.O. Box 67, Angels Camp, CA 95222. ☏ **800/346-6277** or 209/736-2924. www.oars.com.

Outdoors Unlimited   Outdoors Unlimited offers oar-powered and paddle trips with trip lengths ranging from 5 to 15 days. 6900 Townsend Winona Rd., Flagstaff, AZ 86004. ☏ **800/637-7238** or 928/526-2852. www.outdoorsunlimited.com.

Western River Expeditions   Western River Expeditions offers motorized trips with trip lengths varying from 3 to 6 days. On the shorter trips, helicopters drop participants in the western Canyon, where they begin their trips to Lake Mead. 7258 Racquet Club Dr., Salt Lake City, UT 84121. ☏ **800/453-7450** or 801/942-6669. www.westernriver.com.

5

Camping with a Car in the Grand Canyon Area

This chapter focuses on camping with a car—that is, camping done in or near RVs and automobiles. Most car campgrounds have individual pullouts for parking, grassy spots for tents, picnic tables, fire rings or grills, toilets, and drinking water. A few so-called "primitive" campgrounds lack running water. Located in remote areas, these often consist of little more than open space and a pit toilet. In addition to car campgrounds, the Grand Canyon area is home to a handful of RV parks—places where recreational vehicles can tap into water and electricity during overnight stays.

Numerous car campgrounds and RV parks can be found in and near the developed areas of Grand Canyon National Park (as well as one primitive car campground near the western canyon). In addition to the campgrounds listed in this chapter, you'll find many other car campgrounds and RV parks farther from the canyon, in the gateway communities of Flagstaff, Williams, and Kanab.

Of course, not all camping is done near automobiles, especially not at the Grand Canyon. If you're interested in camping far from the roads and inside the park's backcountry, you'll need to obtain a permit through the park's Backcountry Information Center (© **928/ 638-7875**). The Center can help you reserve a spot at the three backcountry campgrounds—**Bright Angel, Cottonwood,** and **Indian Garden**—that are accessible only via hiking trails into the canyon. For more information, see "Backcountry Campgrounds," in chapter 4.

1 Camping Inside the Park
NEAR THE SOUTH RIM
Desert View Campground 🦉 At dusk, the yips of coyotes drift over this campground in piñon-juniper woodland at the eastern edge of the park. Elevated, cool, and breezy, the peaceful surroundings offer no clue that the bustling Desert View Overlook is within walking distance. The floor of the woodland makes for smooth tent

---

Tips Backcountry Camping

If you're thinking about hiking into the canyon and spending the night in the backcountry, flip to "Preparing for Your Backcountry Trip" and "Backcountry Campgrounds" in chapter 4 for information about getting a backcountry permit, and for details about the best places to camp.

---

sites, the most secluded being on the outside of the loop drive. The only drawback: The nearest showers are 25 miles away at Camper Services in Grand Canyon Village. During high season, this first-come, first-served campground usually fills up by noon. To secure a site, swing through in midmorning and see what's open.

25 miles east of Grand Canyon Village on Hwy. 64. No phone, no advance reservations. 50 sites. $10 per site. No credit cards. Open mid-May to mid-Oct.

Mather Campground 🅖   Despite having 319 campsites in a relatively small area, this remains a pleasant place. Piñon and juniper trees shade the sites, which are spaced far enough apart to afford privacy to most campers. The Aspen and Maple loops are especially roomy. Also, it's good to be near, but not too near, the showers ($1 for 5 min.), located in the Camper Services building next to the campground. If you're too close, hundreds of campers tramp past.

Because Mather is the only campground in Grand Canyon Village, it tends to fill up before the others. You can make reservations up to 5 months in advance by calling the 800 number listed below. For same-day reservations, check at the campground entrance. Even when the campground is booked, sites sometimes become available when campers leave early or cancel. There's no waiting list, however, and no set time for the new spaces to be given away. By coming in morning, however, you can avoid waiting in line at the campground entrance.

From December 1 to March 1, the campground is open on a first-come, first-served basis. No reservations are taken for these months, but sites are easy to obtain.

Near Grand Canyon Village on South Rim. 𝄞 **800/365-2267** (301/722-1257 outside the U.S.) for advance reservations, or 928/638-7851 (for campground-specific information). http://reservations.nps.gov. 319 campsites, 4 group sites. No hookups. $15 Apr 1–Nov 30; $10 Dec 1–Mar 31. $4 tent only (no car). DISC, MC, V.

Trailer Village   The neighbors are close, the showers far (0.4 mile) away, and the vegetation sparse. In surroundings like this, you might want to draw the curtains and stay in your RV. The beauty of a hookup is that it lets you do that. If, however, you'd like to venture outside during your stay, scout the property before taking a site. A few sites at the north end of the numbered drives have grass, shade trees, room for a tent, and one neighbor-free side. If you'd like to leave your RV altogether, you can catch a shuttle bus at a stop near the campground.

Like the lodges inside Grand Canyon National Park, Trailer Village is overseen by Amfac—and therefore subject to the same rules as the lodges (except pets are allowed here). That means reservations can be made in advance. If you don't have reservations, check at the campground entrance even if the sign says no openings exist. A few spots open up in the late mornings when campers depart early. (Because reservations are guaranteed by credit card, few additional spots come open at night.)

Grand Canyon Village, P.O. Box 699, Grand Canyon, AZ 86023. ℂ **303/297-2757** (advance reservations) or 928/638-2631, ext. 6035 (same-day reservations, campground questions). Fax 928/638-9247. 84 sites. 84 full hookups. $24 per site, plus $1.75 for each additional adult (17 and over) after the first 2. AE, DISC, MC, V. Open year-round.

NEAR THE NORTH RIM

North Rim Campground 🏕🏕🏕 Shaded by ponderosa pines and situated alongside Transept Canyon (part of Grand Canyon), this is a delightful place to pass a few days. The pines, which shade a soft, smooth, forest floor, are spaced just far enough apart to allow for a vigorous game of Wiffle ball, among other activities.

But there's more here than a field of dreams. The 1.5-mile-long Transept Trail links the campground to Grand Canyon Lodge. The North Rim General Store, a Laundromat, and showers ($1.25 for 5 min.) are all within walking distance. The most spectacular sites are the rim sites, which open onto the canyon. These cost an extra $5 but are worth it, being some of the prettiest anywhere.

With only 83 sites, the North Rim Campground fills up for much of the summer. You can book a spot up to 5 months in advance. If you show up without a reservation only to find the SORRY, CAMPGROUND FULL sign on the entry booth, don't be afraid to ask what seems a stupid question. The gatekeepers often neglect to remove the sign after receiving cancellations, and you may just end up with a campsite. The best time to show up and ask about openings is at 8am. That's when sites made available by the previous night's cancellations go up for sale.

Grand Canyon Area Campgrounds

Bright Angel Campground **8**
Cameron Trading Post RV Park **15**
Cottonwood Campground **6**
DeMotte Park Campground **4**
Desert View Campground **9**
Diamond Creek Campground **1**
Flintstone Bedrock City **14**
Grand Canyon Camper Village **12**
Indian Garden Campground **7**
Jacob Lake Campground **3**
Kaibab Camper Village **2**
Kaibab Lake Campground **16**
Mather Campground **11**
North Rim Campground **5**
Ten X Campground **13**
Trailer Village **10**

103

Campgrounds in the Grand Canyon Area

Campground	Rim	Total Sites	RV Hookups	Dump Station	Toilets	Drinking Water	Showers	Fire Pits/ Grills	Laundry	Public Phones	Reserve	Fees	Open
Cameron Trading Post RV Park	South	48	48	yes	no	yes	no	no	no	yes	yes	$15	year-round
DeMotte Park Campground	North	23	no	no	yes	yes	no	yes	no	no	no	$12	mid-June to mid-Sept
Desert View Campground	South	50	no	no	yes	no	yes	no	no	no	no	$10 per site	mid-May to mid-Oct
Diamond Creek Campground	South	open tent camping	no	no	yes	no	no	yes	no	no	no	$7 per person	year-round
Flintstone Bedrock City	South	unlimited tent sites	27	yes	yes	yes	yes	no	yes	yes	yes	$12 two-person tent, $14 electric hookup, $16 water/electric, $2 each additional person	Feb–Nov
Grand Canyon Camper Village	South	300	250	yes	yes	yes	yes	yes	no	yes	yes	$26 full hookup, $24 water/electric, $22 electric, $18 tent sites, $20 teepees	year-round

Campgrounds in the Grand Canyon Area

Campground	Rim	Total Sites	RV Hookups	Dump Station	Toilets	Drinking Water	Showers	Fire Pits/ Grills	Laundry	Public Phones	Reserve	Fees	Open
Jacob Lake Campground	North	53	no	no	yes	yes	no	yes	no	no	no	$12	year-round
Kaibab Lake Campground	South	74	no	no	yes	yes	no	yes	no	no	no	$12	Apr–Oct
Kaibab Camper Village	North	130	70	yes	yes	yes		yes	yes	yes	no	$22 hookups, $12 dry sites, $12 tent sites	May 15–Oct 15
Mather Campground	South	323	no	yes	yes	yes	yes	yes	yes	no	Mar–Nov	$15 Apr–Nov, $10 rest of year	year-round
North Rim Campground	North	87	no	yes	yes	yes	nearby	yes	nearby	yes	yes	$15–$20 site, $4 tent only, no car	May 15–Oct 15
Ten X Campground	South	70	no	no	yes	yes	no	yes	no	no	no	$12	Apr–Oct
Trailer Village	South	84	84	nearby	yes	yes	nearby	yes	no	nearby	yes	$24 plus $1.75 each additional person	year-round

The campground sometimes stays open on a limited basis after October 15, but few services are available in the park.

On Grand Canyon North Rim (44 miles south of Jacob Lake on Hwy. 67). ℂ 800/ 365-2267 advance reservations, or 928/638-9389 same-day reservations. http://reservations.nps.gov. 83 sites, 4 group sites. No hookups. $15–$20 per site; $4 for tent only (no car). DISC, MC, V. Open May 15–Oct 15.

NEAR THE EASTERN ENTRANCE & THE WESTERN CANYON

Diamond Creek Campground ★   This primitive campground at the confluence of Diamond Creek and the Colorado River at the western end of the canyon is the only place where you can drive to the river inside the Grand Canyon. The gravel road, descending from 4,600 feet in Peach Springs to 1,350 feet at the campground, sometimes gets washed out, but high-clearance vehicles can negotiate it during dry weather. (Don't risk it during monsoon season.) Surrounded by cliffs of granite and schist, the campground is at a lovely spot. People who couldn't otherwise make it to the inner canyon will probably appreciate it most.

But there are some real drawbacks. You probably won't be alone; the beach serves as a popular pullout for raft trips, and the Hualapai River Runners begin their trips in the far western canyon here. If you don't commandeer one of the three metal ramadas, you could end up broiling in the midday sun. (Located just above the canyon's lowest point, this is one of its hottest places.) You'll need to bring your own drinking water and pack out your own garbage. Seldom pumped, the lone portable toilet tests the will.

Hualapai Indian Reservation (18.1 miles from Peach Springs, 19 miles from Hwy. 66 on the Diamond Creek Rd.). ℂ 928/769-2210. Open tent camping. $10.50 per person for camping; $5.50 for sightseeing only. AE, DISC, MC, V. Open Mar–Oct. Pay and register before entering at the Hualapai River Trips Office, open daily 6am–6pm at Hualapai Lodge in Peach Springs. Closed in winter.

2 Camping Outside the Park
NEAR THE SOUTH RIM

Flintstone Bedrock City *(Kids)*   Cartoon lovers will be curious about this Flintstones-themed campground, restaurant, and store, whose multihued, faux-stone buildings cling like putty to the windswept land at the intersection of highways 64 and 180. In addition to peddling the ubiquitous Grand Canyon T-shirts and dead-scorpion paperweights, the gift shop sells all manner of Flintstones paraphernalia, including bibs, sweatshirts, T-shirts, key chains, and magnets. Fred's Diner serves up dishes such as the "Chickasaurus Sandwich" and the "Bronto Burger" for under $3.

One advantage to having a prehistoric theme is that no one can tell whether your campground is run-down. The buildings here seem about as old as caves. So nothing looks out of character. One problem, however, is obvious: the proximity of some tent sites to Highway 64. Services here include a small store, volleyball court, coin-op laundry, TV, and game room.

In Vallé (at junctions of Hwy. 180 and 64). HCR 34 Box A, Williams, AZ 86046. ℂ 928/635-2600. Unlimited tent sites, 27 hookups. $12 2-person tent; $14 electric hookup; $16 water/electric hookup; $2 each additional person after the first 2. AE, DISC, MC, V. Open Mar 1–Oct 31.

Grand Canyon Camper Village
This campground's advantage is its location: Just a mile south of the park entrance, it lies within easy walking distance of stores and restaurants on one side and of Kaibab National Forest on the other. Its disadvantages are its relatively narrow (average width: 27 ft.) campsites and the noise from the nearby Grand Canyon National Park Airport, whose constant daytime helicopter takeoffs, together with the throngs of people at the campground itself, may bring back memories of Woodstock. At least the rest rooms are clean, and the showers (75¢ for 6 min.) hot. There's also a playground and a gravel basketball court.

In Tusayan (1 mile south of the park on Hwy. 64), P.O. Box 490, Grand Canyon, AZ 86023-0490. ℂ 928/638-2887. 50 tent sites, 250 hookups. $18 tent sites; $20 teepees; $22 electric; $24 water/electric; $26 full hookups. AE, DISC, MC, V. Open year-round. Pets allowed.

Kaibab Lake Campground 𝄐𝄐
The campsites at this Forest Service campground are on a forested hillside above the reddish waters of Williams Lake. There's no swimming in the lake, a reservoir for Williams, but the fishing for bottom-feeders isn't bad.

4 miles north of Williams on Hwy. 64. ℂ 928/699-1239. 74 sites, no hookups. $12 per site. No credit cards. Open Apr–Oct.

Ten X Campground 𝄐𝄐
Large, wooded campsites make this Forest Service campground the most peaceful open-air accommodations within 20 miles of the South Rim. With plenty of distance between you and your neighbors, this is a great place to linger over a fire. All sites have fire pits and grills, and the campground host sells wood. Later, you'll find the soft, needle-covered floor perfect for sleeping. This campground does sell out. If you're driving up

from Flagstaff or Williams, consider snagging a site before going to the canyon for the day.

2 miles south of Tusayan on Hwy. 64. ☏ **928/638-2443**. 70 sites, no hookups. $10 per site. No credit cards. Open mid-Apr to Oct 1.

NEAR THE NORTH RIM

DeMotte Park Campground ★★ Bundle up for the nights at this Forest Service campground. It's 8,760 feet high (10 ft. higher than Telluride, Colo.), in Spruce–Fir forest, so you're sure to be cool. It's so cool, in fact, that it closes in mid-September because the pipes freeze. The road through the campground curves sharply and some of the spaces are small, so this place may not work for large RVs. Because this campground is relatively small and located just outside the park entrance, it tends to fill up early. Try to get a site on your way *into* the park, instead of on your way out.

5 miles north of the park boundary on Hwy. 67. ☏ **928/643-7298**. 23 sites, no hookups. $12 per site. Open mid-June to mid-Sept.

Jacob Lake Campground ★★ Nestled into rolling hills covered with ponderosa pine forest, this is a beauty of a Forest Service campground. Towering pines shade sites only a short drive from the services at Jacob Lake Lodge. This campground has regular naturalist programs.

U.S. 89A, just north of Jacob Lake. ☏ **928/643-7298** or 928/643-7395. Fax 928/643-7770. 53 sites, no hookups. $12 per site. Open mid-May to mid-Oct.

Kaibab Camper Village ★★ Compared to the South Rim RV parks, where sagebrush is often the largest plant in sight, this North Rim RV park is like a fairy tale. Everywhere inside the campground, ponderosa pines dust the sky like Jack's mythical beanstalk. Some campers even have a view past the trees to the puddle known as Jacob Lake. The setting makes this easily the prettiest RV park in the Grand Canyon area.

Tent campers will also be comfortable here, especially if they pay the extra $3 for one of the improved sites, which have sand rings and views of Jacob Lake. The use of generators is forbidden, so everyone can enjoy the quiet.

The owners recently added two public showers ($1.50 for 5 min.). Now the only thing missing is flush toilets. Several signs stress the fact that the current toilets are hooked up to a larger septic system. Still, they resemble portable toilets in every other conceivable way, including the fact that they're dark as caves at night.

0.5 mile west of Hwy. 67, just south of Jacob Lake. P.O. Box 3331, Flagstaff, AZ 86003. ℂ 928/643-7804 (when open); 800/525-0924 or 928/526-0924 (when closed). www.canyoneers.com. 50 tent sites, 80 RV sites (70 hookups, 10 dry sites). $22 for hookups (up to 4 people); $12 for dry sites (up to 4 people); $12 for tent sites (up to 2 people), plus $2 for each additional person. MC, V.

NEAR THE EASTERN ENTRANCE & THE WESTERN CANYON

Cameron Trading Post RV Park   This is no-frills RV camping near the eastern entrance of the park: Hookups are in a field, with no showers available and only a few cottonwood trees for shade. A few sites at the north end of the campground overlook the Little Colorado River gorge—especially scenic when the river is flowing. Although there's nothing in the way of recreation at the campground, the Cameron Trading Post, with its restaurant and Native American art, is across the street.

U.S. 89 across from Cameron Trading Post (P.O. Box 339), Cameron, AZ 86020. ℂ 800/338-7385 or 928/679-2231. No tent sites, 48 full hookups. $15 per site. AE, DISC, MC, V. Open year-round.

DISPERSED CAMPING IN KAIBAB NATIONAL FOREST

Park visitors can camp for free simply by driving out of the park and into the **Kaibab National Forest** ☆☆. The Forest Service's rules are simple: Camp at least a quarter mile from paved roads, campgrounds, and water, but never in meadows. (No camping is allowed near Hull Cabin or Red Butte.) Pack out your garbage, including used toilet paper, and remove any signs that you've been there. Bury human waste in holes 4 inches deep, 6 inches across, and at least 100 yards from water or creek beds. Completely douse campfires before leaving. If the forest seems dry, check with a local Forest Service office about burn restrictions.

The dispersed camping in the National Forest on the North Rim is among the best anywhere. Here, a number of Forest Service roads lead to canyon overlooks where you're free to spend the night. The most accessible of these used to be the East Rim Overlook, just 4.4 miles off of Highway 67 on FS Road 611. But the Forest Service, citing overuse, closed the rim area to motorized vehicles. Visitors can still park nearby and walk to the overlook, which opens onto views of the Marble Platform and the eastern Grand Canyon. Other overlooks, such as Crazy Jug Point and Parissawampitts Point, remain open to vehicles and have lovely views of the central Grand Canyon, but they require long, bumpy drives. For maps and

information on dispersed camping on the North Rim, visit the
Kaibab Plateau Visitor Center (© **928/643-7298**) in Jacob Lake.

3 Picnic & Camping Supplies

If possible, stock up on your camping items at a large grocery store
in a larger city such as Flagstaff. In general, prices are lowest in
Flagstaff and rise steadily as you near the canyon, peaking at The
Canyon Village Marketplace inside the park.

SOUTH RIM

The Canyon Village Marketplace ★   Located in the business
district of Grand Canyon Village, the general store on the South
Rim is the largest and most complete retailer in the park, selling
groceries, canyon souvenirs, liquor, electronic and automotive
goods, provisions for camping, and hiking and backpacking gear.
Some of the camping equipment can be rented for overnight use.

In Grand Canyon Village. © **928/638-2262.** June–Sept 8am–8pm; Oct–May
8am–7pm.

Desert View Store   The Desert View Store has souvenirs, beer
and wine, and a limited selection of groceries.

At Desert View (off Hwy. 64). © **928/638-2393.** Summer 8am–7pm; rest of year
9am–6pm or 9am–5pm.

NORTH RIM

North Rim General Store   The North Rim General Store is
small but well supplied with groceries, beer and wine, and a very
limited supply of camping equipment. Unlike the General Store on
the South Rim, the North Rim general store cannot outfit aspiring
backpackers.

Adjacent to North Rim Campground. © **928/638-2611,** ext. 270. 8am–8pm daily
(may vary).

6

Where to Stay & Eat in Grand Canyon National Park

This chapter lists accommodations and dining available inside Grand Canyon National Park. Many other hotels and restaurants exist in the nearby communities of Tusayan, Williams, and Flagstaff, AZ, and in Kanab, UT. Rooms in Flagstaff, Williams, and Kanab—all three of which are more than 50 miles from the park—generally cost less than comparable ones inside the park. Tusayan, 1 mile from the park's south entrance, tends to be more expensive than the park. When planning a visit to Grand Canyon, I recommend reserving a place inside the park for at least one night. This lets you savor the twilight hours at the canyon without driving far in the dark.

If you're hoping to spend the night at or near the rim, be sure to call in advance of your stay. During busy years, the lodges inside the park and in Tusayan frequently fill up, forcing would-be lodgers to backtrack away from the park.

If you tire of relatively new rooms with Southwestern motifs, a few historic hotels and lodges do remain. In the park, stay at **Grand Canyon Lodge** (on the North Rim), the **Bright Angel Lodge,** or the **El Tovar Hotel.** Protected by law, these historic structures cannot be gutted during renovation, so their rooms and cabins remain entertainingly quirky—unlike the other park lodging, which tends to be uniform.

See chapter 7, "Gateway Towns," for more information on where to stay and eat, and what to do outside of Grand Canyon National Park.

1 South Rim Lodges

EXPENSIVE

El Tovar Hotel 🐾🐾   Designed as a cross between a Swiss chalet and a Norwegian villa, the El Tovar is a dark, cool counterpoint to the warm, pueblo-style buildings of Mary Colter. Completed in 1905 to accommodate the influx of tourists on the Santa Fe

Reserving a Room Inside the Park

Lodging inside the park is handled by **Amfac Parks and Resorts**, 14001 E. Iliff, Aurora, CO 80014 (© **303/297-2757** or fax 303/297-3175; www.Amfac.com). Beginning on the first of the month, you can reserve a room for the next 23 months. For example, on January 1, 2001, you could have reserved rooms through the end of December 2003. Amfac accepts American Express, Discover, MasterCard, and Visa. Amfac can take reservations up to the minute of your arrival, but you can also make same-day reservations by calling the properties themselves. Pets are not allowed in accommodations inside the park.

On the South Rim, the hotels themselves can be contacted through the same switchboard (© **928/638-2631** or fax 928/638-9247) and mailing address (P.O. Box 699, Grand Canyon, AZ 86023). The phone number for **Grand Canyon Lodge** on the North Rim is © **928/638-2611**. The hotels do not have specific street addresses. When you enter the park, you will receive a map locating all the hotels.

Most of the rooms in the park have relatively new furnishings, and all but a few have telephones and televisions. None have air conditioning. The only conspicuous difference in furnishings is at the El Tovar, where the furniture is more luxurious. Other than that, the buildings themselves are what differ most within the park.

Railroad, the El Tovar, situated roughly 100 yards from the rim, casts a long shadow over Grand Canyon Village. A pointed cupola sits like a witch's cap above its three stories of Oregon pine and stone, and spires rise above an upstairs deck. Nothing seems summery—from a distance, even its broad porches seem to recede into shadows.

The building's interior is as unforgettable as the outside. Moose and elk heads hang on varnished walls, dimly lit by copper chandeliers. Take away the modern-day tourists and the El Tovar probably looks much as it did at its inception, when it offered guests all manner of luxury, including a music room, art classes, and a roof garden.

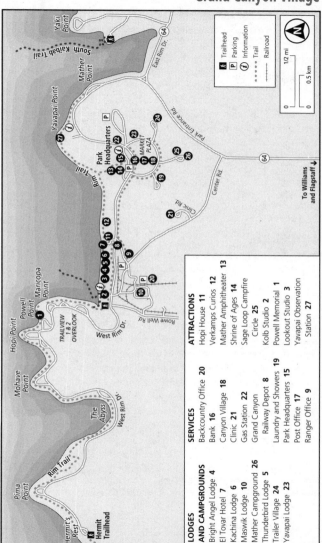

Grand Canyon Village

Trailhead
P Parking
i Information
······ Trail
─── Railroad

0   1/2 mi
0   0.5 km

Yaki Point

South Kaibab Trail

Mather Point

Yavapai Point

East Rim Dr.

64

P

i

Park Headquarters

27

24

23

22

15 i 16
13 14 P 17 18

MARKET
PLAZA

25
26

19

Park Entrance Rd.

Center Rd.

64

To Williams
and Flagstaff →

21

Clinic Rd.

Rim Trail

12

11

7
3 4 5 6
2
i 1

8
9

P

P

10

20

TRAILVIEW
1 & 2
OVERLOOK

Rowe Well Rd.

West Rim Dr.

Powell
Point

Maricopa
Point

Hopi Point

Mohave
Point

The
Abyss

West Rim Dr.

Pima
Point

Rim Trail

Hermit's
Rest

Hermit
Trailhead

LODGES
AND CAMPGROUNDS

Bright Angel Lodge **4**
El Tovar Hotel **7**
Kachina Lodge **6**
Maswik Lodge **10**
Mather Campground **26**
Thunderbird Lodge **5**
Trailer Village **24**
Yavapai Lodge **23**

SERVICES

Backcountry Office **20**
Bank **16**
Canyon Village **18**
Clinic **21**
Gas Station **22**
Grand Canyon
  Railway Depot **8**
Laundry and Showers **19**
Park Headquarters **15**
Post Office **17**
Ranger Office **9**

ATTRACTIONS

Hopi House **11**
Verkamps Curios **12**
Mather Amphitheater **13**
Shrine of Ages **14**
Sage Loop Campfire
  Circle **25**
Kolb Studio **2**
Powell Memorial **1**
Lookout Studio **3**
Yavapai Observation
  Station **27**

While these amenities have gone the way of the Flagstaff-to-Grand Canyon stagecoach, the hotel is still the most luxurious at the canyon and the only one to offer room service and a nightly turndown. At its inception, the rooms were larger, with shared baths at the end of each hall. When private bathrooms were installed, the rooms became smaller and more idiosyncratic. Today, many of the standard rooms are too small for a rollaway. The deluxe rooms are roomier than the standard rooms, but the most stunning accommodations by far are the four view-suites, each of which has a sitting room and a private deck overlooking the canyon. These suites, which cost $286, often fill up a year or more in advance.

✆ **928/638-2631** (main switchboard) or 303/297-2757 (reservations only). Fax 303/297-3175. 78 units. Standard rooms $118–$132; deluxe rooms $176; suites $201–$286. AE, DISC, MC, V. **Amenities:** Restaurant (Continental) in a stunning dining room, lounge with veranda overlooking the rim; concierge; tour desk; room service. *In room:* TV.

MODERATE

Maswik Lodge ✦ *Value*   Built in the 1960s, Maswik Lodge is in a wooded area, a 10-minute walk from the rim. If you're not up to walking, you can catch a free shuttle directly in front of the lodge. The lodge has a cafeteria, sports bar, and gift shop.

The guest rooms are in 16 two-story wood-and-stone buildings known as Maswik North and South. Most Maswik North rooms have vaulted ceilings, private balconies, and forest views, making them among the most pleasant in the park. Rooms in Maswik South are 5 years older, a bit smaller, and have less pristine views. With only one window each, they can also be hot during summer. However, the Maswik South rooms were renovated in 2001, and their low cost—$43 less than Maswik North—makes them a good value despite their shortcomings. During summer, Maswik also rents out 40 guest rooms in ten rustic, thin-walled cabins. If you're staying anywhere at Maswik, bring a flashlight, as the area is dark at night.

✆ **928/638-2631** (main switchboard) or 303/297-2757 (reservations only). Fax 303/297-3175. 278 units. Maswik South $76; Maswik North $119; cabin rooms $64. Winter rate $64. AE, DISC, MC, V. **Amenities:** Cafeteria, sports lounge; tour desk. *In room:* TV, hair dryer (Maswik North only).

Thunderbird and Kachina Lodges ✦   Although the park's master plan preordained the destruction of these rim-side lodges in 1995, no one seems sure when the wrecking ball will actually hit. (Suffice to say that the demolition is on roughly the same timetable as the park's light rail service.) In the meantime, fans of '60s-era dormitory architecture can still admire the flat roofs, decorative concrete panels, and metal staircases on the buildings' exteriors, and the brick walls within.

Inside, the rooms are surprisingly pleasant, with windows as wide as the rooms themselves. Although Amfac refuses to guarantee a canyon view, most of the upstairs units on the more expensive "canyon side" have at least a partial view of the canyon. Check-in for the Thunderbird is at the Bright Angel Lodge; for the Kachina, it's at the El Tovar.

Ⓒ **928/638-2631** (main switchboard) or 303/297-2757 (reservations only). Fax 303/ 297-3175. 55 units at Thunderbird, 49 at Kachina. Park side $116; Canyon side $126. AE, DISC, MC, V. *In room:* TV.

Yavapai Lodge   The largest lodge at the canyon, Yavapai is a mile from the historic district but close to Bank One, the post office, and the Canyon Village Marketplace. Built between 1970 and 1972, the A-frame lodge has a large cafeteria and gift shop. The 358 rooms are in ten single-story buildings known as Yavapai West and six two-story wood buildings known as Yavapai East. Most rooms in Yavapai West have cinder-block walls, and all are compact, but they do afford guests the luxury of driving to the door. Yavapai East's units are larger, and many have views of the forest. Most travelers would agree that they're worth the extra $14. The gravel paths connecting the buildings are very dark at night, so bring a flashlight.

Ⓒ **928/638-2631** (main switchboard) or 303/297-2757 (reservations only). Fax 303/ 297-3175. 348 units. $89 Yavapai West; $103 Yavapai East. Winter $64. AE, DISC, MC, V. **Amenities:** Cafeteria. *In room:* TV, hair dryer (Yavapai East only).

INEXPENSIVE

Bright Angel Lodge & Cabins 𝄞   Guests of Bright Angel Lodge stay in tightly clustered buildings along the rim west of the main lodge. In the 1930s, the Fred Harvey Co. needed to develop new, affordable lodging for the many visitors who had begun driving to the canyon. At the company's request, Mary Colter designed both the lodge and the cabins alongside it. The cabins were built around several historic buildings, including the park's old post office and the Bucky O'Neill Cabin, the oldest continually standing structure on the rim.

Low-end accommodations start with clean, spare rooms in two long buildings adjacent to Bright Angel Lodge. At $48 a night, the "hiker rooms" are the least expensive in the park. Each has a double bed and desk but no television or private bathroom. Other lodge rooms have double beds and toilets but no showers. Still others are appointed like standard motel rooms, only with showers instead of tubs.

Rooms in the historic cabins cost only about $10 more than the most expensive lodge rooms and are worth the extra money. These freestanding cabins, most of which house two guest rooms, recall a time when the canyon was a refuge from civilization. Most rooms have open-frame ceilings, brightly painted window frames, and windows to spare. The rooms nearer the rim are quieter than the ones along the Village Loop Road, where bus traffic can be heavy. At the high end of the price range are the four rim-side cabins, which have partial views of the canyon and cost from $102 to $123. The luxurious Bucky O'Neill Cabin, one of the oldest structures in the park, boasts a fireplace, wet bar, and canyon views. It goes for $236. The rim-side cabins tend to fill up far in advance.

© **928/638-2631** (main switchboard) or 303/297-2757 (reservations only). Fax 303/297-3175. 34 units, 14 with bathroom (10 with sink only, 10 with sink and toilet); 55 cabin units. $48 double with sink only; $54 double with sink and toilet only; $66 double with bathroom; $76 historic cabin; $102–$123 historic rim-cabins; $236 rim-side Bucky O'Neill Suite with fireplace. AE, DISC, MC, V. **Amenities:** Dining room (American), snack bar, lounge (worth seeing), tour desk. *In room:* TV in most rooms.

2 Lodging Inside the Canyon

Phantom Ranch 🏃🏃 Accessible only by floating down the Colorado River or by hiking or riding a mule to the bottom of Grand Canyon, Phantom Ranch is the only park lodging below the canyon rims, and it sometimes sells out on the first day of availability—more than 23 months in advance. To reserve a spot, call as early as possible. If you arrive at the canyon without a reservation, contact the **Bright Angel Transportation Desk** (© **928/638-2631**, ext. 6015) for information about openings the next day.

The reason for the booked slate? Clean sheets never felt better than at the bottom of the Grand Canyon, cold beer never tasted this good (not even close), and a hot shower never felt so, well, miraculous. Phantom Ranch is the only place below the rims inside the park that has these amenities.

The ranch's nine evaporatively cooled cabins are a simple pleasure. A famous Grand Canyon architect, Mary Colter, designed four of them—the ones with the most stone in the walls are hers—using rocks from the nearby Bright Angel Creek. Connected by dirt footpaths, they sit, natural and elegant, alongside picnic tables and under the shade of cottonwood trees. Inside each cabin, there's a desk, concrete floor, and four to ten bunk beds, as well as a toilet and sink. A shower house for guests is nearby.

While most of Phantom Ranch was completed in the 1920s and '30s, four 10-person dorms, each with its own bathing facilities, were added in the early 1980s. Used mostly by hikers, these are ideal for individuals and small groups looking for a place to bed down; larger groups are better served by reserving cabins, which provide both privacy and a lower per-person price than the dorms.

During the day, some guests hike to Ribbon Falls or along the River Trail, while others relax, read, or write postcards that, if sent from here, will bear the unique stamp, "Mailed by mule from the bottom of the Grand Canyon." In the late afternoon, many guests and hikers from the nearby Bright Angel Campground gravitate to the canteen, which sells snacks when not serving meals. (For more on dining at Phantom Ranch, see "Where to Eat Inside the Canyon," later in this chapter.)

Located at the bottom of the canyon, 0.5 mile north of the Colorado River on the North Kaibab Trail. © **928/638-2631** (main switchboard) or 303/297-2757 (reservations only). Fax 303/297-3175. 7 4-person cabins, 2 cabins for up to 10 people; 4 dorms of 10 people each. $23.95 dorm bed; $70.20 cabin (for 2); $11.70 each additional person. Most cabins are reserved as part of mule-trip overnight packages. (See "Mule Trips," in chapter 4, for details.) AE, DISC, MC, V. **Amenities:** Canteen (American). *In room:* Evaporative coolers.

3 Lodging on the North Rim

Grand Canyon Lodge 𝓡𝓡   Like the North Rim itself, Grand Canyon Lodge attracts little attention. Its architect, Gilbert Stanley Underwood, was best known for designing edifices such as train stations and post offices. Although Union Pacific Railroad built the lodge in 1928, the train never came closer than Cedar City, UT. A few tourists came there on "triangle" bus tours that also stopped at Bryce and Zion canyons, but most went to the South Rim. Most still do.

After burning in 1932, the lodge reopened in 1937 and now seems to have grown into the landscape. Its roof of green shingles goes with the needles on the nearby trees, its log posts match their trunks, and its walls of Kaibab limestone blend with the rim rock itself. In its expansive lobby, a 50-foot-high ceiling absorbs sound like the forest floor. Beyond it, the octagonal "Sun Room" has three enormous picture windows opening onto the canyon. Two long decks with imitation-wood chairs flank the sunroom, overlooking the canyon. The lodge also houses a saloon, a snack bar, a meeting room, and an excellent dining room.

Made of the same materials as the lodge, 140 cabins have sprouted like saplings around it. There are four types, all with private bathrooms. With wicker furniture, gas fireplaces, bathtubs, and small vanity rooms, the Western Cabins and Rim Cabins are the most luxurious. The Western Cabins cost $10 less than the four Rim Cabins, which have stunning views of Bright Angel Canyon. The Rim Cabins generally fill up on their first day of availability, nearly 2 years in advance.

The two other types—Pioneer and Frontier—are far more rustic inside. Tightly clustered along the rim of Transept Canyon, they have walls and ceilings of exposed logs, electric heaters, and showers instead of bathtubs. The Frontier Cabins each have one guest room with a double bed and a twin bed. The Pioneer Cabins, meanwhile, each have two guest rooms—one with a double bed and a twin bed, the other with two twins. For $94, a family of five can stay in comfort in one of the Pioneer Cabins.

Tip: If your reservations are for a Frontier or Pioneer cabin, ask for one that has partial view of Transept Canyon. The lodge may be able to accommodate you, and there's no extra charge for the view.

A few motel rooms are also available. Although they're well maintained and were remodeled in 1999, their atmosphere doesn't compare to the cabins.

At North Rim, 214 miles north of South Rim on Hwy. 67. ☎ **928/638-2611** (main switchboard) or 303/297-2757 (reservations only). Fax 303/297-3175. 208 units. $80 Frontier Cabin; $87 motel unit; $94 Pioneer Cabin; $99 Western Cabin; $109 Rim-View Cabin. AE, DISC, MC, V. **Amenities:** 2 restaurants (1 excellent dining room serving Continental fare, 1 snack bar), lounge.

4 Where to Eat on the South Rim

Arizona Room 🐾🐾 STEAKS   Lining up before this restaurant's 4:30pm opening isn't a bad idea. Instead of arriving after sunset to find an hour's wait, you can watch the changing colors through the long, canyon-facing windows. Or, when the days are longer, finish the meal in time to step outside for the evening's show. Either way, make sure you land a table, because the Arizona Room dishes up the most consistently tasty dinners on the South Rim. Entrees include broiled or blackened hand-cut steaks, mustard and rosemary crusted prime rib, marinated chicken breast, and pan-seared salmon with melon salsa. My favorite, the sage-rubbed grilled chicken breast with apple honey glaze, tastes sweet and juicy. To accompany your meal, you can choose from a variety of mid-priced California wines.

At Bright Angel Lodge. ☎ **928/638-2631.** Reservations not accepted. Entrees $16.50–$20.25. AE, DC, DISC, MC, V. 4:30–10pm daily. Closed in winter.

Bright Angel Restaurant *(Kids)* AMERICAN   Although one longtime canyon resident described the food here as "consistently terrible," it struck me as average American coffee shop food. (Perhaps we're both right.) The breakfast fare, including omelets, French toast, and pancakes, tastes inoffensive. At lunch, the burgers, hot sandwiches, and salads usually pass muster. (If not, you can pass the mustard.) At dinner the restaurant supplements the lunch menu by adding palatable entrees such as grilled New York strip steak, chicken Alfredo, and stuffed shells.

This is also a good place for families, who can dine here without worrying much about the children's behavior. The games on the **kid's menu** should distract the small fries until the French fries arrive.

Still, this restaurant, one of the busiest in Arizona, doesn't merit high marks. In addition to absorbing dust from throngs of tourists, it seems to serve as a training camp for new Amfac employees who are destined either to be fired or promoted to the fancy El Tovar Hotel. Besides, comparable food can be found for less money at Yavapai cafeteria.

Located in Bright Angel Lodge. (© **928/638-2631.** Reservations not accepted. Breakfast $4.75–$7.40; lunch $6.35–$9; dinner $6.70–$15. AE, DC, DISC, MC, V. 6:30am–10pm daily.

Desert View Trading Post Cafeteria CAFETERIA   The premade sandwiches and burgers here will sustain you until you make it back to Grand Canyon Village. The breakfast offerings, including eggs and French toast, draw campers from nearby Desert View Campground.

At Desert View, 25 miles east of Grand Canyon Village on Hwy. 64. (© **928/638-2360.** Reservations not accepted. $2–$4.70. No credit cards. Summer 8am–7pm; rest of year 9am–6pm.

El Tovar Restaurant *(Finds)* CONTINENTAL   More than 95 years after opening its doors, this restaurant remains a unique dining experience. Best of all is the stunning room—walls of Oregon pine graced with murals depicting the ritual dances of four Indian tribes and banks of windows at the north and south ends.

At dinner, a Southwestern influence spices the Continental cuisine. One tasty appetizer is the chicken black bean tamale. For an entree, meat eaters will enjoy the flame-broiled peppercorn crusted filet mignon in roasted garlic sauce. Meanwhile, vegetarians can munch the *Clesan-Du-Klish* (Native American vegan blue corn tamales).

The Grand Canyon After Dark

Most people visiting the Grand Canyon don't picture any-thing other than a campfire when they think of evening entertainment, but in fact there's quite a bit of nightlife. On the South Rim, **Maswik Lodge** has a spacious sports bar with a big-screen TV and a pool table. If your favorite team is on the tube at a time when you'd like to dine, grab a tray of food from Maswik Cafeteria, then consume it in the adjoin-ing sports bar. Open from 5pm to 11pm daily, this bar is particularly popular with canyon locals. In 2001, it was also the only canyon bar that allowed smoking. However, Amfac's new contract with the National Park Service calls for an end to smoking in all canyon bars in the near future.

The lounge at the **El Tovar Hotel** (11am–11pm) is the most luxurious watering hole at the canyon, with copper lanterns, stained glass, and cushy furniture. Best of all, however, is its veranda, which overlooks an expanse of lush grass, the rim-side sidewalk, and a slice of the North Rim of the canyon. On a hot afternoon at Grand Canyon Village, cool off here over an iced tea, draft beer, or a prickly pear Margarita (a standard Margarita, but with the sweet juice from a prickly pear cactus). The interior of the lounge is smoke-free, but puffing is allowed on the veranda.

During daytime, the **Bright Angel Lounge** (open 11am–11pm daily) often feels more like a waiting room than a

The El Tovar accepts reservations for dinner only, but it's also open for breakfast and lunch. If you're traveling on a budget or prefer the dinner menu at the Arizona Room (as I do), try dining here during nondinner hours, when you can enjoy the lovely surroundings for just a dollar or two more than you'd spend at the other canyon restaurants. At breakfast, be sure to sample the coffee, the best inside the park, and order the eggs Benedict with smoked salmon.

In the El Tovar Lodge. ✆ **928/638-2631**, ext. 6432. Reservations accepted for dinner only. Breakfast $3.70–$10; lunch $6.95–$14.95; dinner entrees $16.50–$23. AE, DC, DISC, MC, V. 6:30–11am, 11:30am–2pm, and 5–10pm daily.

The Delicatessen at Marketplace _Value_ DELI Many Park Service employees duck into this delicatessen for lunch. Here you watering hole. People use this dark bar room to kill time when their traveling partners are dawdling on hikes or in the nearby shops. Yet the lounge has character in abundance, from its 1958 mural of Anglo tourists by the famous Hopi artist, Fred Kabotie, to the historic photos and postcards suspended in the clear coating on the bar top.

On the North Rim, you'll find a full-service bar, the Rough Rider Saloon at **Grand Canyon Lodge.** Photos of Theodore Roosevelt on the North Rim grace the walls of the saloon, where, come evening, off-duty mule wranglers sometimes swap stories with tourists. When the night really starts hopping, someone usually ponies up for a round of "mule shots"—bourbon topped with Amaretto. Like the bar itself, this drink sweetens a Western tradition. If you'd like to take your beverage onto one of the lodge's decks, you're free to do so.

In addition, Rangers deliver more traditional evening programs on the Grand Canyon (see *The Guide* for details). From May through September, Rangers explore a different topic nightly at Mather Amphitheater near park headquarters on the South Rim. They also lead stargazing programs at Mather Point. On the North Rim, evening ranger presentations are offered at both the Campground Amphitheater and inside Grand Canyon Lodge.

can sit in a corner booth, read the paper, and watch the tourists pass. The deli serves pre-made sandwiches, salads, pizza slices, and hot dishes, including fried chicken, but the best offerings are often the daily specials.

In the South Rim's Canyon Village Marketplace (at Market Plaza). © 928/ 638-2262. $2–$5. No credit cards. 8am–6pm daily.

Maswik and Yavapai Cafeterias *Value* CAFETERIA   For the price of a burger, fries, and a soft drink at the Tusayan McDonald's, you can eat a full meal at either Maswik or Yavapai cafeterias. Though the food costs about the same at either place, there are some key differences between the two. Maswik more closely resembles a food court, where meals come complete with side dishes. One

Maswik station serves Mexican fare; another has hot sandwich plates; a third offers spaghetti and burgers; and a fourth serves barbecue chicken and steak.

At Yavapai, you can mix and match from a variety of stations, picking up a piece of fried chicken from one, a slice of pizza from another, a dish of mashed potatoes from another. (A case of indigestion, when you put it all together.) For $2.25, you can also assemble your own dinner salad at the salad bar. When dining here, try the turkey potpie.

Compared with Maswik's food, Yavapai's fare tastes less institutional. If you're hungry for a burger, however, go to Maswik, where the meat is grilled instead of fried.

Located at Maswik and Yavapai lodges, respectively. ☎ **928/638-2631.** Reservations not accepted. Breakfast $2–$5.25; lunch and dinner $2.75–$7. AE, DC, DISC, MC, V. Maswik 6am–9pm daily; Yavapai 6am–10pm daily (may fluctuate seasonally; closed in low season).

5 Where to Eat Inside the Canyon

Phantom Ranch 🐸🐸 AMERICAN   At the bottom of the Grand Canyon, pretty much anything tastes good, so it's hard to say whether the food at Phantom Ranch would taste as great on the rim as alongside Bright Angel Creek. Whether you arrive by mule or on foot, the food almost always tastes fine.

If you want dinner served your way, however, bring a camp stove. Every evening, just three options are offered: a steak dinner at 5pm, a vegetarian dinner at 5pm, and a hearty beef stew at 6:30pm. The vegetarian plate consists of lentil loaf and the side dishes to the steak dinner: vegetables, cornbread, baked potato, and salad. With either dinner, the dessert is chocolate cake.

The family style, all-you-can-eat breakfasts are also excellent, with heaping platters of eggs, bacon, and pancakes laid out on the long tables in the canteen. The only disappointment is the sack lunch, whose meager offerings (bagel, summer sausage, juice, apple, peanuts, raisins, pretzels, cookies, and apple juice) don't seem worth the $8.50 price. Pack your own lunch and, if necessary, supplement it with snacks from the canteen.

Because the number of meals is fixed, hikers and mule riders must reserve them ahead of time through Amfac (see earlier in this chapter) or at the Bright Angel Transportation Desk. As a last resort, inquire upon arrival at Phantom Ranch to see whether any meals remain. Up until 4pm this can be done in the canteen itself. After 4pm, ask at the side window behind the canteen. Between 8am

(8:30am in winter) and 4pm and from 8 to 10pm, anyone is allowed in the canteen, which sells snacks, soda, beer, wine, basic first-aid items, souvenirs and film.

Inside the canyon 0.5 mile north of the Colorado River on the North Kaibab Trail. To reserve meals more than one day in advance, call *C* 303/297-2757; to reserve meals for the next day, contact the Bright Angel Transportation Desk at 928/638-2631, ext. 6015. Steak dinner $29.35; stew $19.05; vegetarian $19.05; sack lunch $8.50; breakfast $15.85. AE, DC, DISC, MC, V (for advance reservations: AE, DISC, MC, V only).

6 Where to Eat on the North Rim

Grand Canyon Lodge Dining Room *★★* CONTINENTAL Long banks of west- and south-facing windows afford views of Transept Canyon and help warm this room, where the high, open-framed ceiling absorbs the clamor of diners. This is, without question, one of the most scenic dining rooms anywhere. Now, thanks in part to a food and beverage director from Utah's posh Deer Valley resort, the cuisine pleases diners nearly as much as the surroundings do.

At dinner, pesto lovers will enjoy the Pasta Lydia—fresh asparagus and potatoes tossed in pesto sauce with bow-tie pasta. Other excellent choices are the pan-seared Atlantic salmon topped with blueberry chardonnay sauce, and the Four Corners lime chicken— a sautéed chicken breast with artichokes and capers in white wine sauce. The restaurant also offers steaks, prime rib, and salmon, as well as a varied wine list.

The lunch menu consists of mostly burgers, sandwiches and salads. I loved the Asian chicken and noodle salad—stir-fried chicken slices, mixed vegetables, and peanut chili sauce over Asian noodles and mixed greens. At breakfast, a full buffet costs under $9, but the most delectable choice may be the artichoke and asiago cheese omelet.

Tip: Because of the volume of diners, the staff here does not accept reservations for window seats. However, they can often accommodate people who are willing to wait.

At Grand Canyon Lodge. *C* 928/638-2611, ext. 160. Reservations required for dinner, not accepted for breakfast and lunch. Breakfast $2.20–$7.85; lunch $4.75–$9.50; dinner $14.25–$22.50. AE, DC, DISC, MC, V. 6:30–10am, 11:30am–2:30pm, and 4:45–9:30pm daily.

Café on The Rim AMERICAN The cafe serves the best pizza on the North Rim, or so the joke goes. That speaks well for the pizza, which could just as easily—and no less truthfully—be called the worst. At $2.65 a slice, it's an economical alternative to firing up the camp stove; though not an ethereal experience. The snack bar also serves calzones, burgers, salads, made-to-order sandwiches, and breakfasts. If all you desire is good coffee and a muffin, stop by the saloon, where an espresso bar operates daily from 5:30 to 9am. Its prices are high—a tall double mocha runs $4—but the java is the strongest in the park. The saloon continues to serve espresso, minus the pastries, after the bar opens at 11am.

In the west wing of Grand Canyon Lodge. ✆ **928/638-2611.** Reservations not accepted. Breakfast $1.85–$4.80; lunch and dinner $2.65–$6.70; 14-in. Hawaiian-style pizza $16.80. AE, DISC, MC, V. 7am–9pm daily.

Gateway Towns

The Grand Canyon isn't the only wonder in northern Arizona. The surrounding area on the Colorado Plateau is among the most stunning in the world, a sparsely populated landscape of 12,000-foot-high volcanoes and 3,000-foot-deep red-rock canyons—linked by the largest ponderosa pine forest on the planet. Lonely highways lace the countryside, inviting exploration. During your travels, you can track California condors, or watch elk wander the forests. You can walk the same paths and stand in rooms used for centuries by America's indigenous peoples, then learn about the cultures of their modern descendants. You can chat with cowboys in Williams or venture to Flagstaff's cultural attractions, including the Lowell Observatory and the Museum of Northern Arizona. The many diversions won't detract from your trip to the canyon; they'll simply enhance your appreciation of this area, with the canyon at its heart.

1 Flagstaff ✶✶

150 miles N of Phoenix; 32 miles E of Williams; 78 miles S of Grand Canyon Village

Home to Northern Arizona University, the Museum of Northern Arizona, and the Hansen Planetarium, as well as dozens of excellent restaurants and clubs, Flagstaff lets you nurture your intellect, dine on gourmet food, and dance to live music without losing sight of the more important things—the 12,000-foot-high San Francisco Peaks, which rise just north of town. Its historic downtown, with its many shops and galleries, attracts a mix of students, locals, and tourists. Freight trains regularly clatter past, shaking cappuccinos and drowning out street musicians before continuing to points less desirable. Flanked by motels with colorful names such as the Pony Soldier, Geronimo, and El Pueblo, Route 66 parallels the tracks.

ESSENTIALS

GETTING THERE **By Car** Flagstaff is on I-40, one of the main east-west interstates in the United States. I-17 also starts here and heads south to Phoenix. U.S. 89A connects Flagstaff to Sedona

Flagstaff

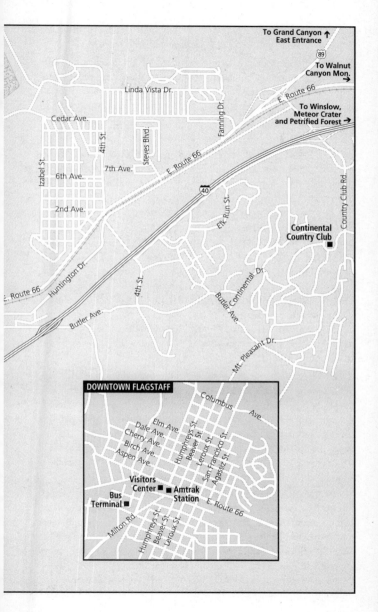

by way of Oak Creek Canyon. U.S. 180 links Flagstaff with Grand
Canyon Village, and U.S. 89 goes from Flagstaff to Page.

By Plane   Flagstaff's Pulliam Airport, which is located three miles
south of town off I-17, is served by **America West Express** (📞 800/
235-9292) from Phoenix.

By Train   Flagstaff is also served by **Amtrak** (📞 800/872-7245
for reservations, or 928/774-8679 for station information only)
from Chicago and Los Angeles. The train station is at 1 E. Rte. 66.

VISITOR INFORMATION   The **Flagstaff Visitor Center,** at 1 E.
Rte. 66 (📞 800/842-7293 or 928/774-9541; www.flagstaff.az.us), is
open daily from 8am to 5pm.

GETTING AROUND   Car rentals are available from **Avis**
(📞 800/831-2847 or 928/774-8421), **Budget** (📞 800/527-0700 or
928/779-5255), **Enterprise** (📞 800/736-8222 or 928/526-1377),
Hertz (📞 800/654-3131 or 928/774-4452), **National** (📞 800/
227-7368 or 928/779-1975), and **X-Press Rent A Car** (📞 800/
522-0773).

   If you need a taxi, call **Friendly Cab** (📞 928/774-4444 or 928-
214-9000), **Sun Taxi & Tours** (📞 800/483-4488 or 928/774-7400),
or **Arizona Taxi & Tours** (📞 928/779-1111).

   Pine Country Transit (📞 928/779-6624) provides public bus
transit around the city every day except Sunday. The fare is 75¢ for
adults.

ORIENTATION   Downtown Flagstaff is located just north of I-40.
Milton Road, which at its southern end becomes I-17 to Phoenix,
passes Northern Arizona University on its way downtown where it
merges with Route 66. Part of Route 66, Santa Fe Avenue, parallels
the railroad tracks, linking the city's historic downtown with its east
side. Downtown's main street is San Francisco Street, while
Humphreys Street leads north out of town toward the San Francisco
Peaks and the south rim of the Grand Canyon.

SUPERMARKETS & GENERAL STORES   If you want to stock
up on food before you hit the road, here are several places to stop:
Albertson's, 1416 E. Rte. 66 (📞 928/773-7955), open daily 6am
to midnight; **Basha's,** 2700 Woodlands Village Blvd. (📞 928/
774-3882), open daily 5am to 1am; **Basha's,** 1000 N. Humphreys
St. (📞 928/774-2101), open daily 6am to 10pm; and **Fry's,** 201 N.
Switzer Canyon Dr. (📞 928/774-2719), open daily 6am to
midnight.

Bus Service to the Canyon

For those without cars, **Nava-Hopi Bus Lines** (© 800/892-8687 or 928/774-5003) provides regular bus service linking Grand Canyon National Park with Flagstaff. During high season, buses from Flagstaff to Grand Canyon leave daily at 7:45am and 2:45pm, arriving at Maswik Transportation Center inside the park about two hours later. The one-way Flagstaff-to-Grand Canyon fare is $14 plus a $6 park entrance fee.

WHAT TO SEE & DO

Lowell Observatory ⊕ *Kids* Percival Lowell, an amateur astronomer, realized that Flagstaff's dry, thin air made the town a choice location for observing the heavens. Hoping to find life on Mars, the Boston aristocrat built an observatory atop a hill here in 1894, then used it to study the skies for the next 22 years. Though he never found life on Mars, the research done at his observatory has contributed greatly to our knowledge of the heavens. In the past century, Lowell Observatory helped discover Pluto, map out the moon, and provide evidence of an expanding universe.

Today, in addition to conducting research, the observatory's 15 Ph.D.-level astronomers educate and entertain the public. It's most fun to come here on clear nights, when they'll help you peer through telescopes at stars far across the galaxy. (Call for a schedule of nighttime programs.) During daytime, tours of the observatory and historic rotunda library are offered. And, the Steele Visitor Center has exciting, state-of-the-art interactive displays, suitable for both adults and kids. They make a trip here worthwhile, any time.

1400 W. Mars Hill Rd., Flagstaff. © **928/774-2096.** www.lowell.edu/. Admission $4 adults, $3.50 seniors and students, $2 ages 5–17, free for children 4 and under. AE, MC, V. Visitor center open 9am–5pm daily Apr–Oct; noon–5pm daily Nov–Dec and Mar; noon–5pm Wed–Sun Jan–Feb. Nighttime hours vary (call for specific program information).

Museum of Northern Arizona ⊕⊕⊕ Founded in 1928 by a Flagstaff couple concerned about the widespread removal of artifacts from the area, this museum explores the history, science, and cultures of the Colorado Plateau. Its **Geology Room** has displays on the unique landforms in the area, and the **Special Exhibits Gallery** frequently shows art from the region. But the best attraction here— one of the best anywhere—is the display of Native American artifacts, culled from the museum's five-million-piece collection.

Always beautiful and occasionally moving, they are arranged in a context that illuminates the history and spirit of the Native American people.

3101 N. Fort Valley Rd. (U.S. Hwy 180), Flagstaff. © **928/774-5213**. www.musnaz. org. Admission $5 adults, $4 seniors, $3 students with ID, $2 children ages 7–17, free for children 6 and under. AE, DISC, MC, V. Daily 9am–5pm.

Sunset Crater Volcano National Monument 𝒜

Sunset Crater formed in 1064 atop a weak spot in the earth's crust. An underground gas chamber exploded, spewing tons of cinders around the newly created vent in the earth. Within a few months of the explosion, cinders had piled up to form a 1,000-foot-tall pyramid-shaped crater. Lava poured intermittently from openings near the bottom of the crater for the next 200 years, snaking across the land before ossifying in choppy mounds that to this day look viscous. In one final flourish of activity, small eruptions deposited red and yellow ash atop the otherwise black cone.

The activity produced a landscape of eerie shapes and striking, subtle colors. During an expedition in the late 1800s, the explorer John Wesley Powell saw this colorful cone, perhaps in the low light in which it is most striking, and named it Sunset Crater. Today, the national monument has a picnic area, visitor center, and several walking trails. Try visiting here in early morning or late afternoon, when the colors are richest.

15 miles north of Flagstaff on Hwy. 89. © **928/526-0502**. www.nps.gov/sucr. Admission $3 adults, free for children under 16. Fee also covers entrance to Wupatki National Monument. Cash or National Park passes at entrance gate. Summer 8am–6pm daily; spring and fall 8am–5pm daily; winter 9am–5pm daily.

Walnut Canyon National Monument 𝒜𝒜

The Sinagua (a subgroup of the Ancestral Puebloans) occupied this wooded canyon for roughly 125 years from 1125 to 1250. They built hundreds of dwellings under natural rock overhangs on sunny east- and south-facing cliffs, and tucked granaries into the smallest openings. Atop the canyon rims, they dug out terraces and check dams that would help keep their crops moist, and erected pit houses and pueblo-style dwellings.

Although most of the terraces and check dams have collapsed, 300 rooms remain. Twenty-five are on the **Island Trail,** a 1-mile-long loop that descends 185 feet (with over 100 steps) below the visitor center. Many others are visible from the trail, on the canyon walls. Another, relatively flat 0.7-mile trail travels along the rim of

> **Tips Planning Tip**
>
> Using Flagstaff as a home base, one can easily visit Walnut Canyon, Sunset Crater, and Wupatki monuments in a long, rewarding day.

the canyon, affording views of the cliff dwellings in addition to skirting the rim-top ruins.

This is a lovely canyon and, with just 125,000 visitors annually, one of the quietest national monuments. By coming off-hours, you can sometimes find yourself alone here, and that's a great way to experience the world of the Ancestral Puebloans.

10 miles east of Flagstaff off I-40 (exit 204). ✆ **928/526-3367.** www.nps.gov/waca/. Admission $3 adults, free for children under 17. Cash only at entrance gate. Summer 8am–6pm daily; spring and fall 8am–5pm daily; winter 8am–5pm daily.

Wupatki National Monument ✦   As their population grew in the 1100s, a large number of the Sinagua people moved onto the land north of Sunset Crater. Today, 800 ruins from this period are scattered across Wupatki National Monument. Some of the most remarkable are near the visitor center, including a mysterious ball court with walls 6 feet high, and pueblo ruins made from the same Moenkopi Sandstone atop which they're built. A blowhole, which releases air from underground caverns, may have had a special significance to the Indians who settled nearby. Other ruins are scattered along the road that loops through the monument, usually in elevated spots with expansive views of both the Painted Desert and San Francisco Peaks. Most of the Sinagua left in the 1200s and are believed to have become the modern-day Hopi (and perhaps Zuni).

35 miles north of Flagstaff on Hwy. 89. ✆ **928/679-2365.** www.nps.gov/wupa/. Admission $3 adults, free for children under 16. Fee also good for Sunset Crater Volcano National Monument. Cash only at entrance gate. Visitor center June 1–Sept 30 8am–6pm daily; Oct 1–May 31 8am–5pm daily.

WHERE TO STAY
EXPENSIVE TO MODERATE
A recommended, expensive chain hotel in Flagstaff is **Radisson Woodlands Hotel Flagstaff** (✆ 928/773-8888), 1175 W. Rte. 66. A recommended, mid-price chain hotel in Flagstaff is the **Holiday Inn Flagstaff** (✆ 928/714-1000), 2320 E. Lucky Lane (off I-40 Exit 198). In addition, a recommended B&B in Flagstaff is **Jeanette's**

Bed and Breakfast (© 800/752-1912 or 928/527-1912), 3380 E. Lockett Rd.; double $115 to $145.

Comfi Cottages ★★ *Kids*   In the 1970s Pat Wiebe, a nurse at the local hospital, began purchasing and renovating small homes in Flagstaff. Today, she rents out six of these quaint cottages, all but one of which were built in the 1920s and '30s. They're old but not ancient, the type of places that have laundry chutes, flour bins, ironing boards that fold into the walls, see-through cupboard doors, and hardwood floors. Wiebe has modernized the cottages somewhat, adding thermostat-controlled fireplaces, televisions, VCRs, and washer/dryers. And, she goes out of her way to make them comfortable. In every unit you'll find fresh-cut flowers, antiques, cupboards stocked with breakfast foods, and rag dolls from her personal collection. Outside of each cottage is a picnic table and gas grill, and most have bicycles and sleds in the garage. These cottages, which sleep from two to six people, can make you feel as if you've acquired a new home, where kids are welcome. My favorite unit is the two-bedroom, one-bathroom cottage at 710 W. Birch Street. Like most of the others, it's just a short walk from the historic business district. And it's beautiful.

1612 N. Aztec St., Flagstaff, AZ 86001. © **888/774-0731** or 928/774-0731. Fax 928/ 773-7286. www.comficottages.com. 6 cottages in different locations in Flagstaff. $110–$250 double. Extra $10 per person, per night, if more than 2 people. Rates include breakfast. DISC, MC, V. Inquire about pets. **Amenities:** Free use of bicycles. *In room:* A/C (in 2 cottages only), TV, kitchen, fridge stocked with breakfast foods, coffeemaker, iron, washer/dryer.

The Inn At 410 Bed & Breakfast ★★ *Finds*   Peering into each of the nine guest rooms at the Inn At 410 is like flipping the pages in an issue of *House and Garden.* Each expertly decorated room is daringly different, yet tasteful. Collectively, they make this 1894 home owned by Sally and Howard Krueger one of the most stunning B&Bs anywhere. One room, "Monet's Garden," is reminiscent of a French country garden. Sections of its walls have been painted to resemble broken plaster (far more appealing than the real thing, found in some Rte. 66 motels), while other areas have reproductions of Monet works brushed upon them. My favorite, "The Dakota Room," celebrates the cowboy way of life. It has barn wood on one wall, and wallpaper with a cowpoke motif on others. Atop the armoire sits a cowboy hat that once belonged to Sally Krueger's grandfather; her grandmother's old cowgirl boots rest on the mantle.

All but one of the guest rooms here have gas fireplaces, and three of them have jetted tubs.

410 N. Leroux St., Flagstaff, AZ 86001. © 800/774-2008 or 928/774-0088. Fax 928/774-6354. www.inn410.com. 9 units. $135–$190 double. MC, V. *In room:* A/C, fridge, coffeemaker, hair dryer, no phone.

Fall Inn To Nature Bed & Breakfast ⚝ *Value*   Annette Fallaha, owner of Fall Inn To Nature, celebrates a different animal species in each of the three guest rooms. In the Butterfly Room, for example, you'll find butterfly *everything,* including clocks, cards, collages, puzzles, lamps, crafts, wallpaper, articles (about, not by), comforters, and sheets. There's also a "Rabbit Room," where the decorations seem to have multiplied, as well as a guest unit celebrating birds and the Southwest. The rooms also come with their share of creature comforts, including robes and fresh-baked cookies.

Built in the late 1990s, the bright, immaculate house has windows opening onto views of the San Francisco Peaks. Its location, seven miles northeast of Flagstaff's historic downtown, makes it a convenient starting point for tours of Walnut Canyon, Wupatki and Sunset Crater Volcano monuments.

8080 N. Colt Dr., Flagstaff, AZ 86004. © 888/920-0237 or 928/714-0237. Fax 928/714-0237. www.bbonline.com/az/fallinn/. 3 units, 2 with private bathroom (1 bathroom has a shower only). $65–$95 double. AE, MC, V. Children under 6 not permitted. **Amenities:** Jacuzzi. *In room:* TV/VCR (2 rooms), coffeemaker, hair dryer, iron.

Little America Hotel ⚝⚝ *Value*   Strangely enough, the most luxurious chain-hotel accommodations in Flagstaff adjoin a truck stop. Little America's rooms are enormous—they have sitting areas, dressing areas, dining tables, and oversized tubs. They're lavishly decorated in the French Colonial style (think Versailles). And they're quiet—especially the ones farthest from I-40.

An even better surprise is the surroundings: 500 largely wooded acres, owned by the hotel, providing access to Flagstaff's urban trail system and, farther out, the Arizona Trail. Closer to the rooms, there's a large outdoor pool, sand volleyball courts, horseshoe pits, and a 1.75-mile jogging trail. And if, by chance, you need 60 gallons of diesel, a mesh baseball cap with an enormous forehead, or coffee in an imposing Styrofoam cup, you won't have to go far. It's almost weird.

2515 E. Butler (off I-40 Exit 198), Flagstaff, AZ. © 800/352-4386 or 928/779-7900. Fax 928/779-7983. www.flagstaff.littleamerica.com. 244 units; 2 apt suites, 1 executive suite. Jan 1–Mar 8 $79–$89 double; Mar 9–Apr 30 and Nov 1–Dec 24 $89–$99 double; May 1–Oct 31 and Dec 25–31 $119–$129 double. AE, DC, DISC,

MC, V. **Amenities:** 3 restaurants (deli, coffee shop, and fine dining); lounge; outdoor pool; exercise room; jogging trail; outdoor Jacuzzi; playground; concierge; business center; shopping arcade; room service (6am–11pm); massage; coin-op washers/dryers; executive level rooms. *In room:* A/C, TV with pay movies, dataport, fridge, coffeemaker, hair dryer, iron.

INEXPENSIVE

A recommended, inexpensive chain motel in Flagstaff is **Super 8 Motel** (© **888/324-9131** or 928/526-0818; fax 928/526-8786), N. Kasper Ave (on Rte. 66, 1 mi. west of I-40 Exit 201).

Hotel Weatherford *(Value)*   Constructed in 1898, this hotel in downtown Flagstaff has some fascinating common areas. An upstairs sitting room features quirky antiques such as a cider press and antique sewing machine, as well as panoramic photos of turn-of-the-century Flagstaff. The Zane Grey Room, on the hotel's third floor, has a hand-carved Brunswick bar next to a fireplace and across from an original painting by the legendary 19th-century landscape artist Thomas Moran. Patrons of the Zane Grey Room can also enjoy the new wrap-around balcony, overlooking the downtown streets.

The guest rooms, only two of which have private bathrooms, are varied and eccentric. My favorite, no. 57, has hardwood floors, an Art Deco style bedroom set, and three 10-foot-high windows that date to its days as the hotel's sun parlor. A transom opens onto the hallway, helping create a draft. The main advantage to this hotel is its lively atmosphere. However, this can also become a drawback when loud partyers walk from the downstairs bar, where live music plays most nights, to the Zane Grey Room, which is situated just a few yards from some of the guest rooms. If you're planning to stay here, rest up plenty in advance and then join the party, starting with a meal at the hotel's restaurant, Charly's. For the least noise, get a room (like no. 57) at the end of the building farthest from the Zane Grey Room.

23 N. Leroux, Flagstaff, AZ 86001. © **928/779-1919.** www.weatherfordhotel.com. 8 units, 6 with shared bathrooms. High-season $45–$60 double; low-season $35–$45 double. AE, DC, DISC, MC, V. Parking mostly on the street, with a few private spaces behind the hotel. **Amenities:** Restaurant (Southwestern/American); 3 delightful bars. *In room:* No phone.

WHERE TO EAT
EXPENSIVE

Black Bart's Steak House, Saloon, and Musical Revue ⭐ *(Kids)*
AMERICAN   Initially I was less than enthralled by the prospect of dining at a steak house and musical revue named for a legendary robber. Past experience had convinced me that people who sing near

steaks sing badly, and that people who cook near singers cook badly, and that people who run steak houses offering bad singing and bad cooking were themselves legendary robbers. But this restaurant surprised me. First, the music is nicely performed by music students from Northern Arizona University. They capably croon country, blues, and cabaret songs, then hurry back to the tables they're serving. Even more surprising is the fact that the food—an assortment of hand-cut steaks and prime rib, salmon, grilled tuna, and ribs—can be pretty tasty. The highlight is the all-you-can-eat sourdough biscuits with honey butter, served with every meal.

2760 E. Butler Ave., Flagstaff. ☏ 928/779-3142. Reservations accepted. Dinner $11–$26. AE, DC, DISC, MC, V. Daily 5–9pm.

Monsoon ☏ NEW ASIAN   With seating for 122, Monsoon sprawls like an L.A. hotspot—and it feels like one too. A sharp-looking waitstaff, dressed in black, dashes through the three dining rooms faster than people in northern Arizona have heretofore been known to move. They speed past bamboo sticks in large vases, ceremonial gowns from China, paintings from Susan Rene's "Desert Dog" collection, and a wall-length print of a 150-year-old Chinese lithograph. The food, which fuses Chinese, Japanese, Korean, and Pacific Island fare, has generated a buzz around town, even though people don't always understand it. Highlights include scallops on crispy spinach, and Thai spicy shrimp with green beans in brown sauce.

1551 S. Milton Dr., Flagstaff. ☏ 928/774-2266. Reservations accepted. Main courses $9.95–$17.95. AE, MC, V. Mon–Thurs 5–10pm; Fri–Sat 5–11pm; closed Sun.

Chez Marc Bistro ☏☏☏ COUNTRY FRENCH   Come to this country French restaurant if you'd like to splurge on a great meal. The talented chef, Marc Balocco, has cooked for luminaries such as Margaret Thatcher and Queen Elizabeth II, but he seems to take nearly as much pride in feeding everyday tourists and Flagstaff locals. Served by waiters in formal attire, you can dine in the bistro's brick-walled, wooden-floored interior, where magnums of champagne line the walls, or, during warm weather, on its outside terrace, surrounded by lovely gardens. You'll savor food that's superb not only in taste, but also in texture and appearance. Start with the *crepe de saumon fume au caviar* (Norwegian smoked salmon rolled in a crepe with cucumber relish, sour cream, and topped with caviar), then try the *faison aux champignon sauvage* (breast of pheasant sautéed with a forest mushroom fricassee laced in a creamy Chablis sauce). For dessert, the restaurant staff recommends the crème brûlée. Cap it with French-pressed coffee and (what the heck) an after-dinner drink.

503 Humphreys St., Flagstaff. (C) **928/774-1343**. Reservations recommended. Lunch $7.50–$13.95; dinner $19.95–$29.95. AE, DC, DISC, MC, V. Fri–Sun 11:30am–2:30pm (summers only); daily 5–9pm (year-round).

MODERATE

Charly's ☞ SOUTHWESTERN/AMERICAN Charly's is spacious and cool, both inside, where the 12-foot-high ceilings of the Hotel Weatherford (built in 1897) provide breathing room, and on the sidewalk, a favorite place for summertime dining. Besides steaks, fish, and burgers, the restaurant offers a number of vegetarian dishes that make for perfect light dining. Try the Durango Tacos—soft tacos with avocado, cilantro, and onions, filled with your choice of beef, chicken, fish, or grilled vegetables. After dinner, you can dance at the hotel bar, which features live entertainment nightly and has 20 beers on tap.

In the historic Hotel Weatherford, 23 N. Leroux, Flagstaff. (C) **928/779-1919**. Reservations accepted. Lunch $5.95–$8.95; dinner entrees $11.95–$16.95. AE, DC, DISC, MC, V. Daily 11am–11pm (10pm in winter).

Dara Thai ☞☞ Value THAI Among the 80-some entrees served at Dara Thai are many fine curry, noodle, vegetarian, and fish dishes. Everything I've had here has been delectable, but you should order cautiously nonetheless. Your server will ask you to select the spiciness level for many sauces, and if you choose the highest level you may soon find your tongue hotter than Phantom Ranch in July. Fortunately, the restaurant provides Thai beer and white rice to cut the heat. Decorated with plants (some real, others painted on the cinder block walls), the dining area seems to have a psychological cooling effect, if not a physical one.

14 S. San Francisco St., Flagstaff. (C) **928/774-0047** or 928/774-8390. Reservations accepted for parties of 4 or more. Lunch items $5.75–$7.95; dinner main courses $6.50–$12.95. MC, V. Mon–Sat 11am–10pm; closed Sun.

INEXPENSIVE

The Black Bean Burrito Bar and Salsa Company ☞ Value MEXICAN The best burritos seem to turn up in the plainest environments. At the Black Bean, you'll eat out of plastic drive-in baskets while sitting at a counter that opens onto a pedestrian walkway. Sure enough, the burritos, which come with a choice of six different salsas, are delicious. A favorite among Northern Arizona University students, the Black Bean offers seven house specialty wraps (steamed or stir-fried food wrapped in tortillas), including exotic flavors such as Thai peanut tofu and roasted jalapeño chicken, as well as traditional bean, chicken, and steak burritos. Wrapped in aluminum foil, the burritos have the heft of hand weights. But with most under $5, they won't burden you financially.

12 E. Rte. 66, Gateway Plaza Suite 104, Flagstaff. © **928/779-9905**. Reservations not accepted. $1.25–$5. MC, V. Summer Sun noon–8pm, Mon–Sat 11am–9pm; call for winter hours.

Cafe Espress ★★ NEW AMERICAN   Like Macy's (see review in this section), Cafe Espress serves great vegetarian fare and displays paintings by local artists. But if the two restaurants were pastries, Macy's would be a nut bran muffin, while Cafe Espress would be a croissant. With hardwood floors and 12-foot ceilings, the interior of Cafe Espress seems brighter than Macy's, and its furniture, unlike the furnishings at Macy's, doesn't resemble something from a Rathskeller. Cafe Espress's food is slightly more refined, in terms of both preparation and ingredients. It may not be as healthful as the food at Macy's, but it sure tastes good. The breakfast fare includes delicious omelettes, huevos rancheros, and pancakes, with tofu available as a substitute for eggs. The lunch and dinner menu is a hodgepodge of soups, sandwiches, salads, and Southwestern fare. The most delectable items, however, are house specials like the rata-touille and veggie kabobs. Don't forget to order a slice of cheesecake or carrot cake, as the desserts here are among the best in town.

16 N. San Francisco St., Flagstaff. © **928/774-0541**. Reservations accepted. Breakfast and lunch $2.75–$7.95; dinner entrees $7.95–$13.95. MC, V. Daily 7am–9pm.

Macy's European Coffee House Bakery & Vegetarian Restaurante ★ *Finds* VEGETARIAN/BAKED GOODS   A refreshing breeze always seems to blow through this restaurant, skimming the dust off the elaborately drawn menus on the chalkboards and stirring aromas of patchouli, spices, and coffee. Macy's may not be able to save the world, but its fine vegetarian food, fresh pastries, and great coffee encourage people to slow down and smell the latte. It's a place where vegans are welcomed, where bikes lean against the building, and where the staff will (literally) carry your meal across a busy street for you. A cashier here earnestly told me that she loves everything on the menu. In addition to the standard menu items such as tempeh tuna and "tofurkey" (tofu made to taste like, but not too much like, turkey) sandwiches, Macy's serves daily specials, including a pasta of the day.

14 S. Beaver St., Flagstaff. © **928/774-2243**. Fax 928-774-4242. Reservations not accepted. Main courses $3–$8.25. No credit cards. Sun–Wed 6am–8pm; Thurs–Sat 6am–midnight.

2 Tusayan ✴

1 mile S of Grand Canyon National Park; 60 miles N of Williams; 80 miles NE of Flagstaff; 340 miles N of Tucson

More a tourist outpost than a town, Tusayan has almost no houses. Most residents live in apartments or trailers behind the town's businesses. Employers pay a lot to house (or lure) workers, and to convince suppliers to lug their goods 60 miles off the interstate. So Tusayan isn't cheap. A cup of coffee costs about $1.50, and rooms generally go for about $20 more than in Williams or Flagstaff. Although most of the accommodations here are pleasant, the food is often bland, and the service can be unpredictable. Still, Tusayan's location makes it the next best thing to being inside the park.

ESSENTIALS

GETTING THERE   By Car   If you drive, make sure and fill your gas tank before setting out for Tusayan and the Grand Canyon; there's only one service station between Tusayan and Flagstaff, the nearest major city, which is almost 80 miles away. From Flagstaff, it's possible to take U.S. 180 and 64 directly to Tusayan.

By Plane   Grand Canyon National Park Airport in Tusayan is served by two airlines flying out of Las Vegas: **Air Vegas** (✆ 800/ 255-7474 or 702/736-3599), which charges $278 round-trip; and **Scenic Airlines** (✆ 800/634-6801 or 702/638-3300), which charges $227 round-trip.

Other than these options, you'll have to fly into Phoenix, Las Vegas, or Flagstaff and then arrange ground transportation to Tusayan and the national park.

By Bus   Bus service between Phoenix, Flagstaff, Tusayan, and Grand Canyon Village is provided by **Nava-Hopi Tours** (✆ 800/ 892-8687 or 928/774-5003). From mid-March through late October, **Grand Canyon Coaches** (✆ 928/638-0821) operates a shuttle between Tusayan and Grand Canyon Village. The shuttle stops hourly in Tusayan at the airport, Best Western Grand Canyon Squire Inn, IMAX Theater, Tusayan General Store, the Grand Hotel, Moqui Lodge, and in Grand Canyon Village at the Maswik Transportation Center. Cost for a one-way ticket is $4 for adults (16 and under ride free) plus a $6 park entrance fee. The shuttle schedules are posted at each stop. An all-day pass costs $7.

GETTING AROUND   By Car   From April 1 through October 31, **Enterprise** (✆ 928/638-2871) rents cars at Grand Canyon National Airport. At other times, the nearest available rental cars are in Flagstaff. There's one **service station** in Tusayan; another just north of town at Moqui Lodge, a quarter mile outside the park's south entrance; and a third at Desert View inside the park's east entrance (this station is seasonal). Be forewarned that gas at these stations costs about 25¢ more per gallon than in Flagstaff, downtown Williams (away from I-40) or Cameron, so make sure to top off in those places.

By Taxi   Fred Harvey offers 24-hour **taxi service** to and from the airport, trailheads, and other destinations inside the park (© **928/ 638-2631**). **Grand Canyon Shuttles** (© **928/638-0821**) offers year round taxi service around Tusayan and into the park.

A SUPERMARKET   Tusayan General Store is located 1 mile south of the park entrance on Highway 180/64 (© **928/ 638-2854**). It's open daily 7am to 10pm in summer, and 8am to 8pm during the slower times of the year. Or, try the larger **Canyon Village Marketplace** inside the park's business district.

WHAT TO SEE & DO
Grand Canyon IMAX Theater 🔎 *Kids*   If you quibble over facts, you'll detect flaws in the 34-minute IMAX presentation, *Grand Canyon—the Hidden Secrets,* which has been showing hourly in Tusayan since 1984. For example, it shows the ill-fated members of General Powell's crew leaving the expedition by going down a side drainage that is clearly *not* Separation Canyon. But if you concentrate on the big picture—and the picture here is very, very big— you'll love the IMAX. Every inch of the six-story-high, 82-foot-wide screen is taken up by stunning footage of the canyon. Among the highlights: whitewater rafting that makes you feel as if you might drown, insects blown up to the size of buildings, and aerial footage from inside some of the canyon's rock narrows.

Located on Highway 64 in Tusayan, 1.5 miles south of the park's south entrance. © **928/638-2203**. www.grandcanyonimaxtheater.com. $10 adults, $7 ages 3–11, free for children under 3. Mar–Oct daily 8:30am–8:30pm; Nov–Feb daily 10:30am–6:30pm. Showings at half past the hour every hour.

WHERE TO STAY
EXPENSIVE
Best Western Grand Canyon Squire Inn 🔎🔎   There's a lot to do at this hotel, which prides itself on being the only full-service resort at Grand Canyon. You can play tennis, rent a mountain bike, get a haircut, or pause to consider the three-story-high mural and waterfall in the lobby. The kids will love the family recreation center, which features bowling and video games. Adults may gravitate to

the Saguaro Food & Spirits Sports Bar, the most popular watering hole in Tusayan.

Costing $15 to $25 extra, the deluxe rooms are nearly spacious enough to justify their extra phones—found in the bathrooms, next to the oversized tubs. Thick-walled and quiet, they're among the most comfortable in town. The standard rooms, in two older buildings left from the Squire Motor Inn (1972), are no larger than the rooms at the other area motels, but they do offer amenities such as hair dryers and coffeemakers. And with so much activity at this inn, you probably won't spend as much time in them as you might elsewhere.

P.O. Box 130 (1.5 miles south of the park on Hwy. 64), Grand Canyon, AZ 86023. © **800/622-6966** or 928/638-2681. Fax 928/638-2782. 250 units. Mar 1–Nov 18 $99–$150 double; Nov 19–Feb 28 $65–$135 double. AE, DC, DISC, MC, V. **Amenities:** 2 restaurants (coffee shop and dining room); 2 bars (lounge and sports bar); tennis courts; exercise room; Jacuzzi; bike rental; concierge/tour desk; coin-op washer/dryer; executive level rooms. *In room:* A/C, TV, dataport, fridge, coffeemaker, hair dryer, iron.

Grand Canyon Quality Inn and Suites 🏵🏵

In summer, guests here sun themselves around the large outdoor swimming pool and hot tub. In winter, they head for the hotel's atrium, where tropical plants and palm trees shade an 18-foot-long spa with a waterfall. As the area's hot tubs go, this one is the grandest, with jets to massage every aching joint. When the guests finally finish soaking, they find themselves occupying some of the most pleasant accommodations in town, including a number of rooms with private decks and refrigerators. A few rooms bordering the atrium have only tiny windows to the outside (and larger ones facing the atrium). Ask for a room with a large exterior window if dark rooms bother you.

Open from 6:30am to 9pm daily, the family style restaurant offers three buffets, which are popular with tour groups, as well as menu selections. The Wintergarten lounge, open only during high season, is situated in the pleasant confines of the hotel's atrium.

P.O. Box 928 (on Hwy. 64, 1 mile south of the park entrance, next to the IMAX Theater), Grand Canyon, AZ 86023. © **800/221-2222** (reservations only) or 928/638-2673. Fax 928/638-9537. www.grandcanyonqualityinn.com. 288 units. Apr 1–Oct 20 $118 double; Oct 21–Mar 31 $78 double. AE, DC, DISC, MC, V. **Amenities:** Restaurant; lounge (seasonal); outdoor pool; 2 Jacuzzis. *In room:* A/C, TV, minibar (60 rooms), fridge (56 rooms), coffeemaker, hair dryer, iron.

Grand Hotel 🏵

This newest hotel in Tusayan is also its most stylish. Modeled after a lodge of the old West, the hotel's lobby features an enormous fireplace, hand-woven carpets, and hand-oiled, hand-painted goatskin lanterns. Imitation ponderosa pine logs rise from the stone-tile floors to the high ceiling. The rooms are also pleasant, though perhaps not large enough to justify the high price charged for them. The choicest ones are the third-story rooms that have balconies facing away from the highway.

The **Canyon Star Restaurant,** specializing in mesquite smoked barbecue and Southwestern cuisine, serves three meals daily and has nightly entertainment in summer. (See review in this chapter.) Among Tusayan's upscale bars, the most appealing by far is the **Canyon Star Saloon.** Below its stamped copper ceiling, patrons belly up to the bar; one of the stools is an old saddle.

P.O. Box 331 (on Hwy. 64, 1.5 miles south of the park entrance), Grand Canyon, AZ 86023. ℂ 888/634-7263 or 928/638-3333. Fax 928/638-3131. www.gcanyon.com/index.cfm?fuseaction=grandhotel. 121 units. High-season $139 standard, $148 balcony; low-season $80 standard, $89 balcony. AE, DISC, MC, V. **Amenities:** Restaurant (Regional); bar; indoor pool; exercise room; Jacuzzi. *In room:* A/C, TV, dataport, coffeemaker, hair dryer, iron.

MODERATE

A mid-priced chain hotel in Tusayan is **Grand Canyon Rodeway Inn Red Feather Lodge** (ℂ **800/538-2345** or 928/638-2414), on Highway 64, one mile south of the park.

Moqui Lodge   Amfac may soon close this lodge, parts of which have structural problems. If the property remains open, the rooms will be overdue for a remodel. At least the guests here can still enjoy the bar, which serves good meals, the surrounding forest, and the 1960s-era A-frame lodge, where a chimney of flagstone and petrified wood climbs to a high ceiling supported by unpeeled logs.

P.O. Box 369 (on Hwy. 64, 0.25 mile south of the park), Grand Canyon, AZ 86023. ℂ 303/297-2757 (advance reservations) or 928/638-2424. Fax 928/638-2895. 136 units. $100 double. AE, DISC, MC, V. Closed Nov 1–Mar 31. **Amenities:** Bar. *In room:* TV.

INEXPENSIVE

7-Mile Lodge ⚘ (*Value*   Instead of taking reservations, the owners of this motel start selling spaces at around 9am and usually sell out by early afternoon. If you need a reasonably priced place to stay, think about stopping here on your way into the park. Don't be put off by the motel's cramped office—surprisingly, the rooms are quite pleasant and large enough to hold two queen beds. Built in 1984, they have two-inch doors and walls thick enough to muffle the noise of planes from the nearby airport.

P.O. Box 56 (1.5 miles south of park entrance on Hwy. 64), Grand Canyon, AZ 86023. ℂ **928/638-2291.** Reservations not accepted. 20 units. High-season $80 double; low-season $48 double. AE, DISC, MC, V. *In room:* A/C, TV, coffeemaker, no phone.

Grand Canyon Inn *(Value)*   Travelers can sometimes save $30 on a room simply by driving 23 miles south from Tusayan to this family run motel in Vallé, at the dusty crossroads of highways 180 and 64. The best deals here are the standard rooms. Built in the mid-'80s, they're as large and pleasant as the slightly newer deluxe rooms, but they cost $10 less because their entrances open onto the parking lot instead of a hallway. Located inside a '50s-era motel across Highway 64 from the main inn, the motel's budget rooms are cheaper still, but they're nowhere near as desirable and cannot be booked ahead. If you're looking for a variety of activities outside the motel, keep driving to Williams or Flagstaff.

P.O. Box 755 (in Vallé, at the junction of Hwy. 180 and 64), Williams, AZ 86046. *(C)* **800/635-9203** or 928/635-9203. Fax 928/635-2345. www.grand-canyon-inn. com. Aug 1–Oct 31 $69–$89 double; Nov 1–Apr 30 $49–$69 double; May 1–July 31 $59–$79 double. AE, DISC, MC, V. **Amenities:** Restaurant; outdoor pool. *In room:* A/C, TV, dataport.

WHERE TO EAT

Cafe Tusayan AMERICAN/SOUTHWESTERN   Since opening Cafe Tusayan in spring 1999 in a space formerly occupied by Denny's, the restaurant's owners have wisely kept the menu small. They serve a few varieties of salads; appetizers such as jalapeño poppers and sautéed mushrooms; and a half dozen entrees, including salmon with herb butter, baked chicken, and stroganoff. Perhaps because the chefs are able to focus on just a few dishes, the food is some of the best in Tusayan. However, the servers tend to lose their focus when busy, and the decor screams "chain restaurant."

Located next to the Rodeway Inn (1.5 miles south of the park on Hwy. 64), Tusayan. *(C)* **928/638-2151.** Reservations not accepted. Breakfast $3.75–$9.25; lunch $4.95–$8.95; dinner $8.95–$16.95. MC, V. 6:30am–10pm daily during high-season; hours vary during low season.

Canyon Star Restaurant REGIONAL   The entertainment at this sprawling restaurant seems designed to give foreign tourists exactly what they hope to find in the American West. Most nights, a lonesome cowboy balladeer and spiritual Native American dancers take turns performing for the visitors. In case anyone gets bored with the show, video clips of the canyon play constantly on monitors above the dance floor. The distractions—especially the dances, which can be captivating—are more than enough to make a person forget the food, even the mesquite smoked barbecue.

In the Grand Hotel on Hwy. 64 (1.5 miles from the park's south entrance), Tusayan. ℂ 888/634-7263 or 928/638-3333. Reservations not accepted. Breakfast $4.50–$8.95; lunch $3.95–$10.95; dinner entrees $12.95–$22.95. AE, DISC, MC, V. Daily 6:30am–10pm.

Coronado Dining Room ⓕ CONTINENTAL   My last meal at the Coronado Room felt like a guest appearance in the '70s TV series "Fantasy Island." The nattily attired waiters, combined with the high-backed wooden chairs and the dimly lighted metal chandeliers, made the room seem far more formal than other Tusayan eateries. The busboy kept my water full all night, and used tongs to plop a lemon wedge in my glass (but only after asking permission). And the staff seemed to never stop watching. There were other nice touches: tiny tabletop lamps; ample room between tables; and moist, delicious dark bread.

This restaurant serves tasty steaks, chicken, and seafood, with a few southwestern dishes thrown in. The most delicious entree may be the elk tournedos—broiled elk tenderloin medallions served with cornbread timbale and finished with roasted shallot demi. The tasty food and attentive service together make this the best restaurant in Tusayan. The adjoining, family oriented Canyon Room offers breakfast and lunch year-round and serves a dinner buffet for $14.95 during high season.

In the Best Western Grand Canyon Squire Inn (1.5 miles south of the park on Hwy. 64), Tusayan. ℂ 928/638-2681, ext. 4419. Reservations accepted. Entrees $13.95–$24.95. AE, DC, DISC, MC, V. Daily 5–10pm.

We Cook Pizza and Pasta ⓚⁱᵈˢ ITALIAN   In this restaurant's lengthy name, the owners neglected to mention how much they charge. Prices here are high, even by Grand Canyon standards, especially for a place without table service. A large four-item pizza runs $22.25, and pasta dishes range in cost from $10 to $14. After paying dearly for your food, you'll have to sit at one of the long picnic tables and wait for your number to be called.

Since you can't reserve tables here, the only way to shorten your wait is by ordering your pizza by telephone ahead of time. At least the food, when it comes, is palatable. Pasta dishes such as the spicy shrimp linguine and the Cajun chicken fettuccini taste especially delicious to people who are salt-deprived, and the pizza pleases most diners, including locals.

On Hwy. 64 (1 mile south of the park entrance), Tusayan. ℂ 928/638-2274. Reservations not accepted. Pizza $7.95–$23.95. Pasta and calzones $9.25–$13.95. Credit cards not accepted. Summer 11am–9:30pm; winter 11am–8pm.

3 Williams ✦✦

59 miles S of Grand Canyon; 32 miles W of Flagstaff; 220 miles E of Las Vegas

With timber above it, ranches below it, and railroads running through it, this town of 2,700 attracted one of the most raucous crowds in the West after being incorporated in 1892. Cowboys, loggers, prospectors, trappers, and railroad workers all frequented the brothels, gambling houses, bars, and opium dens on the town's infamous Saloon Row. Although quieter now, Williams has done an especially good job of packaging its lively past. Much of Saloon Row and many other 19th-century buildings have been restored. The town's newly renovated train depot now serves as the start and finish for the daily runs of the Historic Grand Canyon Railroad. And Route 66, which splits the town's business district, has been enshrined in the T-shirts and caps sold by local businesses. To entertain the tourists, gun-slinging cowboys stage raucous shoot-outs in the streets every summer night. All told, this is a great town for families hoping to experience the old West without battling the traffic of the new West.

ESSENTIALS

GETTING THERE   By Car   Williams is on I-40 just west of the junction with Highway 64, which leads north to the South Rim of the Grand Canyon.

By Train   Amtrak (© 800/872-7245) recently established a new, unstaffed stop in Williams. A free shuttle bus brings departing passengers from the drop-off into town, to the station for the **Grand Canyon Railway.** The **Historic Grand Canyon Railway** (© 800/ 843-8724) offers daily round-trip service linking Williams and Grand Canyon Village. For more on this historic railway, see "What to See & Do," below.

By Bus   Greyhound (© 800/231-2222) has daily bus service from Williams to Flagstaff for $18 round-trip.

VISITOR INFORMATION   For more information on the Williams area, contact the **Williams–Grand Canyon Chamber of Commerce,** 200 W. Railroad Ave., Williams, AZ 86046-2556 (© 800/863-0546 or 928/635-4061; www.thegrandcanyon.com). The visitor center here is open 8am to 6pm daily (5pm in winter). A vending machine located outside the building sells entrance permits to the park.

GETTING AROUND   There are no car rental agencies in Williams. Taxi service is available through **Smitty's Taxi** (© 928/ 635-9825).

SUPERMARKET   Safeway is located at 637 W. Rte. 66 (© 928/ 635-0500); it's open daily from 5am to 10pm (hours may vary in winter).

WHAT TO SEE & DO

Grand Canyon Railway 🐾🐾 *Kids*   In 1968, the automobile helped end the Santa Fe Railway's service between Williams and Grand Canyon. By 1989, when service resumed on the 65-mile-long line, automobiles were clogging the park's narrow roads. Thousands of visitors discovered that the historic train not only spared them the headache of driving, but was big-time fun. Today, the 100-year-old railroad carries more than 160,000 passengers annually, many of whom buy package tours that include transportation to Williams.

The trip starts at the historic Williams Depot and the original Fray Marcos Hotel. Built in 1908, this concrete building, on the National Register of Historic Places, survives today only because the railroad realized in the 1970s that to demolish it would cost more than to leave it standing. It now houses a gift shop, coffee shop, and a free museum tracing the history of the Grand Canyon Railway.

At 9:30 every morning, after local cowboys stage a Wild West gunfight outside the depot, conductors help passengers board the train. Coach passengers sit in restored 1923 Harriman coaches with Pullman windows, Art Deco–style lamps, and tiny ceiling fans. For $20 more, you can purchase an upgrade to the Club Car, with a fully stocked mahogany bar. For $55 more than coach fare, you can enjoy First Class treatment, including continental breakfast in the morning and champagne and appetizers on the trip home—all while sitting in comfortable recliner chairs. If you really want to savor the views of the high desert, however, I recommend purchasing a seat in the Deluxe Observation class, whose seats are in a glass dome atop the car. These seats cost $75 more than Coach Class. I even prefer the Deluxe Observation class to the most expensive service, the Luxury Parlor Car, which boasts an open-air rear platform.

From Memorial Day through Sept. 30, a rare steam engine pulls the train at speeds up to 30 miles per hour. (A vintage diesel locomotive often helps pull the train. In winter, only the diesel is used.) While the train chugs across the high desert, musicians wander through the compartments, playing folk and country standards. The trip *to* the canyon ends at the historic Grand Canyon Depot in Grand Canyon Village. From here, passengers can lunch at the historic El Tovar Hotel or take Fred Harvey bus tours of the rim. You can sign up for bus tours while reserving train tickets. Though I've never enjoyed traveling in a group, I savored the train ride. It's a great way to break up your travel routine and to focus on the people you love.

Williams Depot, 235 N. Grand Canyon Blvd. (take I-40 Exit 163, go 0.5 mile south), Williams. © **800/843-8724.** Fax 928/773-1610. www.thetrain.com. Round-trip coach tickets are $54.95 adult, $24.95 children 2–17 (plus tax and $8 National Park Service entry fees for ages 17–61), free for children under 2; upgrades cost $20–$85 per person. AE, DC, DISC, MC, V. Train departs daily at 10am and arrives at Grand Canyon at 12:15am. Leaves Grand Canyon at 3:30pm, arriving in Williams at 5:45pm.

Western-Style Gun Fights 𝄐𝄐 (Moments)   The same bad guys, sheriffs, and deputies who battle every morning near the Grand Canyon Railway Depot shoot at one another all over again at 7pm on summer nights in downtown Williams. The free show, which moves to a different block of Route 66 each night, entertains thousands of visitors every year. If you're in town, don't miss it. These guys seem like real gunslingers, only they're funny. To find out where the show will be on a given night, consult one of the schedules available at the **Williams–Grand Canyon Chamber of Commerce** (© **800/863-0546** or 928/635-4061) or at businesses throughout town.

At various locations in William. © **800/863-0546.** Free admission. Memorial Day–Labor Day 7pm nightly.

WHERE TO STAY
EXPENSIVE

Williams has one expensive chain hotel: **Best Western Inn of Williams** (© **928/635-4400**), 2600 Rte. 66, Williams, AZ 86046.

Fray Marcos Hotel 𝄐   Named for a Franciscan monk believed to have been the first white person in the region, this sprawling, luxurious hotel replaces the original Fray Marcos Hotel. (Located next door, the original hotel now houses a gift shop and the museum for the Grand Canyon Railway.) In the lobby of the new hotel, oil paintings of the Grand Canyon adorn the walls, and cushy chairs surround a flagstone fireplace. Bellhops carry luggage to the spacious, comfortable, Southwestern-style rooms.

The Grand Canyon Railway, which starts and ends its daily runs next to the hotel, has become hugely popular with tour groups, many of whom stay at the Fray Marcos. Its success has translated into rapid growth for the hotel, which now has 196 rooms. Although this is a quality hotel providing good service, it inevitably feels less intimate and more commercial than other area lodges. **Spenser's Lounge,** which features a beautiful 100-year-old bar imported from Scotland, offers simple dining and top-shelf liquor.

235 N. Grand Canyon Blvd., Williams, AZ 86046. ℭ **928/635-4010.** Fax 928/635-2180. www.thetrain.com/fares.cfm#fares_sub_fraymarcoshotel. 196 units. Mar 16–Oct 15 $119 double; Oct 16–Mar 15 $79 double. AE, DISC, MC, V. **Amenities:** Restaurant (American); lounge; indoor pool; exercise room; Jacuzzi. *In room:* A/C, TV.

Sheridan House Inn 🐾🐾   A display case just inside the front door of this inn holds ancient clay figurines from China and Central America, as well as tiny oil lamps from the Middle East. Beyond that, the home's interior bristles with bronze sculptures (including replicas of Remingtons) and shimmers with original paintings. Guest rooms are ultraluxurious, with brass beds, glass-topped coffee tables, TVs, stereos, VCRs, and refrigerators stocked with cold drinks. Outside, under the ponderosa pines at the end of this quiet, dead-end street (a short walk from downtown Williams), the hot tub awaits. Making this setting all the more enjoyable are the innkeepers, Steve and Evelyn Gardner. Unassuming and down-home friendly, they wouldn't seem the least bit out of place at the Daytona 500, even though their home more closely resembles the Louvre. In addition to dishing up hearty breakfasts, they also serve nightly cocktails in a downstairs bar with a slate billiard table. For an additional fee, they'll also fix dinner.

460 E. Sheridan Ave., Williams, AZ 86046. ℭ **888/635-9345** or 928/635-9441. Fax 928/635-1005. www.thegrandcanyon.com/sheridan/. 12 units. $135–$225 double. Rates include full breakfast and evening social hour. AE, DISC, MC, V. Ask about pets in advance. **Amenities:** Exercise room, Jacuzzi, billiard table, washer/dryer. *In room:* A/C, TV/VCR, stereo.

A Terry Ranch Bed and Breakfast 🐾   The most striking element of this 1994 Victorian Country home is the wood: walls of lodgepole pine; hardwood floors; and cherry and oak antiques. The wooden interior seems to inhale fresh air from the nearby mountains—each of the four guest units has large windows, a ceiling fan, and a private entrance with a screen door that opens onto the lodge's wrap-around veranda. The interior and exterior blend so easily, you may find yourself wandering outside wearing one of the inn's terrycloth robes (free for guests). I know I did. This B&B does not allow alcohol.

701 Quarterhorse (near Rodeo Rd.), Williams, AZ 86046. © **800/210-5908** or 928/635-4171. Fax 928/635-2488. www.terryranchbnb.com. 4 units. $139–$172 double for 1-night stay, $122–$155 double for multi-night stays. AE, DISC, MC, V. Inquire about kids. *In room:* A/C, TV/VCR, hair dryer, thermostat-controlled gas fireplace. Phone with dataport and fridge are available in the common area.

MODERATE

Recommended mid-priced chain hotels in Williams include **Quality Inn Mountain Ranch Resort** (© **928/635-2693**), 6701 E. Mountain Ranch Rd. (8 miles east of Williams on I-40, exit 171); and **Holiday Inn Williams** (© **928/635-4114**), 950 N. Grand Canyon Blvd. (off I-40 exit 163).

The Red Garter Bed and Bakery ★★ *Finds*   In the early 1900s, this Victorian Romanesque building had a brothel upstairs, a saloon downstairs, and an opium den in the back. The innkeeper, John Holst, has worked hard to preserve both the building, built in 1897, and its colorful history. A general contractor specializing in restoration work, he fully refurbished the structure, which served as tire storage in the early 1970s. Using early county and city records, he also fleshed out the building's history, which he gladly shares with visitors.

Each of the four guest rooms has custom-made (by Holst himself) moldings, a 12-foot-high ceiling, a ceiling fan, and antique furnishings. My favorite guest room, **The Best Gals' Room,** overlooks Route 66 and is the largest and most luxurious of the four. Its two adjoining rooms were once reserved for the brothel's "best gals," who would lean out of the Pullman windows to flag down customers.

137 W. Railroad Ave. (P.O. Box 95), Williams, AZ 86046. © **800/328-1484** or 928/635-1484. www.redgarter.com. 4 units, all with private bathroom (1 with shower only). $85–$125. Rates include continental breakfast. AE, DISC, MC, V. Closed Dec–Jan. *In room:* A/C, TV.

Mountain Country Lodge B&B ★ *Value*   Peeling paint, an out-of-order pay phone on the porch, and a location mere yards from Route 66 in historic Williams combine to make this 1909 house seem like an unlikely place for luxury. The surprise comes when you open the door to a guest room. Decorated in seemingly random themes such as "Alaska," "Route 66," and "Lavender," the nine recently refurbished guest units all have plush sofas or easy chairs, TVs with VCRs, refrigerators, and charming decor. My room, "The Cowboy Room," had metal cut-outs of cowboys, a replica of a sign from an old general store, and denim-colored linens. In addition to being luxurious, the room boasted its original trim and doors, exposed pine beams, and a brick hearth left over from the days when it served as the house's parlor. The innkeepers offer 20 percent discounts for Internet bookings and for people who reserve ahead and mention the Internet discount. For people who receive the discount, this is one of the best lodging values near Grand Canyon.

437 W. Route 66, Williams, AZ 86046. (C) 800/973-6210 or 928/635-4341. Fax 928/635-1450. www.stayon66.com. 9 units, all with private bathroom and shower. $59–$119 double, $47–$95 double (for Internet bookings). Rates include breakfast. *In room:* A/C, TV/VCR, fridge.

Canyon Motel *Value* In addition to having 18 rooms in historic flagstone cottages, this motel offers a total of five guest rooms in two railroad cabooses and one former Grand Canyon Railway coach car. From the outside, the cabooses resemble, well, cabooses, only with private decks. They even sit on segments of train track. Inside, however, my caboose seemed to morph into a single-wide trailer with a low ceiling, a compact bathroom and shower, and two narrow sleeping areas connected by a hallway. If you want to take the train, reserve one of the two largest guest rooms in the Grand Canyon Railway car. Unlike the caboose rooms, these rooms have windows that open and enough space to accommodate a queen bed and futon. Still, the cottage rooms are the best deal at this motel and a wise choice for travelers on a budget.

1900 E. Rodeo Rd., Williams, AZ 86046-9527. (C) 800/482-3955 or 928/635-9371. Fax 928/635-4138. canyonmotel@thegrandcanyon.com. 18 cottage units, 5 train-car units (15 with shower only). Cottage unit $49–$69 double; train-car unit $79–$119 double. AE, DISC, MC, V. Pets accepted in smoking rooms only for $5 extra. **Amenities:** Indoor pool (may close seasonally). *In room:* A/C (11 units), TV, fridge (18 units), microwave (18 units)., no phone.

INEXPENSIVE

Inexpensive chain hotels in Williams include **Travelodge** ((C) 928/635-2651), 430 E. Rte. 66; **Motel 6 East** ((C) 928/635-4464), 720 W. Rte. 66, **Motel 6 Premier** ((C) 928/635-9000), 831 W. Rte. 66.

El Rancho Motel *Value* This two-story 1966 Motor Court between the eastbound and westbound lanes of Route 66 is one of the best lodging values in Williams. Guests can swim in the outdoor pool, cook out on barbecue grills, or recline in the spotless rooms, which were refurbished in 1996 and come with a host of amenities. The only drawback is the proximity of certain rooms to the westbound traffic. As for the decor, one owner aptly describes it as "blue."

617 E. Route 66, Williams, AZ 86046. (C) 928/635-2552. Fax 928/635-4173. www.thegrandcanyon.com/elrancho/. 26 units. Winter $26–$35 double; summer $52–$67 double. AE, DISC, MC, V. One small pet allowed per room for $5 extra. **Amenities:** Outdoor pool; barbecue grills. *In room:* A/C, TV/VCR (videos available for $2 each), fridge, coffeemaker.

WHERE TO EAT

Cruisers Cafe 66 ⊛ *Kids* AMERICAN   Built in an old Route 66 gas station, this restaurant is jammed with gas-station memorabilia, including stamped glass, filling-station signs, "Sky Chief" gas pumps, and photos of classic stations. Served up with plenty of napkins as well as drinks in unbreakable plastic mugs, the road-house-style food will fuel you for days to come. Start with the sampler of appetizers—wings, chicken strips, mozzarella sticks, and fried mushrooms—served on a real automobile hubcap. The burgers are tasty, but the best choice, if you really want to fill up, is the pork back ribs. Even the help calls to mind the road trips of years past—on a busy day, the waitresses can be as slow with your change as those old gas station attendants used to be.

233 W. Rte. 66, Williams. © **928/635-2445**. Reservations not accepted. Lunch and dinner $5.95–$17.95. AE, DISC, MC, V. Daily 3–10pm (may vary seasonally).

Rosa's Cantina ⊛ *Finds* MEXICAN   Unless you thrill to the sight of inflatable beer bottles hanging from the roof of a former bowling alley, don't come to this restaurant for its ambience. But come anyway, in order to dine on traditional Mexican cuisine that, given the surroundings, deserves a score of 300. Never mind that a local might just tell you which lane you're sitting in. Concentrate on the delightful tastes of the fajitas, enchiladas, and (best of all) chile rellenos; sooth your nerves, if not your eyes, by drinking a neon-colored margarita; and marvel at the immensity of the portions.

411 N. Grand Canyon Blvd., Williams. © **928/635-0708**. Reservations not accepted. $3.25–$12. AE, DISC, MC, V. Tue–Thurs 11am–9pm; Fri–Sat 11am–10pm; Sun 11am–8pm; closed Mon.

Pine Country Restaurant ⊛ *Value* AMERICAN   Many locals who dine at this no-frills restaurant in downtown Williams eat their pie first, and then order dinner. One taste of any of this restaurant's 31 varieties of fresh-baked pie—including unusual flavors such as banana peanut butter and strawberry cream cheese—will convince you that the pie-eaters have their priorities straight. But pie is just a slice of the offerings. Dinner entrees like roast beef, pork chops, and fried shrimp all cost under $8 and taste like meals your mother should have made. The lunch menu mostly consists of burgers and hot sandwiches. One winner: the turkey melt with bacon, green chiles, and Swiss cheese on grilled sourdough.

107 N. Grand Canyon Blvd., Williams. © **928/635-9718**. Reservations accepted. Breakfast $2.25–$5.95; lunch $3.95–$5.95; dinner $6.95–$10.95. AE, DISC, MC, V. Daily 5:30am–9pm.

Rod's Steak House &&& STEAKS   If you're a steak lover, brake for the cow-shaped sign on Route 66 as you would for real livestock. This landmark restaurant, sprawling across a city block between the highway's east- and westbound lanes, has hardly changed since Rodney Graves, an early member of the U.S. Geological Survey, opened it in 1946. Printed on a paper cutout of a cow, the menu is still only about 6 inches across—more than enough space for its laconic descriptions of the restaurant's offerings. You can choose nonsteak items such as "beef liver grilled onions and bacon" and "jumbo fantail shrimp tempura battered"; or prime rib in three sizes, from the 9-ounce "ladies lite cut" to the 16-ounce "cattleman's hefty cut." But the best choices are probably the corn-fed mesquite-broiled steaks, which have kept this place humming for a half-century. For dessert, try the mud pie.

301 E. Rte. 66, Williams. (© **928/635-2671.** Reservations accepted. $7–$24. MC, V. Daily 11:30am–9:30pm. Closed first 2 weeks of Jan and Sun Oct–Feb.

4 Cameron

51 miles N of Flagstaff on U.S. 89, and 30 minutes from Desert View and the eastern entrance to the park

Cameron is a convenient place to stay if you plan on exploring the eastern end of the park or visiting destinations inside the Navajo Nation.

SUPERMARKET   Simpson's Market (© **928/679-2340**) is located at the junctions of highways 89 and 64, next to the Chevron. It's open daily from 6am to 9:30pm (7am to 8:30pm in winter).

WHAT TO SEE & DO

The **Cameron Trading Post** (© **800/338-7385** or 928/679-2231), at the crossroads town of Cameron (where Hwy. 64 to Grand Canyon Village branches off U.S. 89 on the Navajo Reservation), merits a stop. When here, be sure to visit the original stone trading post. Built in the 1910s, this historic building now houses a gallery of museum-quality Native American artifacts, clothing, and jewelry. Even if you don't have $10,000 or $15,000 to drop on an old rug or basket, you can still look around. The main trading post is a more modern building and is the largest trading post in northern Arizona. If you shop here, you will probably pay a little more than you should, but you won't pay way too much. Even so, I prefer taking my chances at the open-air stands scattered along highways 64 and 89, where you can sometimes chat with the artists or their families.

WHERE TO STAY

Cameron Trading Post Motel 𝒜   Renovated in the early 1990s, the rooms in this motel are among the most stylish in the Grand Canyon area. Each features its own unique Southwestern-style furnishings, many of them handmade by the motel's staff. The motel's Hopi building borders a terraced garden with stone picnic tables, a fountain, and a large grill. The campground opposite the motel offers full hookups for $15 per night.

P.O. Box 339 (54 miles north of Flagstaff on Hwy. 89), Cameron, AZ 86020. ℂ **800/ 338-7385** or 928/679-2231. Fax 928/679-2350. www.camerontradingpost. com/hotel.htm. 66 units. Jun 1–Oct 15 $89–$119 double; Oct 16–Jan 31 $59–$79 double; Feb 1–Mar 1 $49–$69 double; Mar 2–May 31 $69–$99 double. AE, DC, DISC, MC, V. Pets accepted. **Amenities:** Restaurant (Regional); trading post. *In room:* A/C, TV, coffeemaker.

WHERE TO EAT

Cameron Trading Post Dining Room REGIONAL   The menu at this restaurant draws upon a variety of cultures. As you might guess from the location, the Navajo dishes are the tastiest—particularly the hot beef, available only at lunch. A taste of the seafood, meanwhile, might remind you the ocean is a long way away.

On U.S. 89, Cameron. ℂ **800/338-7385** or 928/679-2231. Reservations not accepted. Breakfast $4–$9; lunch $4–$8; dinner $6–$17. AE, DC, MC, V. Summer 6am–10pm daily; winter 7am–9pm.

5 Towns & Outposts Near the North Rim

The area surrounding Grand Canyon north of the Colorado River is some of the most sparsely populated—and scenic—in the continental United States. Highway 89A crosses the Colorado River at the northeastern tip of Grand Canyon—just 5 miles downstream of **Lee's Ferry,** where most river trips in the canyon begin. Continuing west from the bridge on Highway 89A, you'll pass three lonely lodges—**Marble Canyon Lodge, Lees Ferry Lodge,** and **Cliff Dwellers Lodge**—each a few miles apart, at the base of the aptly named Vermilion Cliffs. This eerie desert landscape, which features balancing rocks and other striking landforms, gives way to forest when you begin the 4,800-vertical-foot climb from the Marble Platform to the Kaibab Plateau. Because the area surrounding the park's North Rim is largely National Forest, you may have to travel a ways if you fail to find a room inside the park. The closest lodging to the park's northern entrance is at **Kaibab Lodge,** 18 miles north of the North Rim on Highway 67, and at **Jacob Lake,** 44 miles

---

Tips **A View from the Bridge**

The old Navajo Bridge, completed in 1928, now serves as a footbridge over Marble Canyon. When traveling on Highway 89A near Lee's Ferry, park your car in one of the lots on either side of the gorge, then walk across the old bridge. More than 800 feet across, it affords stomach-churning views straight down 467 feet to the Colorado River, and several miles to the south down Marble Canyon (the northeastern tip of Grand Canyon).

---

north of the North Rim. If those two lodges are full, you may have to drive as far north as Fredonia, Arizona, or Kanab, Utah, to find a room.

WHERE TO STAY & EAT
NEAR THE PARK

Jacob Lake Inn ✿   In 1922, Harold and Nina Bowman bought a barrel of gas and opened a gas "stand" near the present-day site of the Jacob Lake Inn. Seven years later they built this inn at the junction of highways 67 and 89A. Today, Jacob Lake Inn is the main hub of activity between the North Rim and Kanab, UT. To serve the growing summer crowds, the Bowmans' descendants and their friends travel south from their homes in Utah. Together, they run the Inn's various businesses: the bakery, churning out excellent fresh-baked cookies; the soda fountain, which serves milkshakes made from hard ice cream; the gift shop, which features museum-quality pieces by Native American artists; not to mention the restaurant, the motel, and the full-service gas station. *Note:* The ATM at the inn is the nearest one to the North Rim.

Lodgers can choose between motel units and cabins. Though pleasant inside, the motel rooms in the front building are not nearly as peaceful as the rooms and cabins behind the lodge. Built in 1958, the motel rooms in back are solid and clean. The bathrooms have showers but no tubs, and many of them drain onto the same tile floor as the bathroom itself—a curious design. Most people prefer the rustic cabins, which cost less than the motel rooms. The cabin floors creak, the guest rooms (from one to four per cabin) are cramped, and most smell like soggy pine needles. In other words, they're exactly how cabins should be. (Unfortunately, two have been lovingly restored and therefore ruined.) Another advantage to the cabins is that each has its own private porch, either attached to the building or standing alone in the Ponderosa pine forest.

The **Jacob Lake restaurant** 𝒜, with both a U-shaped counter and a dining room, serves burgers, sandwiches, and steaks, but the most appetizing entree may be the grilled trout. A delicious lunch item is the cranberry cream cheese chicken sandwich. Even if you don't need a meal, it's worth stopping at Jacob Lake Inn to buy a few home-baked cookies or a real milkshake.

Junction of Hwy. 67 and 89A, Jacob Lake, AZ 86022. ℭ **928/643-7232.** Fax 928/643-7235. www.jacoblake.com. 12 motel units; 27 cabins (all with shower only). May 14–Nov 30 $72–$90 double; Dec 1–May 13 $52 double. Pets accepted for $10 extra. **Amenities:** Restaurant; playground. *In room:* No phone.

Kaibab Lodge   The main lodge here feels as warm and comfortable as a beloved summer camp. It has an open-framed ceiling and enormous pine beams that date from its construction in the 1920s. Perhaps because the guest rooms lack phones and all but two lack televisions, guests tend to congregate in the Adirondack-style chairs in front of the 5-foot-wide fireplace, in the small television room, or at the tables across from the counter that doubles as front desk and beer bar.

Each cabinlike building houses 2 to 4 of the 24 guest rooms, which sleep from two to five people. The rooms are spare but clean, with paneling of rough-hewn pine. Most have showers but not tubs. One luxury room, added in 1999, has a queen bed, microwave, refrigerator, and coffeemaker. Because the walls of the older units are very thin, it's best to share a cabin with friends. Located roughly a quarter mile from the highway, the rooms open onto the broad expanse of DeMotte Park, one of the large, naturally occurring meadows on the Kaibab Plateau.

Like most summer camps, this lodge isn't perfect. Parts of its exterior are biodegrading; the front desk occasionally finds itself overwhelmed, and the food lacks consistency. But the surrounding meadows soothe the mind.

HC 64, Box 30 (26 miles south of Jacob Lake on Hwy. 67), Fredonia, AZ 86022. ℭ **928/638-2389** May 15–Nov. 1; 800/525-0924 or 928/526-0924 rest of year. Fax 928/638-9864. www.canyoneers.com/KL.html. 29 units. $80–$95 double. DISC, MC, V. **Amenities:** Restaurant; bar. *In room:* No phone.

NEAR LEE'S FERRY

Cliff Dwellers Lodge 𝒜 *(finds*   Cliff Dwellers Lodge sits in the most spectacular setting in the Marble Canyon area. It's just a few hundred yards from an eye-catching area of balancing rocks (formed when boulders, having toppled off the nearby Vermilion Cliffs, "capped" the softer soil directly underneath them, thereby slowing its erosion). Against the side of one of these boulders, two former New Yorkers built a house in the 1920s and began serving dinner and drinks to the occasional passerby. Known simply as "Old Cliff Dwellers," the house still stands—barely.

The "new" Cliff Dwellers, which dates from the '50s, is set back 50 yards or so from the highway, so the rooms are very quiet. Unless you strongly prefer a bathtub to a shower, ask for a room in one of the older buildings, some of which have carports and recessed patios. Located in the oldest building, my favorite rooms have wood paneling even on the ceilings and in the bathrooms, which look a bit like saunas. The pace at the lodge is very relaxing, making it my favorite place to sleep in this area.

The best known fishing guide service in the area, Lee's Ferry Anglers Fly Shop and Guide Service, recently relocated here from Lee's Ferry Lodge. There's also a restaurant and package liquor store on the premises. Cliff Dwellers also rents a nearby, three-bedroom house for $175 per night.

HC 67-30 (9 miles west of Navajo Bridge on North Hwy. 89A), Marble Canyon, AZ 86036. (800/433-2543 or 928/355-2228. Fax 928/355-2271. www.leesferry. com. 20 units. $60–$70 double. DISC, MC, V. Often closed in mid-winter. **Amenities:** Restaurant; fly shop; package liquor store. *In room:* A/C (or evaporative cooler), no phone.

Lee's Ferry Lodge ⭐   Some of the world's best porch-sitting can be enjoyed on the patios outside the low sandstone buildings of this 1929 lodge, a popular stopping place for trout fishers trying their luck above Lee's Ferry. The patios, like those at nearby Cliff Dwellers, afford stunning views south across the highway toward greenish-pink Marble Platform or north to the Vermilion Cliffs. Although the motel sits close to the road, traffic is slow at night.

The older rooms, which are small and rustic, have been redecorated in themes ranging from cowboy to—yes—fish. Double rooms in newer, prefab style buildings are available for groups. When you tire of porch-sitting, shamble a few feet to the adjacent bar and grill, which serves the best food near Lee's Ferry.

The only thing not restful are the showers, which erupt like Old Faithful, only less faithfully.

After rigging boats for trips down the Colorado, many river guides come to the restaurant here, the **Vermilion Cliffs Bar & Grill** ⭐⭐, and not just because it stocks nearly 130 types of bottled beer. They also come for nicely prepared steaks, chicken, and fish, and for imaginative sandwiches such as the "Turkey in a Straw"— sliced turkey breast, sauerkraut, and Swiss cheese grilled on sourdough bread and served with Thousand Island dressing. The staff provides low-key, friendly service, in a dining room whose wood walls, tables, chairs, and bar seem to all have been sawed from the same tree. The restaurant can be very crowded at dinnertime during peak fishing periods (generally fall and spring).

HC 67-Box 1 (4 miles west of Navajo Bridge on North Hwy. 89A), Marble Canyon, AZ 86036 (located in the tiny "Arizona designated place" of Vermilion Cliffs). ☎ **928/355-2230** or 928/355-2231. www.leesferrylodge.com. 11 units. $53 double. MC, V. Pets accepted. **Amenities:** Excellent restaurant; bar; flyshop; artist's guild with on-site silversmith. *In room:* A/C, coffeemaker, no phone.

Marble Canyon Lodge The closest to Lee's Ferry, this lodge frequently fills up with rafters eagerly awaiting the journey into the canyon or fishermen stocking up for their next excursion. The traffic gives the place a busier, less personal feel than at the nearby Cliff Dwellers and Lee's Ferry lodges. The rooms here vary, but the ones in the 300 building are brightest and most pleasant. Although a restaurant and lounge are on the premises, I usually come here to browse the selection of unusual books on the region. Marble Canyon Lodge also rents eight two-bedroom apartments at prices ranging from $125 to $142.

P.O. Box 6001 (0.25 mile west of Navajo Bridge on Hwy. 89A), Marble Canyon, AZ 86036. ☎ **800/726-1789** or 928/355-2225. Fax 928/355-2227. 60 units. $60–$70 double. AE (lodge only), DISC, MC, V. **Amenities:** Restaurant; lounge; coin-op washer/dryer. *In room:* A/C, TV, no phone.

6 Kanab, Utah ✪

78 miles NW of Grand Canyon National Park; 80 miles S of Bryce Canyon National Park; 42 miles E of Zion National Park; 303 miles S of Salt Lake City

The Navajo ran off the first Mormon settlers in this area. The second group, who arrived in the 1870s, managed to hold on. Brigham Young himself surveyed the land in Kanab and helped lay out the downtown, which remains largely unchanged today. For years Kanab survived on ranching. Later, in the 1960s, uranium mining boosted the economy. So did film crews who shot Westerns in the spectacular red-rock canyons that surround the town. Today, tourism drives the economy, as throngs of travelers stay here while visiting Grand Canyon, Bryce, and Zion parks, not to mention the comparatively new Grand Staircase-Escalante National Monument. The town doesn't even have a bar that serves liquor, but the people are friendly, the food wholesome, and the nights serene. Seven miles south of Kanab is the smaller town of Fredonia, Arizona. Fredonia has all the sagging trailers, junk cars, dusty lots, and rusting bulldozers that one expects to find in rural Arizona. That's the downside. The upshot is that it also feels like a place where people measure time in sunrises and sunsets instead of seconds.

ESSENTIALS

GETTING THERE   By Car   Kanab is located on U.S. 89 at the junction of U.S. 89A, which crosses into Arizona just 7 miles south of town. To reach Fredonia from the North Rim, take Highway 67, 44 miles north to Jacob Lake, then take Highway 89A, 29 miles northwest to Fredonia.

Highway 12 between Boulder, UT, and Tropic, UT, crosses the north end of the monument, and Highway 89 between Kanab, UT, and Page, AZ, clips the monument's southernmost tip. Linking these highways are a number of gravel roads, which travel through the heart of the monument. If your aim is simply to cross the monument's boundary, drive 12 miles east of Kanab on Highway 89. To really experience it, however, do one of the following: Eight miles east of Kanab on Highway 89, turn north on the Johnson Canyon road. After 16 miles, turn right onto the gravel Skutumpah Road. The Skutumpah Road leads to some of the best areas for hiking in the area—not to mention some incredible scenery. Or, visit "The Toadstools"—an area of hoodoos and balancing rocks near the Paria Contact Station, 43 miles east of Kanab on Highway 89. Or, picnic near the Paria Movie Set, where rainbow-like cliffs of clay rise above a replica movie set. To reach the movie set, drive 37 miles east of Kanab on Highway 89A, then five miles on the bumpy dirt road. (*Note:* Do not attempt this road during rainy weather or in an RV.) Be sure to obtain additional information from locals about the roads and trails going into the heart of the monument (see below).

VISITOR INFORMATION   The **Kane County Travel Council and Film Commission** is located at 78 S. 100 E., Kanab, UT 84741 (© **800/SEE-KANE** or 435/644-5033; www.kaneutah.com).

The **Kane County Office of Tourism** (© **800/733-5263** or 435/644-5033), 78 South 100 East, Kanab, Utah 84741, has more information on the many movie sets around Kanab.

GETTING AROUND   The only way to reach Kanab (easily) is by automobile. The nearest car rental agencies are in St. George, UT, and Cedar City, UT. Ground zero in Kanab is where Center and Main streets intersect. U.S. 89 comes in from the north on

300 West Street, turns east onto Center Street, south again on 100 East Street, and finally east again on 300 South. U.S. 89A follows 100 East Street south to the airport and, after about 7 miles, the smaller town of Fredonia, AZ.

FAST FACTS   The **Kane County Hospital & Skilled Nursing Facility** is at 355 N. Main St. (© **435/644-5811**). In an **emergency,** dial © **911.** The **post office** is at 39 S. Main St. (© **435/644-2760**). **Glazier's Food Town** is located at 264 S. 100 E. (© **435/644-5029**), open daily 7am to 10:30pm (10pm during low season). A slightly larger store, **Honey's Jubilee Foods,** is at 260 E. 300 South (© **435/644-5877**). It's open daily 7am to 10:30pm (10pm during low season).

WHAT TO SEE & DO

The citizens of Kanab are starting to acknowledge the existence of the sprawling, 1.9-million acre **Grand Staircase-Escalante National Monument** *(ⒶⒶ)*, whose southwest boundary stretches to within just a few miles of town. Many Kanab residents still believe that protecting this area will interfere with southern Utah's economic development. So far, there are few developed areas for visitors to this rugged desert landscape, where erosion has carved out narrow canyons, broad mesas, amphitheaters, spires, and arches. There are, however, a few bumpy, beautiful roads through the area and many tantalizing places to hike. Before venturing into this mazelike country, the best thing to do is gather maps and advice from locals. **The Bureau of Land Management Kanab Field Office** (© **435/644-4600**), 318 N. 100 East in Kanab, sells USGS maps of the area and can help you plan your excursion. If you're considering hiking, stop at **Willow Creek Books Coffee and Outdoor Gear** (© **435/644-8884**), 263 S. 100 East in Kanab. The shop's friendly staff dispenses advice, maps, outdoor gear, books (including guidebooks of the area), and—in case you lack incentive—espresso.

Frontier Movie Town *(Kids)*   Come here to visit pieces of old movie sets from Westerns shot around Kanab; to dress up as a cowboy or cowgirl (cost: $5); and to admire the many autographed photos of actors who visited Kanab while filming Westerns. On nights when groups are visiting, Frontier Movie Town employees dress in period clothing and stage a Wild West drama that culminates in a deafening shootout. Because most of the participants in this drama are pulled from the audience, the acting is as wooden as on the USA network, but your kids probably won't care. Best of all, it's free. Frontier Movie Town also has an outdoor cook shack that serves buffalo wings, burgers, and steaks; an ice cream parlor; and a gift shop. Call ahead to find out when a shoot-out might take place.

297 W. Center St., Kanab. © 800/551-1714. Free admission. Daily 10am–10pm (may vary seasonally). No food Mon.

WHERE TO STAY
EXPENSIVE

Kanab has one expensive chain hotel: **Holiday Inn Express Kanab** (© 435/644-8888), 815 E. Hwy. 89.

Viola's Garden Bed and Breakfast 🏵🏵   In 1912, a sheep rancher named James Swapp built this home using a $640 kit from the Sears Roebuck catalog. All the components of the home, including pre-cut beams, siding, roofing, and paint, were delivered by train from Chicago to Marysvale, UT, then carried an additional 200-odd miles on a buckboard wagon to Kanab. Today, Swapp's granddaughter, Nileen Whitlock, and her husband, Von, welcome guests to a remarkably comfortable B&B in the home. Nileen's influence is evident in the many silk flowers, floral patterns, and lace curtains. Von serves up heavenly breakfast fare, including French toast stuffed with either baked apples or cherries and cream cheese. Two guest rooms—The English Garden Room and The Rose Garden Room—are in the original home, while three others are in an addition. My favorite, the English Garden Room, has a fully tiled shower, dormers, a Victorian-style bed, and, best of all, a private second-story balcony. The Rose Garden Room, meanwhile, boasts a claw-foot bathtub painted in a fairy motif, among other luxuries.

250 North 100 West, Kanab, UT 84741. © 435/644-5683. www.violas-garden. com. 5 units, each with private bathroom (shower only in 4 units). $115 double. Rates include gourmet breakfast. MC, V. Older children acceptable. **Amenities:** Jacuzzi. *In room:* No phone.

MODERATE

Kanab has three moderately priced chain hotels: **Best Western Red Hills** (© 435/644-2675), 125 W. Center St; **Shilo Inn Kanab** (© 435/644-2562), 296 West 100 North; and **Super 8 Motel** (© 435/644-5500).

Parry Lodge 🏵   Many of the older rooms (known as "movie units") in this 1929 Colonial-style lodge display plaques bearing the names of stars who stayed in them while filming Westerns (Dean Martin, Gregory Peck, and Sammy Davis, Jr., among others). One unit (no. 131) was built specially to house Frank Sinatra's mother-in-law while the famed crooner starred in *Sergeants Three.* (Sinatra stayed in an adjoining room.) The movie units are smaller and closer to Center Street than the motel's newer rooms, but they're far more charming. Most have tile bathroom floors and classic American furnishings inside, and they're shaded by hardwood trees. (If you want a bathtub, you'll have to take a newer unit.) At Parry Lodge, you do pay a little extra to stay where the stars once stayed—other, comparable motels in town cost less. Open from April 1 through October 30, the lodge's restaurant serves good breakfasts.

89 E. Center St., Kanab, UT 84741. ℭ **800/748-4104** or 435/644-2601. Fax 435/644-2605. www.infowest.com/parry. 89 units. May 1–Oct 31 $52–$77 double; Nov 1–Apr 30 $30–$60 double. AE, DISC, MC, V. Pets accepted for $5 extra. **Amenities:** Restaurant (seasonal); outdoor pool (heated); Jacuzzi. *In room:* A/C, TV.

INEXPENSIVE

Clean, inexpensive rooms can also be found at **Grand Canyon Motel and Old Travelers Inn** (ℭ **928/643-7646**), 175 S. Main St. (Hwy. 89A), Fredonia; **Crazy Jug Motel** (ℭ **928/643-7752**), 465 S. Main St. (Hwy. 89A), Fredonia, **Blue Sage Motel and RV Park** (ℭ **928/643-7125**), 330 S. Main St. (Hwy. 89A), Fredonia.

Treasure Trail Motel 🐾   Built in the 1950s and '60s, this family-run motel recalls the days when enormous gas guzzlers that were not SUVs prowled the American West. Its showers, which pre-date today's water-saving plumbing, slam you like fire-hose spray; surrounded by lounge chairs and beached floatation toys, the tiny swimming pool calls to mind a 5¢ post card; and the gaudy neon motel sign would look right at home in a Rat Pack movie. Best of all, the motel remains clean, comfortable, and relatively quiet. My favorite rooms—the corner units in the older, one-story building—have space to spare and feel as solid as pyramids. Built in the 1960s, the adjacent two-story building has central air-conditioning—as opposed to wall units in the one-story building—but it feels less sturdy.

150 West Center St., Kanab, UT 84741. ℭ **800/603-2687** (reservations only) or 435/644-2687. Fax 435/644-2754. treasure@xpressweb.com. 29 units (showers only). May 15–Oct 31 $40–$58 double; Nov 1–May 14 $32–$44 double. AE, DC, DISC, MC, V. 1 small pet per room for $5 extra. **Amenities:** Swimming pool (heated); coin-op washer/dryer. *In room:* A/C, TV.

WHERE TO EAT

Rocking V Café 🐾🐾 *Finds* ECLECTIC   In 2000, Vicky Cooper left her stressful job as a TV news reporter to open this eclectic cafe, easily the best restaurant in Kanab. If you're here at dinnertime, start with the bruschetta—a house-baked focaccia topped with freshly sliced Roma tomatoes, slivered garlic, basil, and olive oil. Then, indulge in the chicken and mushroom Alfredo—a creamy Alfredo sauce atop spinach fettuccine, sautéed mushrooms, and grilled chicken. Or try the charbroiled filet mignon encrusted with portobello mushrooms and surrounded with a thyme port demi-glacé. Finish with the raspberry almond torte. The restaurant, which also serves lunch, occupies a glass-fronted 1892 building that has seen duty as a general store, mortuary, grocery, and bank. The wine cellar occupies the old safe.

97 W. Center St. ✆ 435/644-8001. Reservations accepted. Lunch $6–$7.50; dinner $7–$19. V, MC. Daily 11:30am–2:30pm and 5–10pm.

Houston's Trails End Restaurant STEAKS/BURGERS/SEAFOOD

Generations of ranchers have eaten in this restaurant, as evidenced (sort of) by the many rifles, branding irons, and spurs hanging on the walls. While country music plays over the stereo, waitresses wearing their own toy side arms serve up meaty courses, including the house special, a chicken-fried steak, and baby back ribs, which are slathered in sauce and baked all day. The soup is made fresh daily, as are the enormous yeast rolls that come with each dinner. Breakfast includes a choice of omelettes, and lunch consists primarily of burgers and sandwiches.

32 E. Center St. ✆ 435/644-2488. Reservations accepted. Breakfast $4–$6.95; lunch $4–$8; dinner $5.50–$18.75. AE, DISC, MC, V. 6am–10pm daily; closed mid-Nov to Mar 15.

Nedra's Café ✿ MEXICAN

Because this restaurant in Fredonia, Ariz., serves hearty Mexican food at a moderate price, it's a great place to fill up after completing a North Rim backpacking trip. In addition to enchiladas, tostadas, burritos, and tacos, Nedra's serves less-common Mexican dishes such as *carnitas* (seasoned roast pork topped with fresh cilantro and green onions) and *machaca* (shredded beef cooked with tomatoes, onion, green chilies, cilantro, and egg). The only thing missing is beer. In Kanab you'll find a similar restaurant, **Nedra's Too,** but the tastiest Mexican fare in that community is at **Escobar's Mexican Restaurant** (✆ **928/644-3739**), 373 East 300 South.

Hwy. 89A. ✆ **928/643-7591.** Reservations not accepted. Breakfast items $3.25–$8.50; lunch and dinner $2.75–$15.95. AE, DISC, MC, V. 8am–10pm Mon–Thurs; 7am–10pm Fri–Sun (may vary in winter); closed Thanksgiving and Christmas.

Vermilion Espresso Bar and Café *Finds* COFFEE   I've always had mixed feelings about trendy espresso bars cropping up in cow country: It depresses me to know that people who share my yuppified tastes (and who may, in fact, be like me) are becoming ubiquitous; yet I always appreciate java that doesn't resemble water from a rusty bucket. For better or worse, the Vermilion Espresso Bar and Cafe brings dark coffee, teeny ceramic cups, hip music, cushy sofas, Internet connections, and delectable pastries to Kanab—not to mention an "espresso-cam" that broadcasts, over the internet (www.xpressweb.com/~espresso/cam.htm), live images of people standing in line at the counter. All these luxuries may help ease the pain for homesick city dwellers. Then again, they might make you wonder why you left home in the first place.

4 East Center St. *C* 435-644-3886. Coffee $1–$2.85; sandwiches $3.90–$5.25. MC, V. Daily 7am–5:30pm.

Wok Inn HUNAN/SZECHUAN   For the past 11 years this Chinese restaurant has occupied a historic building that in the 1920s served as a rest station for bus passengers traveling between Grand, Zion, and Bryce Canyons. If, as rumored, the building really is haunted, its ghosts are probably gorging on spicy dishes such as Mongolian beef and kung pao chicken; vegetarian fare (including spicy tofu and snow peas with black mushrooms); and sizzling platters of meat and shrimp. In addition to serving good food, this restaurant dispenses liquor—a rarity in Kanab. Be forewarned, however, that the wine list is ghastly. Your choices: Almaden, Almaden, and Almaden.

86 South 200 West (next to Super 8 Motel). *C* 435/644-5400. Reservations accepted. Lunch $4.50–$5.50; dinner $6.95–$15.95. AE, DISC, MC, V. Mon–Fri 11:30am–10pm; Sat 1–10pm; Sun 5–9pm; closed in winter.

7 Havasu Canyon & Supai

70 miles N of Hwy. 66; 155 miles NW of Flagstaff; 115 miles NE of Kingman

In the heart of the 185,000-acre Havasupai Indian Reservation, south of the Colorado River in the central Grand Canyon, you'll find the town of Supai. It's nestled between the red walls of Havasu Canyon, alongside the spring-fed Havasu Creek. Two miles downstream are some of the prettiest waterfalls on earth.

ESSENTIALS
GETTING THERE   By Car   You can't drive all the way to Supai Village or Havasu Canyon. The nearest road, Indian Road 18, ends

8 miles from Supai at Hualapai Hilltop, a barren parking area where the trail into the canyon begins. The turnoff for Indian Road 18 is 6 miles east of Peach Springs and 21 miles west of Seligman on Route 66. Once you're on Indian Road 18, follow it for 60 paved miles to Hualapai Hilltop. There's no gas or water available anywhere in this area, so be sure to top off in either Seligman or Kingman.

By Helicopter   The easiest and fastest (and by far the most expensive) way to reach Havasu Canyon is by helicopter from the Grand Canyon National Park Airport. Daily flights linking Grand Canyon National Park Airport and Supai are operated by **Papillon Grand Canyon Helicopters** (© 800/528-2418 or 928/638-2419). The round-trip fare from Papillon's heliport in Tusayan to Supai is $436, $126 of which goes to the Havasupai tribe. **Skydance Helicopters** (© 800/882-1651) shuttles passengers between Supai and Hualapai Hilltop, the trailhead for Supai and Havasu Canyon, from 10am to 3pm every Sunday, Monday, Thursday, and Friday. One-way fare is $70 (cash only) per person. Seating is first-come, first-served, with tribe members and goods taking priority. Each passenger is allowed to bring one backpack weighing no more than 40 pounds.

By Horse or Mule   The next-easiest and most traditional way to get to Havasu Canyon is by horse or mule. Both you and your luggage can ride either to Havasupai Lodge or to the campground from Hualapai Hilltop. For the 10-mile trip from Hualapai Hilltop to the campground, pack and saddle horses can be rented through the **Havasupai Tourist Enterprise** (© 928/448-2121 or 928/448-2141), which is based in Supai. The cost is $150 round-trip, or $75 one-way. If you're only taking the 8-mile trip to the **Havasupai Lodge,** call the lodge (© 928/448-2111) itself to rent your mule or pack horse. Round-trip fare between Hualapai Hilltop and the lodge is $120; a one-way ride costs $70.

Day tours from the lodge to Havasu Falls are available for $60. Riders must weigh under 250 pounds, be at least 4 feet, 7 inches tall, be comfortable around large animals, and have at least a little riding experience. Be sure to confirm your horse reservation a day before driving to Hualapai Hilltop. Sometimes no horses are available, and it's a long drive back to the nearest town. Entrance ($20 per person) and camping ($10 per person per night) fees are not included in the mule-trip price. Many people who hike into the canyon decide that it's worth the money to ride out, or at least have

---

⌒Tips **Making Reservations**

The Havasupai ask that visitors secure reservations for camping or lodging before arriving at the parking area at Hualapai Hilltop. It's good to make reservations as far in advance as possible, especially for holiday weekends. If you show up in Supai without a reservation, you may be asked to hike all the way back to your car.

---

their backpacks packed out. Pack mules, which can carry up to four articles weighing up to 130 pounds (total), are available for the same price as a mule ride. The gatekeeper at the campground can usually help you arrange for a ride out.

On Foot   To reach Supai on foot, you'll follow a trail that begins at Hualapai Hilltop and descends 8 miles and about 2,000 vertical feet to the village. It covers a shorter vertical drop than the rim-to-river trails in the canyon, but has no drinking water or rest rooms until you reach town. From Supai, it's another 2 miles, mostly downhill, to the campground. The steepest part of the trail is the first 1½ miles from Hualapai Hilltop. After this section it's relatively gradual. See below for more information on the hike to Supai.

FEES & RESERVATIONS   There's a $20 per-person entry fee to Havasu Canyon, effective year-round.

To make camping reservations, contact the **Havasupai Tourist Enterprise** at ℂ **928/448-2141.** The tourist enterprise accepts Visa and MasterCard for both mule and camping reservations. After making reservations, you'll need to check in at the Tourist Enterprise office upon arriving in Supai, 8 miles into your hike.

To make lodging reservations, call **Havasupai Lodge** directly at ℂ **928/448-2111.** Also, be sure to get a map and full trail description of this area before starting your hike. The best is the *Havasu Trail Guide* written by Scott Thybony and published by the Grand Canyon Natural History Association.

HIKING TO SUPAI & BEYOND TO THE WATERFALLS

Initially, the surroundings on the trail to Supai from Hualapai Hilltop aren't particularly pleasant. Helicopters buzz overhead, bits of paper rot alongside the trail or hang impaled on cacti, and phone lines parallel the path. Unannounced by the wranglers trailing them, horses canter past, startling hikers.

The trail drops in switchbacks down the Coconino Sandstone cliffs below Hualapai Hilltop, then descends a long slope to the floor of Hualapai canyon. Most of the hike consists of a descent down the gravelly, gradually sloping creek bed at the bottom of the canyon. Usually dry, this wash is prone to flash flooding, so exercise caution during stormy weather. At the confluence with Havasu Canyon, go left, following the blue-green waters of Havasu Creek downstream into the town of Supai.

When you see the two large hoodoos (rock spires) atop the red-rock walls, you'll know you're near town. The 450 Havasupai Indians living here believe that if either rock falls, disaster will befall their people. Unconcerned, children chase each other through town, ducking barbed wire strung between sticks, cottonwood trees, and metal poles. Prefabricated wood houses, some with windows boarded up, line the dirt paths that crisscross this sleepy community, which has a post office, a small grocery, a lodge (see information below), and a cafe.

Roughly 1½ miles past town you'll come to 75-foot-high **Navajo Falls,** then to 150-foot-high **Havasu Falls.** Just past the campground, more than 10 miles from the trailhead, is 300-foot-high **Mooney Falls,** named for a miner who fell to his death there in 1880. The milky water in the creek seems deceptively clear where shallow. It's turquoise at deeper points and emerald at its deepest, under falls so lovely as to make a swimmer laugh with delight. The creek's milky appearance comes from calcium carbonate, which precipitates around the falls in formations resembling enormous drooping mustaches. These formations are colored brownish red by the mud and iron oxide contained in runoff.

Three miles past the campground is the smaller Beaver Falls. Below them, travertine repeatedly dams the river, forming a series of seductive swimming holes. Getting there requires doing one long and relatively tricky descent down a rock face, using a fixed rope for assistance, and several shorter climbs without ropes. Four miles past these dams, Havasu Creek empties into the Colorado River. The hike downstream from the campground involves numerous river crossings, so bring your river sandals in addition to your hiking boots.

As you travel, remember that tourists often inundate this village, and that many of the Havasupai have grown weary of outsiders. Don't expect all of them to shout cheerful greetings on the trail.

OTHER AREA ACTIVITIES

Grand Canyon Caverns 🐾 *Kids*   In addition to visiting Havasu Canyon, you may want to tour the Grand Canyon Caverns. Discovered by a drunken cowboy in 1927, these caverns are notable not for pristine limestone formations but for sheer size. One cavern room is at least as large as a basketball court—or a football field, if the guides here can be believed.

The 45-minute tour recalls the days when entrepreneurs continually dreamed up new, more creative ways of luring tourists off Route 66. After descending 210 feet by elevator, you'll see an enormous fake ground sloth, a dead mountain lion that presumably fell into the hole and was preserved here, and an emaciated road-killed coyote, which the cavern's owners dragged into the cave in 1958 to test their theories on underground preservation. (They were wrong.) There are even some glowing rocks, which our tour guide told us had been "found elsewhere and brought down here strictly for your viewing."

The adjacent gift shop also has its share of novelties, including sharks' teeth and Hoover Dam placemats. The cafeteria serves burgers and sells cold cans of beer for $1.50.

On Rte. 66 (12 miles east of Peach Springs). © **928/422-3223**. Admission $9.50 adults, $6.75 kids 4–12, free for children under 4. AE, DISC, MC, V. 8am–6pm high-season; 9am–5pm low-season. Tours every 30 min.

WHERE TO STAY
IN HAVASU CANYON

Havasu Canyon Campground 🐾🐾   First, a few reasons for not coming: Dog-haters will want to avoid this campground, where dusty, scarred, but ultimately content canines nap under picnic tables by day and howl at their own echoes by night. The outhouses seldom if ever have paper in them. And, oh yes, the crowds can be thick on weekends. The Havasupai Tourist Enterprise allows 200 campers before cutting off reservations—this is 150 fewer than in the recent past, but still enough to crowd the place. There are no showers, public phones, fire pits, or grills. (Open fires are not allowed.)

When uncrowded, however, the campground is a delight. The milky creek flows past on one side, perfect for cooling off. Drinking water is available at the aptly named Fern Spring, where chlorinated water is now available. The ground, dusty from heavy use, nonetheless is soft enough to make for excellent tenting, and cottonwood trees provide ample shade. And then there are the falls.

During monsoon season, pitch your tent in an area high above the creek. During my last visit, a half-dozen mangled picnic tables in Havasu Creek served as evidence of recent flash floods through the area. If you're seeking solitude, travel farther downstream from the campground's entrance. The camping area is nearly a half-mile long, and few people lug their packs all the way to the end nearest Mooney Falls. However, bear in mind that you may have to walk all the way back to the entrance to find a useable toilet.

10 miles from Hualapai Hilltop on the Havasu Canyon Trail. © 928/448-2141. $20 per person entrance fee, plus $10 per person per night. MC, V. Open year-round.

Havasupai Lodge   For a place halfway to the bottom of the Grand Canyon and 8 miles from the nearest road, this motel is appealing enough. The rooms, which open onto a grassy courtyard, could use new fixtures and drapery. (Simply put, a lot of things are broken.) But they're clean and air-conditioned—a real blessing when the red rock walls around the town begin radiating the mid-summer heat. And, after a long mule ride or hike, the mattresses will feel just right. Even if there were televisions, the coolest entertainment would be the waterfalls, which you can reach on horseback from the lodge for $60, or on foot for free.

The Havasupai Cafe, across from the general store, serves breakfast, lunch, and dinner. It's a casual place where people fritter time over french fries and fry bread. The food is relatively inexpensive despite the fact that most ingredients are packed in by horse.

General Delivery, Supai, AZ 86435. © 928/448-2111. 24 units. $80 double, plus $20 per person entry fee. MC, V.

NEAR HUALAPAI HILLTOP

Grand Canyon Caverns Inn *Value*   The closest lodging to Hualapai Hilltop, this motel sits as far off the beaten path as you can get in the Grand Canyon area. The rooms probably look much the same as they did in the 1950s. In mine, polished rocks and crystals had been mounted, framed, and hung on a wall that had striped wallpaper. The main attractions are the outdoor swimming pool, the nearby caverns, and the space itself. Come sunset, that is more than enough to make the stay enjoyable.

P.O. Box 180 (on Hwy. 66, 12 miles east of Peach Springs, 25 miles west of Seligman), Peach Springs, AZ 86434. © 928/422-3223. Fax 928/422-4470. www.gccaverns. com/GCCInn.html. 48 units. Mar 1–Oct 31 $50 double; Nov 1–Feb 29 $35. AE, DC, DISC, MC, V. Pets accepted. **Amenities:** Outdoor pool. *In room:* A/C, TV (barely).

8

A Nature Guide to Grand Canyon National Park

A photograph of the Grand Canyon may tell a thousand words, but a thousand words don't begin to tell the canyon's story, which spans more than 2 billion years. This chapter tells more of that story. The landscape section discusses the rock layers and how the canyon was carved. The flora section describes common plants, ranging from fir trees on the rims to barrel cacti on the canyon floor. The fauna section covers the creatures that flourish in the canyon's forbidding climes. And the ecology section explores a very recent development—the effects of humans.

1 The Ecosystem

Grand Canyon National Park is a continuation of the land around it—land that's far from pristine. Its air is clouded by distant industry and not-so-distant automobiles, its largest river constricted by dams, its silence shattered by high-flying jets and low-flying sightseeing planes. Theodore Roosevelt's dictum—to "leave it as it is"—now seems oversimplified. In the new millennium, the canyon's ecology depends nearly as much on far-reaching public policy as on nature.

EFFECTS OF THE GLEN CANYON RIVER DAM Some of the most significant changes in the ecology of the Grand Canyon result from the Glen Canyon Dam, which constricts the Colorado River just northeast of Grand Canyon. Finished in 1963, the dam provides large amounts of subsidized hydroelectric power for cities such as Phoenix and recreational opportunities for approximately four million visitors to Lake Powell every year.

In addition to inundating the once majestic Glen Canyon area, the dam has completely altered the biological communities in and around the Colorado River inside Grand Canyon. Water temperatures in the canyon used to fluctuate from near freezing in winter to 80°F or warmer in summer. A mere trickle in winter, the river surged during the spring snowmelt to levels five times higher than the largest floods today. Now, penstocks 230 feet below the surface of Lake Powell take in water that varies only slightly from 48°F year-round, at a rate that hardly changes. And the water itself has been sanitized. In pre-dam days, the Colorado carried tons of reddish silt that had washed into it from the canyons of the Four Corners area (thus the name "Rio Colorado," Spanish for "red river"). Today, that silt settles to the bottom of the torpid waters of Lake Powell, and the river emerges from the dam as clear as snowmelt.

These changes decimated the canyon's native fish, which had evolved to survive in the extreme temperatures, powerful flows, and heavy silt of the old river. Four of the eight native fish species died off, and one—the humpback chub—is breeding only where warmer tributaries enter the Colorado. In their places, rainbow trout, which were introduced below the dam for sport fishing, have flourished. Along the shores, tamarisk and coyote willow choke riverbanks that pre-dam floods once purged of vegetation. This vegetation now is home to a variety of small lizards, mammals, and waterfowl, which, in turn, attract birds of prey such as the peregrine falcon.

Another effect of the dam has been the loss of an estimated 45% of the beaches along the Colorado River. Before the dam was built, the canyon's huge floods lifted sand off the bottom of the river and deposited it in large beaches and sandbars. The post-dam flows are too weak to accomplish this. There's also a shortage of sand: the reservoir captures approximately 95% of the sand that would otherwise come into the canyon from upstream.

In March 1996, the Bureau of Reclamation, the National Park Service, and a group of concerned environmental groups sought to find out whether a man-made flood released from the dam would restore some of the beaches. For 7 days in March and April 1996, the dam unloosed a sustained flow of 45,000 cubic feet per second—the maximum it could safely release. Although the flood packed only a fraction of the force of pre-dam deluges, it temporarily restored parts of 80 canyon beaches, and most scientists initially deemed the experiment—known as the Beach Habitat Restoration Flood—to be a success.

Still, the long-term prognosis for the beaches isn't good. With the dam in place, years can pass before enough sand accumulates for a productive man-made flood. And the beaches created during the 1996 flood eroded faster than expected—85% of them had washed away within 6 months. Today, most scientists value the project for what it taught them about spiked flows, but as little more than a Band-Aid in restoring beaches and natural aquatic habitats.

The Hoover Dam, near Las Vegas, also affects the canyon. The last 35 miles of the Colorado River in the Grand Canyon are submerged in the still waters of Lake Mead, the reservoir above Hoover Dam.

EFFECTS OF AIR TRAFFIC   While the dams control the river, airplanes and helicopters break the natural silence. In a 12-month period spanning 1997 and 1998, 642,000 people took sightseeing flights over Grand Canyon, according to Federal Aviation Administration (FAA) estimates. For years, planes and helicopters were free to fly anywhere over the canyon and below the rims. Then, after a collision between sightseeing aircraft killed 25 people in 1986, the FAA established strict flight corridors for the aircraft and forced helicopters and planes to fly at different altitudes.

Although sightseeing flights have long been forbidden over Grand Canyon Village, their droning is still audible at popular destinations, and public opinion supports reductions in noise. In 2000, the FAA implemented a new set of regulations for sightseeing flights over Grand Canyon. These rules froze the maximum number of air-tour flights per year at the number between May 1997 and April 1998, tightened requirements for the reporting of flights, and replaced one meandering flight route in the western canyon with two straighter ones.

Unfortunately, most visitors won't notice any changes. The busiest flight corridors still thrive, and only a small part of the canyon is out of earshot of aircraft noise, which travels an average of 16 miles laterally from aircraft in the eastern canyon and even farther in the west. However, the cap on flights does ensure that, at the very least, the problem shouldn't worsen much in the future.

By keeping the number of flights relatively constant, the FAA made it easier for researchers to monitor the acoustics in the park. The Park Service and Federal Aviation Administration may use this data in the years ahead, when they discuss ways to achieve Congress's goal of restoring "natural quiet" to at least 50% of the park at least 75% of the time by the year 2008.

The Park Service believes this goal can be safely achieved through a combination of smaller flight corridors, quieter aircraft, and fewer (or shorter) flights. But many obstacles loom. For starters, the Park Service and FAA must agree on exactly what Congress meant. The safety of air traffic over the canyon cannot be compromised. And, while environmental groups press for quiet, representatives from the area's air tour industry are likely to challenge any new limits on their operations.

AIR POLLUTION   Another factor affecting the canyon's ecology is air pollution, which on some days decreases the visibility over the canyon from more than 200 miles to less than 50. In summer, much of the air pollution comes from urban areas in southern California, southern Arizona, Nevada, and northern Mexico. In winter, during periods of calm weather, nearby pollution sources play a more significant role. Overall, ozone levels in the park have been steadily rising, and visibility has declined.

The federal Clean Air Act mandates that natural visibility eventually be restored to all National Parks and Wilderness Areas by 2065. Seeking to accomplish this at Grand Canyon, the National Park Service regularly takes part in a commission that includes state and Environmental Protection Agency regulators, Native American tribal leaders, industry representatives, and other interested parties.

The commission achieved a major victory in 1999, when scrubbers were installed at the Navajo Generating Station in Page, Arizona. This coal-burning station may have been responsible for as much as half of the canyon's air pollution in winter, according to Park Service estimates.

Yet the problem extends far past obvious polluters in the immediate area. For natural visibility to be restored, pollution sources ranging from automobile emissions in Los Angeles to factories in Mexico must be addressed. WRAP (the Western Regional Air Partnership) targeted at least a few of these distant polluters in 2001, when it proposed a declining cap on sulfur dioxide emissions throughout the western states.

FOREST FIRES   Even as National Park Service scientists fret over air quality, they know that more forest fires are needed in the ponderosa pine forest on the canyon rims. Before humans began suppressing forest fires, these areas experienced low-intensity blazes every 7 to 10 years. These fires made the forest healthier by burning excess undergrowth and deadfall, thinning tree stands, and returning nutrients to the soil. After fire suppression began, however, deadfall and excess undergrowth accumulated on the forest floors, and trees grew too close together. With so much "fuel" available, the fires that did occur burned much hotter than before—hot enough, even, to kill old-growth ponderosas, which tend to be fire-resistant. Once dead, stands of these grand old trees were often supplanted by faster-growing aspen and fir trees.

Protecting the Environment

Here are a few things you can do during your stay to protect Grand Canyon National Park:

- **Respect the animals.** When accustomed to handouts, wild animals are nuisances at best, dangerous at worst. Deer will sometimes butt, kick, or gore people who have food; squirrels, which may carry rabies and even bubonic plague, won't hesitate to bite the hand that feeds them. And human food isn't good for wildlife. In recent years, the park has been forced to shoot deer that have become sickly from eating human food. So don't feed the critters. With your cooperation, they can live in the park in something akin to a natural state.

- **Report sightings of California condors and stay at least 300 feet away from them.** The endangered California condor, the largest land bird in North America, was reintroduced to the wild just north of Grand Canyon in 1996. Unafraid of people, many of the condors eventually began venturing to crowded areas on the South Rim. If the condors—identifiable by their grayish-black coloration, orangish heads, and triangular white patches under each wing—become accustomed to people, their survival will be jeopardized. Already, one has been killed by a poacher, another by flying into a power line. The park asks that visitors stay at least 300 feet from the birds and report any sightings to a ranger.

- **Stay on designated trails.** Short-cutting is riskier on steep trails at Grand Canyon than at other parks. Besides falling, people who cut trails often kick off rockfall dangerous to those below. Short-cutting also digs paths that channel water during storms, causing unnecessary erosion of desert soils. Throughout the canyon, off-trail

In the late 1990s, Congress appropriated additional federal funding for land agencies to manage fire for ecological benefits, either through prescribed burns or what the government calls "fire-use fires"—unplanned blazes that are allowed to burn. The new funds will enable the National Park Service to burn more areas, more often, improving the health of its forests. Taking into account hikers frequently trample cryptogamic soils—delicate plants that take as long as 100 years to form.

- **Pack it out.** Even when day-hiking, remember to carry out anything that you bring.

- **Pick up litter and recycle.** Even small bits of litter such as cigarette butts can add up to a big mess in the crowded areas on the rim. Pieces of paper that blow into the canyon can take decades to decay in the dry desert air. So can seemingly harmless organic material such as orange and banana peels and apple cores. Also note that plastic, glass, and aluminum are recycled in bins alongside trash receptacles throughout the park.

- **Leave plants, rocks, and artifacts in place.** Removing any of these things not only detracts from the beauty of the park but is against the law. While it may seem innocuous to pick a flower, imagine what would happen if each of the park's 5 million visitors did so.

- **Use the shuttles.** From March 1 to November 30, Grand Canyon Village, the West Rim Drive, the Canyon View Information Plaza, and Yaki and Yavapai points are accessible via free shuttles, all of which pass through the Maswik Transportation Center. By using the shuttle, you can ease congestion, noise, and air pollution.

If you'd like to do something extra to help the park and make some new friends, sign up for the canyon's **Habitat Restoration Program,** which works to restore the park's natural environment. Activities include seed gathering, the removal of exotic species, and revegetating areas where the soils have been disturbed. During high season on the South Rim, a group usually meets in the morning and works for an hour or two. To find out more, ask at the Canyon View Center.

factors such as air quality, weather, location, fire-danger level, and available manpower, Grand Canyon National Park hopes to eventually do prescribed burns on 7,000 to 10,000 acres per year, far above levels in the early '90s.

Of course, fire use is not an exact science, and in May 2000, a prescribed burn on the North Rim spread faster and farther than expected, blackening over 14,000 acres near Point Imperial on the North Rim and closing parts of the park for weeks. Because the effects of the fire were obvious to visitors, the National Park Service in 2001 devoted much of the North Rim version of *The Guide* to a discussion of the ecological benefits of wildland fires.

2 The Landscape

If you could observe 2 billion years pass in an hour, you'd see the land from which the Grand Canyon is carved wander across the globe, traveling as far south as the equator and perhaps even farther. You'd see it dip below sea level, rise as mountains, dry into dunes, and smother under swamps. You'd watch as different sediments such as silt, mud, and sand, were deposited (usually by water) atop it. Out of sight, compacted from above and cemented together by minerals, these sediments would eventually form *sedimentary* rocks such as sandstone, siltstone, limestone, and shale. Some of these rocks would resurface later, only to be eroded by wind and water. Others would remain safely buried. Because the canyon itself may be as little as 6 million years old, you probably wouldn't recognize it until the last 11 seconds of the hour, when two or more rivers began to cut down through the rocks of the Colorado Plateau. All of human history would require only a quarter second at the end of the hour.

Although you can't personally experience the canyon's two-billion-year history, the layers of rock in the Grand Canyon record much of what happened during that time. Because the rocks are both well preserved and exposed down to very deep layers, the canyon is one of the best places in the world for geologists to learn about the Paleozoic era—and even earlier.

The record starts with the **Vishnu Formation,** consisting of schist, gneiss, and granite. The oldest and deepest layer in the canyon, it's the black rock draped like a wizard's robe directly above the Colorado River. Originally laid down as sedimentary rock, the layer was driven deep into the earth underneath a mountain range more than 1.7 billion years ago. There, it was heated to temperatures so extreme (1,100°F) and under pressure so great that its chemical composition changed, making it a *metamorphic* rock that's much harder and glossier than the others.

The Grand Canyon Supergroup, a group of sedimentary and *igneous* (volcanic) rocks laid down between 1.25 billion and 600 million years ago, appears directly above the schist in numerous locations in the canyon. These pastel-colored layers stand out because they're tilted at about 20°F. **Desert View** is one good place to see them. Once part of a series of small mountain ranges, the Supergroup was shaved off by erosion, disappearing from many parts of the canyon.

Where the Supergroup has disappeared, the **Tapeats Sandstone layer** sits right on top of the Vishnu Formation, even though a gap of over a billion years separates the two layers. Caused by erosion, this huge gap is commonly referred to as the **Great Unconformity.** Because of it, the layers have little in common. While the Vishnu Formation predates atmospheric oxygen, the Tapeats Sandstone contains fossils of sponges and trilobites that date to the Cambrian explosion of life. It also tells us about the beginnings of an incursion of the Tapeats Sea 545 million years ago. At that time, the water was so shallow and so turbulent that only the heaviest particles—sand—could sink. That sand eventually formed the sandstone.

The Bright Angel Shale forms the gently sloping blue-gray layer (known as the Tonto Platform) above the Tapeats Sandstone. It tells of a Tapeats Sea that had become deeper and considerably calmer in this area. Some 530 million years ago, the water was calm enough to let fine-grained sediment settle to the bottom. The sediment formed a muck that eventually became the shale.

Above it is the **Muav Limestone,** which dates back 515 million years. The Muav layer recalls a Tapeats Sea that was deeper still in this area—so deep that feathery bits of shell from tiny marine creatures sank. These bits of shell, together with other calcium carbonate that precipitated naturally out of the water, created lime-stone. Where not stained by the layers above, the Muav appears as a yellowish cliff underneath an obvious layer known as the Redwall Limestone.

About halfway between rim and river, the **Redwall Limestone** forms some of the canyon's steepest cliffs—800 feet in places. This imposing rock layer tells us about a Mississippian-age sea that deposited layers of calcium carbonate across all of what is now North America from 360 to 320 million years ago. Silvery gray under the surface, the Redwall is stained red by iron oxide from the red rocks above. To see the true color of the Redwall, look for places where pieces have recently broken off.

Just above the Redwall is the **Supai Group.** Formed about 285 million years ago, these layers of sandstone, shale, and siltstone were deposited in tidal flats along shorelines. They usually form a series of red ledges just above the Redwall cliffs. Right above them, and even deeper red, is the Hermit Shale, which was deposited in the flood plain of one or more great rivers around 265 million years ago. This soft shale usually forms a gentle slope or platform directly below the **Coconino Sandstone.**

The Coconino may be the easiest layer in the canyon to identify. The third layer from the top, it's the color of desert sand and forms cliffs that are nearly as sheer as those of the Redwall. The Coconino was laid down as dunes in a Sahara-like desert that covered this land about 270 million years ago. Everywhere in this layer, you'll see the slanted lines caused by cross-bedding—places where new dunes blew in atop old ones. While the other layers display fossils that become increasingly complex through time (the Supai contains fossils of insects and ferns, and marine invertebrates are common in the Redwall), the only imprints in the Coconino are lizard and arthropod tracks that always go uphill. This seems odd until you watch a lizard on sand. It digs in while going up, making firm imprints in the process, then smears its tracks coming down. Some of these fossils are visible along the South Kaibab Trail.

On the top sit the canyon's youngest rocks—the yellow-gray **Toroweap Formation** and the cream-colored **Kaibab Formation,** which forms the rim rock. Both were deposited by the same warm, shallow sea from 260 to 250 million years ago, when this land was roughly 100 meters below sea level. Younger rock layers once laid atop the Kaibab Formation, but they have eroded off in most areas around the canyon. However, a few remnants of these layers remain. To see them, look east from Desert View to nearby Cedar Mountain or northeast to the Vermilion and Echo cliffs.

MOVING MOUNTAINS   Today, the ancient rocks are part of the **Colorado Plateau.** Between 65 and 38 million years ago, this land was lifted by a process known as subduction. When a continental plate butts up against an oceanic plate, the heavier, denser oceanic plate slips underneath it. Like an arm reaching under a mattress, this slipping—or subduction—can elevate land (on the upper plate) that's far inland from the continental margins. This happened in the Four Corners area during an event known as the **Laramide Orogeny.** At that time, the Pacific plate was subducted under the North American plate, pushing the 130,000 square miles of land in the present-day Four Corners area to elevations ranging from 5,000 to 13,000 feet. This area, which consists of many smaller individual plateaus and landforms, is today known as the Colorado Plateau. The Grand Canyon area has six plateaus—the

Coconino and Hualapai on the South Rim; and the Kaibab, Kanab, Uinkaret, and Shivwits on the North Rim—that are part of the larger Colorado Plateau.

Because the earth's crust is very thick under the Grand Canyon area, the layers of rock here rose without doing much collapsing or shearing. In those places where significant faulting did take place, the rocks sometimes folded instead of breaking. Places where rocks bend in a single fold are known as **monoclines.** As you drive your car up the 4,800-vertical-foot climb from Lee's Ferry to Jacob Lake on the North Rim, you'll ascend the East Kaibab monocline. As you drive east from Grandview Point, you'll descend the Grandview monocline. In both cases, you'll remain on the same rock layer, the Kaibab Formation, the whole time.

The Colorado Plateau is an excellent place for canyon formation for three reasons. First, it sits at a minimum of 5,000 feet above sea level, so water has a strong pull to saw through the land. This makes the rivers here more active than, say, the Mississippi, which descends just 1,670 feet over the course of 2,350 miles. With an average drop of 8 feet per mile, the Colorado River in Grand Canyon is 11 times steeper than the Mississippi. Second, its desert terrain has little vegetation to hold it in place, so it erodes quickly during rains. Third, those rains often come in monsoons that fall hard and fast, cutting deep grooves instead of eroding the land more evenly, as softer, more frequent rains would.

The different layers and types of rock make the resulting canyons more spectacular, perhaps, than any in the world. In addition to being different colors, the rocks vary in hardness and erode at different rates. Known as **differential erosion,** this phenomenon is responsible for the **stair-step effect** one finds at the Grand Canyon.

Here's how it works: The softer rocks—usually shales—erode fastest, undercutting cliffs of harder rock above them. During melt-freeze cycles in winter, water seeps into cracks in these now-vulnerable cliffs, freezes, and expands, chiseling off boulders that collapse onto the layers below. These collapsed rocks tumble down into boulder fields such as those at the bases of the canyon's temples. The biggest rock slides sometimes pile up in ramps that make foot descents possible through cliff areas. Where soft rock has eroded off of hard rock underneath it, platforms are formed. One such platform, known as the Esplanade, is obvious in the western canyon. The end result is a series of platforms and cliffs.

Runoff drives the process, and more of it comes from the North Rim. This happens for two reasons. First, the land through which the canyon is cut slopes gently from north to south. So runoff from the North Rim drains into the canyon while runoff from the South Rim drains away from it. And more precipitation falls at the higher elevations on the North Rim—25 inches, as opposed to 16 for the South Rim. As this water makes its way—often along fault lines—to the Colorado River, it cuts side canyons that drain into the main one.

These side canyons tend to become longer and more gradual through time. Since the runoff can't cut any lower than the Colorado River, it tends to eat away the land near the top of each side canyon. As this happens, the head of each canyon slowly moves closer to its water source—a process known as headward erosion. If you're standing at Grand Canyon Village looking down the Bright Angel fault, you may notice that the gorge formed along it is longer on the north side of the Colorado River. This is typical of the side canyons in the Grand Canyon. Because more water comes off the North Rim, more erosion has taken place on that side of the river, and longer canyons have been formed.

AND THEN CAME THE FLOODS   The eroded material has to go somewhere. The rocks that fall into the side canyons are swept into the Colorado River, usually by flash floods during the canyon's August monsoon season. While it may be hard to imagine a current this strong in what is usually a dry or nearly dry side canyon, look again at how thousands of tiny drainages converge like capillaries into a single significant creek bed. In most cases, several square miles of hard land drains into one relatively narrow rock chute. When a downpour falls at the canyon, it can generate floods that are immensely powerful and very dangerous.

Below each significant side canyon are boulders, swept into the Colorado River by these floods. These boulders form dams in the larger river, creating rapids where the water spills over them. The water above each set of rapids usually looks as smooth as a reservoir. Below the first rocks, however, it cascades downstream, crashing backward in standing waves against large boulders. Before Glen Canyon dam was built, the Colorado River broke up many of the biggest rocks during its enormous spring floods. These floods, which commonly reached levels five times higher than an average flow today, swept along small rocks, which would in turn chip away and break apart boulders, eventually moving *them* downstream. For the canyon to have reached its present size, the river had to sweep away more than 1,000 cubic miles of debris. Now, with the enormous spring floods a thing of the past, less debris is being moved, and the rapids have become steeper and rockier.

While it's fairly easy to explain how the side canyons cut down to the level of the Colorado River, it's much harder to say how the Colorado cut through the plateaus that form the sides of the Grand Canyon. Unless the river was already in place when these adjoining plateaus started rising roughly 60 million years ago, it would have had to first climb 3,000 feet uphill before it could begin cutting down. The explorer John Wesley Powell, who mapped the Colorado River in 1869, assumed that the river had cut down through the land as the land rose. The river in the eastern canyon may indeed be old enough to have accomplished this. The western canyon, however, is much younger. In fact, there's no evidence of a through-flowing Colorado River in the western Grand Canyon before about five million years ago.

Geologists have proposed a number of theories about how the river assumed its present course, none of which is supported by a strong body of evidence. Most center on the idea of an ancestral Colorado River that flowed through the eastern canyon, exiting the canyon via a channel different from its current one. The ancestral Colorado River would have been diverted onto its present course by another, smaller river that probably reached it via headward erosion. Depending on the theory you choose, this "pirate" river may have cut headward all the way from the Gulf of California, or it may have originated on the Kaibab Plateau during a period when the climate was wetter than it is today. No one is sure what happened, and the debate is still open.

3 The Flora

C. Hart Merriam, an American zoologist who studied the plant life around the canyon in 1889, grouped the species here in geographical ranges that he called "life zones." According to Merriam, different life zones resulted from "laws of temperature control" that corresponded to changes in elevations. Each life zone began and ended at a particular elevation, much like the rock layers that ring the canyon walls.

Merriam's theory was a good one at the time, but he didn't immediately recognize the significance of other variables. Today, naturalists understand that the Grand Canyon's flora are strongly affected by factors such as air currents, water flows, soil types, slope degree, and slope aspect. Most naturalists now prefer to talk about biological communities, avoiding the mistake of fixing species in any particular "zone."

However, if your goal is to identify a few major plant species and the general areas where you might find them, life zones still work fairly well. So we'll use them, with thanks to Dr. Merriam. The canyon's five life zones are: **Boreal,** from 8,000 to 9,100 feet; **Transition,** from 7,000 to 8,000 feet; **Upper Sonoran,** from 4,000 to 7,500 feet; **Lower Sonoran,** from the bottom of the canyon to 4,000 feet; and **Riparian,** along the banks of the Colorado River and its tributaries. Some of the more common or unusual plants in each zone are as follows:

BOREAL ZONE

Douglas fir   Found on the North Rim and on isolated north-facing slopes below the South Rim, the Douglas fir grows up to 130 feet high and 6 feet in diameter. You'll often find it in areas close to the North Rim itself. Its soft 1-inch-long needles generally grow in pairs. Its hanging cones, which grow to about 3 inches long, each have three-pronged bracts between their scales. The Douglas fir is built for cold weather; its branches, while cupped, are flexible enough to slough off snow.

Douglas fir   *White fir*

White fir   You'll know you've moved into Spruce–Fir forest when you start tripping over deadfall and running into low branches. One of the more common trees in this high-alpine forest, the white fir has smooth, gray bark; cones that grow upright to about 4 inches long; and 2-inch-long, two-sided curving needles. The white fir closely resembles the subalpine fir. But the branches of the subalpine fir, unlike those of the white fir, grow to ground level, and its needles are about an inch shorter. Another common tree in this forest is the blue spruce, recognizable by its blue color and sharp needles.

TRANSITION ZONE

Big sagebrush More common on the rims than in the canyons, this fuzzy gray-green plant grows to 4 feet high on thick wood stalks. To make sure you haven't misidentified it as rabbit brush (another gray-green plant of comparable size), look at a leaf—it should have three tiny teeth at the end. Or simply break off a sprig (outside the park) and smell it. If it doesn't smell divine, it's not sagebrush. Some Indian tribes burned sage bundles during purification rituals.

Big sagebrush

Gambel oak

Gambel oak To find Gambel (or scrub) oak on the South Rim in winter, look for the bare trees. The only deciduous tree in the immediate vicinity of the South Rim, its leaves turn orange before falling. To find Gambel oak in summer, look for its acorns, its long (up to 6 in.) lobed leaves, and its gray trunk. It grows in thick clumps that clutter the otherwise open floor of the ponderosa pine forest. A plant with a similar name, shrub oak, grows lower in the canyon and has sharp, hollylike leaves.

Indian paintbrush

Lupine

Indian paintbrush You should be able to identify this plant from the name alone. Many of its leaves are colored red or orange at their tips, making them look as if they've been dipped in paint.

Lupine Common on both rims, this purple flower blooms from spring to late summer. You can spot lupine by its palmate leaves and tiny purple flowers growing in clusters at the top of its main stem.

Ponderosa pine Found on both rims and in isolated places in the canyon, this tree can withstand forest fires, provided the fires come often enough to keep the fuel on the forest floor to a minimum. Its thick bark shields the inside of the tree from the heat. When the fires are over, the ponderosa thrives on the nutrients in the ash-covered soil. Once the tree's low branches have burned off, fires can no longer climb to the crown. So the trees that survive grow stronger. To spot a mature ponderosa pine, look for its thick red-orange bark (younger ones have blackish bark), its 6-inch-long needles in groups of three, and its absence of low branches. Once you've identified one, smell its bark—you'll be rewarded with a rich vanilla-like scent.

Ponderosa pine

Quaking aspen

Quaking aspen The ponderosa pine may smell the best, but tree-huggers should save the last dance for the quaking aspen, which grows alongside it in many North Rim forests. Its cool, dusty white bark feels great against your cheek on a hot day. Its leaves, on long, twisted stems, shudder at the very idea of a breeze. If you hug one aspen you're probably hugging many. Dozens and sometimes hundreds of these trees have been known to sprout from a common root system, meaning they're technically one plant. In fact, one of the world's largest organisms is a quaking aspen in Utah.

UPPER SONORAN

Cliff rose & Apache plume   These flowering shrubs, which grow both on the rims and in the canyon, have much in common. Both are members of the rose family, grow tiny five-lobed leaves, and send up numerous delicate flowers from which feathery plumes sometimes protrude. However, a few differences do exist: Cliff rose is the larger of the two, growing to a maximum of 25 feet, compared to 5 feet for the Apache plume. Its flowers are a creamy yellow, as opposed to white for the Apache plume. And its leaves, unlike those of the Apache plume, are hairless. The Apache plume blooms a few weeks longer—from early spring into October.

Cliff rose   *Apache plume*

Mormon tea   Common throughout the park, this virtually leafless plant has hundreds of jointed, needlelike stems that point skyward. Once the plants are full-grown, they remain largely unchanged for as long as 500 years. Photos of desert scenes taken more than 50 years apart show the same Mormon tea plants with every stem still in place. The only difference between young and old plants is color—the older plants are yellow-green or even yellow-gray; the younger ones are light green. Both the early Mormon pioneers and the Indians used the stems, which contain pseudoephedrine and tannin, for medicine.

Piñon pine   Wherever a new juniper tree sprouts, a piñon pine usually follows, growing to about the same size (30 ft.) as the juniper. Shorter and rounder than most pines, the piñon pine grows 1-inch-long needles, usually in pairs. It commonly takes root in the shadows of juniper trees, which are more heat-tolerant. Their system has worked well. Together, the piñon pine and the Utah juniper dominate much of the high desert in the Southwest. Packing 2,500 calories per pound, piñon (or pine) nuts have always been a staple for Native Americans in this area, and today they're also popular in Italian restaurants, where they're used to make pesto.

Piñon pine

Utah agave & banana yucca   The plants consisting of 3-foot-long spikes are most often agave or yucca. Agave leaves have serrated edges, while yucca leaves have rough, sandpaper-like sides. The Indians in the canyon used fibers and leaves from these plants to make sandals, baskets, and rope. If you were to break off a particularly sharp leaf and peel away the fibers from its edge, you would eventually end up with a thread with a needlelike tip. The agave blooms only once every 15 to 25 years. When it does, it's easy to spot—its spiky base sends up a wooden stalk, about 14 feet high, atop which yellow flowers grow. Because this flourish occurs so rarely, the agave is often referred to as the century plant. After flowering, it dies. Some naturalists theorize that the agave, whose leaves become rich in nutrients just before it flowers, evolved to bloom rarely so animals would not grow accustomed to eating it. This trick didn't fool the Ancestral Puebloans, who discovered that the roasted hearts of the plant were always nutritious. Unlike the agave, the banana yucca blooms every 2 to 3 years, sending up 4-foot-high stalks on which yellow flowers hang. Its fruit, which tastes a bit like banana, ripens later in summer.

Utah agave

Banana yucca

Utah juniper

Utah juniper   This tree, which seldom grows higher than 30 feet, *looks* like it belongs in the desert. Its scraggy bark is as dry as straw, its tiny leaves are tight and scalelike, and its gnarled branches appear to have endured, well, everything. Burned in campfires since the dawn of time, juniper wood releases a fragrant smoke that evokes the desert as much as the yipping of coyotes. Its dusty-looking blue berries are actually cones, each with one or two small seeds inside.

LOWER SONORAN

Barrel cactus   The barrel cactus does indeed resemble a small green barrel. One of the more efficient desert plants, it can survive for years without water. Contrary to the popular myth, however, there's no reservoir of drinking water inside.

Barrel cactus

Blackbrush   The blue-gray color of the Tonto Platform (above the Tapeats Sandstone) doesn't derive solely from the Bright Angel Shale. It also comes from blackbrush, a gray, spiny, 3-foot-high plant that dominates the flora atop the platform. Blackbrush grows leathery half-inch-long leaves on tangled branches that turn black when wet. Because the plant's root system is considerably larger than the plant itself, each blackbrush bush commands plenty of area. There are usually 10 to 15 feet between plants.

Hedgehog cactus   The hedgehog cactus looks like a cluster of prickly cucumbers standing on end. Of the four species in the canyon, the most colorful is the claret cup, which sprouts crimson flowers every spring.

Hedgehog cactus

Honey mesquite

Honey mesquite & catclaw acacia   These two species of tree, which favor the walls above rivers or creek beds, show us the heights reached by the Colorado River's pre-dam floods. After a flood recedes, acacia and mesquite seedlings take root in the moist soil. Later, the maturing trees send pipelike roots down to the river or creek bed. Both species have dark branches and leaves with small paired leaflets, reach heights of about 20 feet, and grow seedpods several inches long. The mesquite's leaflets, however, are longer and narrower than the acacia's. And while the acacia has tiny barbs like cat claws for protection, the mesquite grows paired inch-long thorns where the leaves meet the stems. Mesquite beans were a staple for the Ancestral Puebloans.

Opuntia cactus   Most members of this family are known as prickly pear. Although prickly pears do grow on the South Rim, the most impressive are lower in the canyon. There, the prickly pear's flat oval pads link up in formations that occasionally sprawl across 40 or more square feet of ground. Look closely at each pad and you'll notice that, even in the most contorted formations, the narrow side always points up, cutting down on the sunlight received. Because this cactus tends to hybridize, it produces a variety of yellow, pink, and magenta flowers from April to June. Put a finger inside one of these flowers, and the stamens will curl around it, a reflex designed to coat bees with pollen. Prickly pear pads can be roasted and eaten, and the fruit, which ripens in late summer, is often used to make jelly. There are several species of opuntia, ranging from very prickly (grizzly bear) to spineless (beavertail).

Opuntia cactus/ prickly pear

RIPARIAN

Fremont cottonwood   To cool off, look for the bright green canopy of this tree, which grows near many of the tributaries to the Colorado River but seldom by the large river itself. The tree's spreading branches and wide, shimmering leaves shade many of the canyon's springs. Covered with grooved, ropelike bark, the cottonwood's trunk can grow as wide as a refrigerator. Its flowers, which bloom in spring, drop tiny seeds that look like cotton and can ride breezes to distant water sources. A nice grove of these trees shelters the picnic area at Indian Garden.

Fremont cottonwood

Tamarisk

Tamarisk   This exotic species was once used for flood-bank control by the CCC. Today, it is the plant that boaters and hikers love to hate. Before the Glen Canyon dam was built, the Colorado River's annual spring floods thinned or wiped out most of the tamarisk along its banks. Now tamarisk and coyote willow have taken over many beaches, creating thickets that can make hiking miserable. Other animals don't mind the thickets, as they're home to a diverse population of birds, lizards, and insects. Soft as ostrich feathers, the plant's stems grow tiny scalelike leaves and sprout small white flowers in spring. While young tamarisk consists of skinny, flexible stalks, the older plants have wood trunks.

4 The Fauna

To view wildlife during your stay at Grand Canyon, bring a flashlight. Most desert animals are either *nocturnal* (active at night) or *crepuscular* (active at dawn and dusk). By laying low during the day, they avoid the powerful sun, cutting their water needs and enabling them to forage or hunt without overheating. All have specialized mechanisms to survive this harsh environment, and many, if provoked, can be as prickly as the plants around them.

MAMMALS

Bats The **western pipestral** is the most common bat at Grand Canyon. At sunset you'll see them flutter above the rim, rising and falling as if on strings. Gray with black wings, they send out supersonic sounds that echo differently off of different objects. The bats then "read" the echoes to determine what they're approaching. If it's an insect, they know what to do. They'll sometimes eat 500 bugs in an hour.

Bat

Bighorn sheep

Bighorn sheep If there's a hint of a foothold, a bighorn sheep will find it. Its hooves are hard and durable on the outside but soft and grippy underneath, a perfect design for steep, rocky terrain. You'll often hear them clattering before you spot their stocky, gray-brown bodies and white rumps. Six feet long, the males weigh up to 300 pounds. Their horns are coiled; the females' are straight. Look for bighorn sheep in side canyons that have water, and sometimes on the rims.

Coyote

Coyotes   Coyotes will eat almost anything—bugs, carrion, plants, rodents, and bird eggs included. Their versatile diet has helped them flourish, and today you'll find them all around the canyon. They look like lanky mid-sized dogs. But their noses are more sharply pointed, and their tails hang between their legs when they run. During summer, their bodies are tan, their bellies white, and their legs rust-colored. In winter, the ones on the rims turn mostly gray. If you camp during your visit, you'll probably hear their squeaky yips and howls at sunset. Look for them at dusk in the meadows on the North Rim or at daybreak around the Tusayan garbage dumpsters.

Desert cottontails   Common even in the canyon's most populated areas, these oval-eared rabbits feed on grasses, twigs, juniper berries, and leaves. Their bodies are mostly tan, but sometimes all you'll see is their white tails as they dash away from coyotes and bobcats.

Desert cottontail

Elk

Elk   Merriam's elk, which were native to this area, were hunted off in the 1920s. Transplanted from Yellowstone, Roosevelt elk have flourished on the South Rim. Their bodies are tan; their heads and necks dark brown and shaggy. These long-legged, thick-bodied animals grow to enormous sizes. The bulls weigh as much as 1,000 pounds and stand up to 5 feet high at the shoulders; the cows average 550 pounds. Unlike deer, which prefer bushes and shrubs, elk feed primarily on grasses on the forest floor. Rather than migrate far, they'll dig through snow for forage. Every year the bulls grow large racks, used to battle one another for the cows. In fall, during mating season the bulls can be dangerously aggressive. At this time, you may hear their high-pitched "bugling" inside the park. Herds of elk can often be seen roaming the National Forest on the South Rim near Grandview Point, and less commonly along the North Rim entrance road.

Mountain lions   These solitary cats, whose legs are as powerful as springs, will probably see you before you see them. Sightings around the canyon are rare, even among people who have spent their lives studying them. This isn't because the animals are small—they grow up to 6 feet long and weigh 200 pounds, with cylindrical tails as long as 3 feet. Their coat is tawny everywhere except the chest and muzzle, which are white. Their retractable claws let them alternately sprint across rocks and dig in on softer slopes—bad news for deer and elk, on which they prey. Hunted to near extirpation in this area in the early 1900s, the mountain lion has recovered of late, especially on the North Rim, where over 100 are believed to live.

Mule deer   These tan or gray ungulates, which grow to as much as 200 pounds, are common everywhere in the park, including developed areas. They often summer on the rims, then move into the canyon or lower on the plateaus in winter, when their fur turns grayish-white. Every year the bucks grow antlers, then shed them in March after battling other males during mating season. Mule deer feed on a variety of bushes and shrubs, but their favorite food may be cliff rose. Active at night, they frequently dart in front of cars, making night driving risky.

Mountain lion

Mule deer

Raccoon   *Ringtail*

Raccoons   Recognizable by their black "bandit" masks, their gray bodies, and tails with black stripes, raccoons are common around the rim campgrounds.

Ringtails   A relative of the raccoon, ringtails frequently raid camp-sites near the Colorado River. Their tails have luminous white bands. Their ears are pink and mouselike, their bodies gray-brown. They're smart enough and dexterous enough to untie knots. If cornered, they may spray a foul-smelling mist like skunks do. When not raiding campsites, they feed on mice and other small animals. Look for ring-tails at night on the rafters inside the El Tovar Restaurant. (The hotel has tried unsuccessfully to move the population.)

Kaibab squirrel   *Aberts squirrel*

Squirrels   The Kaibab and Aberts squirrels were once the same species sharing the same ponderosa pine forest. After the canyon separated the squirrels, subtle genetic differences between the groups took hold in later generations. Although both still have tufts of fur above their ears, the Kaibab squirrel, which lives only on the North Rim, is gray with a white tail. The Aberts squirrel, on the South Rim, has a gray body, a reddish back, and a dark tail with white sides. Both still nest in, and feed on the bark of, ponderosa pines, and both are notoriously clueless (even by squirrel standards) around cars. Among the other species, the grayish-brown squirrels seen begging along the rim are rock squirrels. The ones that look like oversized chipmunks are golden-mantled ground squirrels.

BIRDS

Bald eagles   It's hard to mistake a mature bald eagle for any other bird. Dark plumage, a white head and tail, and yellow beak combine to give this bird, with its 6-foot wingspan, a look as distinctive as America itself. During winter, bald eagles frequently sit in trees along the river in the eastern canyon, where they like to fish for trout.

Bald eagle

Common raven

Common ravens   These shiny blue-black birds soar like raptors above the rims when not walking like people around the campgrounds. They're big—up to 27 inches long—and smart. In addition to unzipping packs and opening food containers, they've been known to team up and take trout from bald eagles.

Golden eagle

Great Horned Owl

Golden eagles   Golden-brown from head to talon, this bird is commonly spotted soaring above the rims, its wings spanning to 6 feet or more. Wings tucked, the golden eagle can dive at speeds approaching 100 mph. Although known to kill fawns, it usually prefers smaller mammals. It sometimes can be mistaken for an immature bald eagle.

Great horned owls This bird often perches in trees along the rims. Look for black circles around its eyes, puffy white feathers on its chest, and feathery tufts that resemble horns above its ears.

Peregrine falcon

Red-tailed hawk

Peregrine falcons Identifiable by its gray back, black-and-white head, and pointed, sickle-shaped wings, this bird frequently preys on waterfowl, sometimes knocking them out of the air. Once endangered, the peregrine has benefited from the outlawing of the harmful pesticide DDT. The canyon is now home to the largest population of peregrines in the continental United States.

Red-tailed hawks One of the more commonly sighted raptors, the red-tailed hawk flies with its wings on a plane the way an eagle does, but has a smaller (4-ft.) wingspan. Identifiable by its white underside, reddish tail, brown head, and brown back, the red-tailed hawk sometimes drops rattlesnakes from great heights to kill them.

Violet-green swallow

Swifts and swallows Two small birds—**white-throated swifts** and **violet-green swallows**—commonly slice through the air above the rims, picking off bugs. The swift's black-and-white colored body is uniformly narrow from head to tail. Its wings, which curve back toward its tail, seem to alternate strokes as it flies. The swallow, which has a rounder body and green feathers on its back and head, flies more steadily than the swift.

Turkey vultures   If you see a group of birds circling, their wings held in "Vs," rocking in the wind like unskilled hang-glider pilots, you're watching a group of turkey vultures. Up close, look for the dark plumage and bald red head. California Condors sometimes follow turkey vultures because the vultures have a better sense of smell and can more easily locate carrion.

Turkey vulture

Wild turkey

Wild turkeys   Growing to 4 feet long, the males of this species are easiest to spot. They have bare blue heads, red wattles, and 6-inch-long feathered "beards" on their chests. The females are smaller and less colorful. Common on both rims but seen most often in the meadows on the North Rim, wild turkeys were once raised in pens by the Ancestral Puebloans.

INVERTEBRATES

Black widows   These black spiders often spin their irregularly shaped, sticky webs in crevices in the Redwall Limestone. Although they're most active at night, you can occasionally spy one in the shadows. Their large, round abdomens give them a unique appearance. Only the females, recognizable by the red hourglass shape under the abdomen, are poisonous, with bites lethal enough to endanger small children.

Scorpions   Like a crayfish, each scorpion has two pincers and a long tail that curls toward its head like a whip. At the end of the tail is a stinger. Of the two species commonly found in the canyon, the most numerous by far is the giant hairy scorpion. Three to four inches long, this tan-colored scorpion inflicts a bite that's usually no worse than a bee sting. The bark (or sculptured) scorpion is more dangerous. Up to 2 inches long and straw-colored, it injects a neurotoxic venom much stronger than that of its larger counterpart. These bites are very painful and can be deadly in rare cases. The best way to see scorpions is to shine an ultraviolet light on the canyon floor at night—in this light, they glow!

Scorpion

REPTILES

Chuckwallas Common in the lower parts of the canyon, chuckwallas look as if they've just completed a crash diet, leaving them with skin that's three sizes too big. When threatened, they inflate that loose skin, wedging themselves into crevices in rock piles and cliffs. From 11 to 16 inches long, chuckwallas have blackish heads and forelegs.

Chuckwalla

Collared lizard

Collared lizards At the middle and lower elevations of the canyon, you'll see a variety of collared lizards, all of which grow to 14 inches long and have big heads, long tails, and two black bands across their shoulders. Usually tan, black-collared lizards change shades when the temperature shifts. Western collared lizards are among the more colorful in the park, with blue, green, and yellow markings supplementing the black bands. These lizards are not the least bit shy around people. Sometimes, they'll stare you down for hours.

Rattlesnake

Rattlesnakes   If something rattles at you below the rim, it's probably the Grand Canyon rattlesnake, the most common rattler inside the canyon. Its pinkish skin with dark blotches blends well with the canyon's soil. Like other rattlers, it has a triangular head, heat-sensing pits between its eyes, and a rattle used to warn larger animals. To maintain an acceptable body temperature, this snake becomes active only when the temperature along the ground approaches 78°F. At other times it's sluggish. It may sun itself on a ledge or curl up under a rock pile or log. Although venomous, the Grand Canyon rattlesnake is more reluctant to bite than other rattlesnakes. They're often seen near water, where they prey on small rodents. Other rattlesnake species are found closer to the rims. On the South Rim, the only common rattlesnake is the Hopi rattlesnake; on the North Rim, it's the Great Basin rattlesnake.

Short-horned lizard

Short-horned lizards   These lizards can be found sunning themselves or scurrying across the forest floors on the canyon rims. With horizontal spines on their heads and rows of barbs on their backs, these short, stout lizards look like tiny dinosaurs or "horny toads," as they're commonly called. They'll sometimes ooze blood from their eyes at attackers.

Index

See also Accommodations and Restaurant Indexes, below.

ACCOMMODATIONS

RESTAURANTS

FROMMER'S® COMPLETE TRAVEL GUIDES

Alaska
Alaska Cruises & Ports of Call
Amsterdam
Argentina & Chile
Arizona
Atlanta
Australia
Austria
Bahamas
Barcelona, Madrid & Seville
Beijing
Belgium, Holland & Luxembourg
Bermuda
Boston
British Columbia & the Canadian
  Rockies
Budapest & the Best of Hungary
California
Canada
Cancún, Cozumel & the Yucatán
Cape Cod, Nantucket &
  Martha's Vineyard
Caribbean
Caribbean Cruises & Ports of Call
Caribbean Ports of Call
Carolinas & Georgia
Chicago
China
Colorado
Costa Rica
Denmark
Denver, Boulder & Colorado Springs
England
Europe
European Cruises & Ports of Call
Florida
France

Germany
Great Britain
Greece
Greek Islands
Hawaii
Hong Kong
Honolulu, Waikiki & Oahu
Ireland
Israel
Italy
Jamaica
Japan
Las Vegas
London
Los Angeles
Maryland & Delaware
Maui
Mexico
Montana & Wyoming
Montréal & Québec City
Munich & the Bavarian Alps
Nashville & Memphis
Nepal
New England
New Mexico
New Orleans
New York City
New Zealand
Nova Scotia, New Brunswick &
  Prince Edward Island
Oregon
Paris
Philadelphia & the Amish Country
Portugal
Prague & the Best of the Czech
  Republic
Provence & the Riviera

Puerto Rico
Rome
San Antonio & Austin
San Diego
San Francisco
Santa Fe, Taos & Albuquerque
Scandinavia
Scotland
Seattle & Portland
Shanghai
Singapore & Malaysia
South Africa
South America
Southeast Asia
South Florida
South Pacific
Spain
Sweden
Switzerland
Texas
Thailand
Tokyo
Toronto
Tuscany & Umbria
USA
Utah
Vancouver & Victoria
Vermont, New Hampshire
  & Maine
Vienna & the Danube Valley
Virgin Islands
Virginia
Walt Disney World & Orlando
Washington, D.C.
Washington State

FROMMER'S® DOLLAR-A-DAY GUIDES

Australia from $50 a Day
California from $70 a Day
Caribbean from $70 a Day
England from $75 a Day
Europe from $70 a Day

Florida from $70 a Day
Hawaii from $80 a Day
Ireland from $60 a Day
Italy from $70 a Day
London from $85 a Day

New York from $90 a Day
Paris from $80 a Day
San Francisco from $70 a Day
Washington, D.C., from $80
  a Day

FROMMER'S® PORTABLE GUIDES

Acapulco, Ixtapa & Zihuatanejo
Amsterdam
Aruba
Australia's Great Barrier Reef
Bahamas
Baja & Los Cabos
Berlin
Big Island of Hawaii
Boston
California Wine Country
Cancún
Charleston & Savannah
Chicago
Disneyland

Dublin
Florence
Frankfurt
Hong Kong
Houston
Las Vegas
London
Los Angeles
Maine Coast
Maui
Miami
New Orleans
New York City
Paris

Phoenix & Scottsdale
Portland
Puerto Rico
Puerto Vallarta, Manzanillo &
  Guadalajara
San Diego
San Francisco
Seattle
Sydney
Tampa & St. Petersburg
Vancouver
Venice
Virgin Islands
Washington, D.C.

FROMMER'S® NATIONAL PARK GUIDES

Family Vacations in the National
  Parks
Grand Canyon

National Parks of the American
  West
Rocky Mountain
Yellowstone & Grand Teton

Yosemite & Sequoia/
  Kings Canyon
Zion & Bryce Canyon

FROMMER'S® MEMORABLE WALKS

Chicago	New York	San Francisco
London	Paris	

FROMMER'S® GREAT OUTDOOR GUIDES

Arizona & New Mexico	Northern California	Vermont & New Hampshire
New England	Southern New England	

SUZY GERSHMAN'S BORN TO SHOP GUIDES

Born to Shop: France	Born to Shop: Italy	Born to Shop: New York
Born to Shop: Hong Kong, Shanghai & Beijing	Born to Shop: London	Born to Shop: Paris

FROMMER'S® IRREVERENT GUIDES

Amsterdam	Los Angeles	San Francisco
Boston	Manhattan	Seattle & Portland
Chicago	New Orleans	Vancouver
Las Vegas	Paris	Walt Disney World
London	Rome	Washington, D.C.

FROMMER'S® BEST-LOVED DRIVING TOURS

Britain	Germany	New England
California	Ireland	Scotland
Florida	Italy	Spain
France		

HANGING OUT™ GUIDES

Hanging Out in England	Hanging Out in France	Hanging Out in Italy
Hanging Out in Europe	Hanging Out in Ireland	Hanging Out in Spain

THE UNOFFICIAL GUIDES®

Bed & Breakfasts and Country Inns in:	Florida with Kids	New Orleans
California	Golf Vacations in the Eastern U.S.	New York City
New England	The Great Smoky & Blue Ridge Mountains	Paris
Northwest		San Francisco
Rockies	Hawaii	Skiing in the West
Southeast	Inside Disney	Southeast with Kids
Beyond Disney	Las Vegas	Walt Disney World
Branson, Missouri	London	Walt Disney World for Grown-ups
California with Kids	Mid-Atlantic with Kids	Walt Disney World for Kids
Chicago	Mini Las Vegas	Washington, D.C.
Cruises	Mini-Mickey	World's Best Diving Vacations
Disneyland	New England & New York with Kids	

SPECIAL-INTEREST TITLES

Frommer's Adventure Guide to Australia & New Zealand
Frommer's Adventure Guide to Central America
Frommer's Adventure Guide to India & Pakistan
Frommer's Adventure Guide to South America
Frommer's Adventure Guide to Southeast Asia
Frommer's Adventure Guide to Southern Africa
Frommer's Britain's Best Bed & Breakfasts and Country Inns
Frommer's France's Best Bed & Breakfasts and Country Inns
Frommer's Italy's Best Bed & Breakfasts and Country Inns
Frommer's Caribbean Hideaways

Frommer's Exploring America by RV
Frommer's Gay & Lesbian Europe
Frommer's The Moon
Frommer's New York City with Kids
Frommer's Road Atlas Britain
Frommer's Road Atlas Europe
Frommer's Washington, D.C., with Kids
Frommer's What the Airlines Never Tell You
Israel Past & Present
The New York Times' Guide to Unforgettable Weekends
Places Rated Almanac
Retirement Places Rated